A Thinking Person's

GUIDE *to* ISLAM

A Thinking Person's
GUIDE *to* ISLAM

The Essence of Islam in 12 Verses from the Qur'an

H.R.H. PRINCE GHAZI BIN MUHAMMAD

Foreword by H.M. King Abdullah II ibn Al-Hussein

White Thread
PRESS

TURATH
PUBLISHING

THE PRINCE GHAZI TRUST
FOR QUR'ANIC THOUGHT

ISBN 978-1-90-6949-30-3 (case)
ISBN 978-1-93-3764-15-3 (soft)

Jointly Published by
White Thread Press
White Thread Limited
London, UK
www.whitethreadpress.com

Turath Publishing
79 Mitcham Road
London sw17 9pd
www.turath.co.uk

The publishers do not take responsibility for all of the author's personal opinions
expressed herein.

Distributed in the UK by Azhar Academy Ltd. London
sales@azharacademy.com   Tel: +44 (208) 911 9797

British Library Cataloguing in Publication Data. A catalogue record for this book is
also available from the British Library.

⊗ Printed and bound in the United States of America on premium acid-free paper. The
paper used in this book meets the minimum requirement of ANSI/NISO z39.48-1992
(R 1997) (Permanence of Paper). The binding material has been chosen for strength
and durability.

Cover design and typography by ARM

Cover pattern based on the Hilu family of Fez's Qur'anic frontispiece.
All calligraphy featured in this book is available at www.freeislamiccalligraphy.com

Contents

~

Contents

بِسْمِ اللهِ الرَّحْمنِ الرَّحِيمِ

وَالحَمْدُ لِلّهِ رَبِّ العَالَمِينَ

وَالصِّلَاةُ وَالسَّلَامُ عَلَى خَاتَمِ الأَنْبِيَاءِ وَالمُرْسَلِينَ

ABDULLAH II IBN AL-HUSSEIN

Foreword

The world is at a crossroads today. A tiny minority of Muslims seems to be bent on hijacking the religion of Islam—which comprises about a quarter of the world's population—and bringing it into perpetual conflict with the rest of the world. They are doing this in three main ways. Firstly, through distorting and subverting the teachings of Islam by misunderstanding and thus misinterpreting Islamic scripture. Secondly, by attacking and brutalizing Muslims and trying to terrorize them into joining them. Thirdly, by terrorizing and killing as many non-Muslims as publicly and viciously as they can in order to provoke an overreaction that targets or stigmatizes *all* Muslims, so that more Muslims will in turn join their cause. With God's help, they will not succeed.

In addition to the necessary hard power strategies, the thing that Muslims and non-Muslim alike need most is to have a clearer understanding of Islam as it always was and as it should be. Then, they need to understand how Islam is being distorted and abused, and why this distortion and abuse is spreading. This book, *A Thinking Person's Guide to Islam* aims to explain all of this.

The author is my first cousin, HRH Prince Ghazi bin Muhammad, an Islamic scholar who also currently serves as my Chief Advisor for Religious and Cultural Affairs. I believe Ghazi is unique in having both a PhD from the world's leading Islamic University, the Azhar, and another PhD from one of the Western world's leading universities—Cambridge University, in Great Britain. Ghazi also has long practical experience in both Islamic and interfaith affairs, both in Jordan and internationally. On the Islamic side he has been extremely helpful—and has been personally proactive in—highly successful projects such as the 2004 CE Amman Message (and especially its 'Three Articles'); Altafsir.com (the largest online Qur'anic Commentary website); FreeIslamicCalligraphy.com and W.I.S.E. University in Jordan. On the interfaith side he has been instrumental in setting up the Baptism Site of Jesus Christ ☙ at the River Jordan, and the 2007 CE *A Common Word* initiative, and provided invaluable assistance in establishing the 2010 CE UN World Interfaith Harmony Week.

In 1706 CE, in his *Thoughts on Various Subjects*, Jonathan Swift wrote 'We have just enough religion to make us hate, but not enough to make us love one another.' Sadly, this still seems to be true today so I hope that this book will, to a certain extent, help to rectify this.

ABDULLAH II IBN AL-HUSSEIN

About the Author

~

H.R.H. Prince Ghazi bin Muhammad bin Talal of Jordan (b. 1966 CE) was educated at Harrow School, UK; received his BA Summa cum Laude from Princeton University, NJ, USA; his first PhD from Trinity College, Cambridge University, UK, and his second PhD from Al-Azhar University, Cairo, Egypt. He is a Professor of Islamic Philosophy and his book *Love in the Holy Qur'an* has been widely acclaimed, has gone into ten editions and has been translated into a number of languages. He also serves as Chief Advisor for Religious and Cultural Affairs to H.M. King Abdullah II ibn Al-Hussein of Jordan.

Acknowledgements

This text has been read and improved by a number of excellent editors and outstanding scholars—I wish to thank them and I pray God reward them. Needless to say, any remaining errors are my own—and I pray God forgive me.

A Note on Translation

The translations herein, unless otherwise stated, are generally my own—or have been adjusted so much that I cannot attribute them to anyone else. With the Qur'an, I have relied primarily on the Royal Aal al-Bayt translation (see: www.Altafsir.com) but adjusted it on occasion by selecting phrases from the many different good English translations. I avoided translating a verse or passage entirely anew myself, out of fear of making a mistake.

Introduction

~

Muslims nowadays are constantly having to explain what Islam is not. A tiny minority of Muslims have fundamentally misunderstood Islam and are grossly misrepresenting it. Because of their actions, very few non-Muslims understand the real difference between Islam as it has always been and as it is in the Qur'an, and the distorted perversions of Islam today. What follows is an attempt to positively say what Islam actually is — and always was — as well as what it is not.

Over 12 chapters, 12 verses from the Qur'an are taken as a starting point for 12 critical issues. There are Arabic calligraphy drawings of each of these verses (available for free at www.FreeIslamicCalligraphy.com), and these are displayed at the start of each chapter to give a small but concrete foretaste of the visual and emotional impact that each verse has on Muslims. These 12 verses are generally not the best-known verses in the Qur'an. There are a lot of books that concentrate on the more famous verses of the Qur'an. Perhaps by focusing on verses that are not so well known, the issues can be discussed in a fresh light. And of course, every single verse in the Qur'an is authoritative and authentic.

This book is written in stand-alone chapters, so that people can read whatever interests them in whatever order they like. That is actually how many people read books nowadays. These chapters are generally quite short with the exception of the chapters on the Qur'an and the *shari'ah* (which have to tackle a lot of misunderstandings). There is also a freestanding annex on the first two years of ISIS (aka 'ISIL' or 'IS' or 'Daesh') which is quite extensive and written for people with an interest in politics or current affairs. There are clearly many other things that could have been mentioned, but that would make the book too long. Although the book touches on some important and perhaps complex ideas, the language is not complicated, and there are quite deliberately no footnotes, endnotes or bibliography. There are a lot of quotes from the Qur'an (presented in italics) and the sayings of the Prophet Muhammad ﷺ—and a number from poetry; this is quite usual in Islamic writings. As Aristotle said (*Poetics*, 1451 b1): '[Great] Poetry is something more scientific and serious than history, because poetry tends to give general truths whereas history gives particular facts'.

The book is intended only as an educated primer on Islam—a brief guide to the religion, its outlook and its counterfeits—for anyone willing to think about it a little bit. Unwillingness to think about things is what Muslims who misunderstand Islam, and non-Muslims who distort it, have in common. That is why the book is called *A Thinking Person's Guide to Islam*.

Chapter 1

WHAT IS RELIGION?

Truly this is in the former scrolls,
(Al-A'la, 87:18)

Humanity has never been able to exist without religion. It is true that some people ignore religion all their lives. During the nineteenth and twentieth centuries—for the first time in history perhaps—certain countries became atheist and others became secular. It is also true that some people wish there were no religion. Today perhaps five per cent of the world is atheist and perhaps another 10 per cent is avowedly irreligious. It is even true that religion—or rather the misuse of religion—has caused a lot of suffering. But it is also true that regimes based on atheistic ideologies like Communism and perhaps Nazism have caused even more suffering when they have been in power, and they have often made 'religions' of their own atheistic philosophies. And it is clear that the vast majority of humanity loves religion and has always done so. At any rate, today (1437 AH/2016 CE) about 85 per cent of the world's population of 7.4 billion people belong to a religion.

Currently, the largest religions in the world are—as they have been for the last thousand years—Christianity and Islam. Christians make up about one third of the world. Muslims make up about one quarter of the world. Together they make up 55 per cent of the world's population. So religion has never gone away, despite the coming of modern science and technology during the last 200 years. And today religion seems to be as powerful as ever in shaping history.

Religion must be a part of human nature. There is obviously an innate and profound human need for it—or at least for faith as such—and it obviously fulfils deep human needs. As Emily Brontë (1818–1848) wrote (in 'No Coward Soul is Mine'):

> No coward soul is mine,
>> No trembler in the world's storm-troubled sphere!
> I see Heaven's glories shine,
>> And Faith shines equal, arming me from Fear.

At any rate, religion is a fact of life, and a fact of history. And since it is not going away any time in the foreseeable future, it is essential for everyone in the world to know what it really is. In what follows, we will examine Islam's view of religion, and thus of itself, based upon the Qur'an and the sayings of the Prophet Muhammad ﷺ (the *hadith*). Islam is the world's last major religion, and so the whole world—Muslim and non-Muslim alike—needs to have a concise and accurate explanation of it.

WHAT DOES THE WORD 'RELIGION' MEAN?

The Arabic word for 'religion' is '*din*'. Its original meaning is 'humility', 'restriction' and 'obedience', and it is related to the word for 'debt' ('*dayn*'). The idea is that we must be humble and constrain ourselves, for we are under God's control. Moreover, we owe a debt to God (for having created us), so religion (*din*) is the natural relationship we have with God.

The English word for 'religion' is now a word whose meaning people argue about. Originally, however, it came from the Latin '*re-ligio*' meaning to 're-tie' or 're-bind'—and hence 'bond'—(between man and heaven). This implies a bond that ties us, or re-ties us, to God.

In short, by definition, a true religion is what 'attaches' human beings to God (and hence to salvation and paradise) according to their inherent relationship with God.

In the Qur'an, God mentions that there is a timeless message in the monotheistic religions. God says:

Truly this is in the former scrolls, | the scrolls of Abraham and Moses. (Al-A'la, 87:18-19)

The 'scrolls of Moses' 🕮 are the Torah—the first five books of the Old Testament, which itself is the first part of the Bible. The 'scrolls of Abraham' 🕮 are lost to us now, or perhaps they were absorbed into the Torah. At any rate, we know that they contained essentially the same message.

What was that message? God describes it in the verses leading up to the ones quoted above. God says:

Successful indeed is he who purifies himself, | and mentions the Name of his Lord and prays. | Nay, but you prefer the life of this world, | whereas the Hereafter is better and more lasting. | Truly this is in the former scrolls, | the scrolls of Abraham and Moses. (Al-A'la, 87:14-19)

So the essential message of monotheistic religion consists of : (1) belief in One God; (2) belief in the afterlife (and hence in judgement); (3) prayer and remembrance of God; and (4) purification of the soul from the ego and evil (and hence virtue). One might say that it consists of a doctrine, a method and the practice of virtue.

~

WHY IS IT IMPORTANT TO KNOW ALL THIS?

It is important to know this because it shows that the purpose of religion is fundamentally to *help* people, morally and spiritually. It is meant to help people in this life and the next. It is meant to be a force for *good*. It is also important to know this because it shows that religion is a 'complete programme' for human life: it has a vision of reality, a plan of action, and embraces all of life. This programme is extremely powerful. Where there is great power, there is also great danger. In other words, religion is supposed to be a great force for good, but for that same reason it can be very dangerous if it is abused. So nothing is more important for human beings than a proper understanding of religion.

~

Chapter 2

WHAT IS ISLAM?

Truly I am God—there is no god except Me.
So worship Me and establish prayer to make
remembrance of Me. (Ta Ha, 20:14)

The word 'Islam' has come to have a number of different meanings, and people get confused between them. First, there is the literal meaning of the word *'islam'* in Arabic. Second, there is the religion of Islam, as it is in principle, according to the Qur'an and the *hadith*. It is what Muslims believe, and should do. It is, as it were, what God and the Prophet Muhammad ﷺ have said and done. Third, there are the civilisation and cultures created over the course of history by the religion of Islam. It is what Muslims have said and done, and are doing—rightly or wrongly. It is important to distinguish between the second and third senses of the word. Otherwise, the religion of Islam gets blamed for things it actually condemns, and the few hijack the reputation of the many.

THE MEANING OF THE WORD 'ISLAM'

The meaning of the word *'islam'* in Arabic is: 'to turn oneself over to; to resign oneself; to listen and submit oneself'. This meaning is indicated perfectly in God's words about Abraham ﷺ:

When his Lord said to him, 'Submit', he said, 'I have submitted to the Lord of the Worlds'. (Al-Baqarah, 2:131)

The root of the word *islam* is the triliteral Arabic root *s-l-m*. *S-l-m* basically means two things: (1) 'to be free of blemish' and hence 'security, safety, well-being'; and (2) 'peace' (*'salam'*). So these two root meanings of *s-l-m* are 'built in' to the very concept of the religion of Islam.

1. The Prophet Muhammad 🕮 alluded to the first meaning (of 'safety') in his definition of what a (true) Muslim is: 'The Muslim is a person from whose tongue and hand *all people* are safe (*salima*).' (*Nasa'i; Ibn Majah; Musnad Ahmad Ibn Hanbal*)

2. The second meaning (of 'peace') is shown by the characteristic greeting of Islam, *'Al-Salam 'alaykum'* ('Peace be upon you'). God says in the Qur'an: . . . *But when you enter houses, salute [with a greeting of Peace] ('sallimu') one another with a greeting from God of blessing and purity. . . (Al-Nur, 24:61)*. Actually, in the Qur'an this is the greeting not only of believers (*Al-Nisa'*, 4:94 et al.); but also of pre-Islamic prophets (*Maryam*, 19:15 et al.); of angels (*Al-Nahl*, 16:32); and of God Himself (*Yasin*, 36:58). It is a greeting that conveys Divine Mercy, for God says in the Qur'an:

And when those who believe in Our revelations come to you, say: 'Peace be unto you!' Your Lord has prescribed for Himself mercy, that whoever of you does evil through ignorance and repents of it afterwards and does right, [for him] lo! He is Forgiving, Merciful. (Al-An'am, 6:54)

'Al-Salam' ('The Peace') is also one of the Names of God in the Qur'an (*Al-Hashr*, 59:23), and paradise is called *'dar al-salam'* ('the abode of peace') in the Qur'an (*Yunus*, 10:25 et al.). The implication here is that *'Muslim'* is someone who has submitted to God and has found (inner) peace (*salam*).

It will be noted that the word *'islam'* is different from the word *'istis-lam'* which means 'giving up; abandoning; capitulating, succumbing'. The linguistic implication of the word *'islam'* is only that the *'Muslim'* (the person who lives *'islam'*) voluntarily gives up his or her will—or rather, ego—to God, and so (a) becomes safe and secure (and others are secure from him or her); and (b) finds (inner) peace. He (or she) *does not* capitulate or lose himself (or herself). On the contrary, he (or she) gains his (or her) (true) self.

ISLAM AS A CIVILISATION

Turning to the history and civilisation of Islam, as is well known, the religion of Islam started in around 610 in Mecca, a town in the western part of Arabia. A noble Arab, descended from Ishmael ﷺ the son of Abraham ﷺ, aged around 40, began to receive revelations from God whilst in solitary retreat. He tried to convey the content of the revelations, but the majority of his people, who practised idolatry, rejected him (initially at least). After 13 years of persecution in Mecca, he ﷺ escaped north to the town of Yathrib (later renamed 'Medina'), where he ﷺ was welcome. This event was known as the *Hijra*, and it marks the beginning of the Islamic calendar. There he set up a new community with the people of Medina and with those Meccans and others who believed his message. The Meccans and their allies pursued him even in Medina and waged war on him there. Ten years later he died. By that time, however, most of Arabia had entered his religion. The revelations he received are known as the *Qur'an*. The man was Muhammad bin 'Abdullah ﷺ. No single person has had a greater influence on the history of the world than he.

The religion brought by the Prophet Muhammad ﷺ was called *Islam*. It was a final restatement of the same monotheistic religions brought by the great prophets of the past. It moulded one of the greatest civilisations in history. Within 100 years it spanned much of the Middle East, Asia and Africa, as well as parts of Europe. For the last 1300 years these areas have more or less remained Muslim, and Muslims today make up about a quarter of the world's population. Islam is the second largest religion in history, and today the fastest growing. It is also the most widely practiced in the world—Muslims being generally more religious than the mass of adherents to other religions.

Until the beginning of the nineteenth century and the influence of modern Western science, Islamic civilisation was moulded primarily by the Qur'an. The first word revealed in the Qur'an was *'iqra!'* ('read' or 'recite') (*Al-'Alaq*, 96:1), so Islamic civilisation became a civilisation of learning. This learning was not just confined to religious sciences. Islamic civilisation preserved, translated and developed the classical learning of the ancient Greeks and others. The Prophet Muhammad ﷺ said: 'Wisdom is the stray camel of the believer—wherever he finds it, he has more right to it' (*Tirmidhi*; *Ibn Majah*). Islamic civilisation also developed—*within a Qur'anic worldview and cosmology*—other forms of knowledge deemed useful or beneficial for human beings. These included: astronomy, mathematics, algebra (itself an Arabic word), medicine, pharmacology, optics, agriculture, biology, geography, chemistry, musicology, poetry, sociology, psychology, history, law and many other disciplines. God says in the Qur'an: . . . *Say [unto them, O Muhammad]: are those who know equal with those who know not? But only people of understanding will pay heed* (*Al-Zumar*, 39:9).

In order to preserve the recitation and understanding of the Qur'an, Islamic civilisation developed sciences such as semantics, etymology, hermeneutics, rhetoric, logic, grammar, vocalization, phonetics, melody, harmony, recitation, writing, calligraphy, manuscript and book-making, and painting and colouring. The resulting treasures are prized possessions in many of the world's great museums. The arts in Islamic civilisation also developed around the Qur'an. There are basically two kinds of fine art in Islam: calligraphy and architecture. The one was developed to 'house' the Qur'an in beautiful writing. The other was developed to 'house' the Qur'an in beautiful recitation and prayer. In other words, it was developed for the construction of mosques. Also, in order to preserve and discern the true sayings of the Prophet Muhammad ﷺ, many sciences of historiography, documentation, literary criticism and biography developed.

Because the Qur'an encouraged law and order, trade, written documentation, hygiene, generosity, frugality, spirituality, and (defensive) war, Islamic civilisation was well-ordered and disciplined, mercantile, organized, clean (there were public baths in every city), full of charitable endowments, simple, spiritual, and yet martial. Because believers were brothers (or sisters) in faith (*Al-Hujurat*, 49:10), Islamic society tended to have no formal social classes. Because all Muslims were in theory at least one community (*Al-Baqarah*, 2:143), there was always (until 1924, and for Sunni Muslims at least) a universal leadership (or caliphate), even if in practice it was often only symbolic, and often contested. Because Muslims had to travel for the *hajj* (the pilgrimage to Mecca), there was a lot of travelling and resettling throughout the Islamic world. Finally, because Islamic civilisation had Arabic as a common language—a *lingua franca*—there was a lot of internal communication, even over long distances (through carrier pigeons, and land and sea relays). In short, Islamic civilisation was learned, orderly, balanced, generally stable and content.

After Napoleon's invasion of the Middle East in 1798 and during the colonial age after it, traditional Islamic civilisation changed forever. Indeed, the world changed forever. Napoleon's armies had marched across the world at the same speed as Alexander the Great's 2,000 years earlier. But the next 200 years saw more change in every way than had taken place during the preceding 6,000 years of human high civilisation. Such changes included: electricity, photography, telegraph, trains and railways factories, machines and mass production, steam-powered ships, heavy weaponry and machine guns, radio, telephones, film, television, cars, planes, atom bombs, rockets, submarines and huge discoveries in every conceivable scientific discipline, especially physics, energy production, agriculture and medicine. These inventions themselves came with modern education, secular political culture, global capitalism, popular culture, Western clothes, fizzy drinks and fast food, pop music and Hollywood films and the globalization of Western sports. By the end of the twentieth century they included: computers, space flight, the internet, robots, superconductors, genetic engineering, ubiquitous pornography, personal computers and satellite communication. The first 15 years of the twenty-first century saw: iPhones; the rise of social media, especially Facebook, Twitter and YouTube, global culture, environmental collapse, drones, high-tech limbs and wearable technology, and countless other things. The point is that because of all this, no matter what Muslims or non-Muslims say, the civilisation of Muslims today is no longer, and cannot ever be again, purely spiritually 'Islamic' in all its contents. It did not arise organically out of the Qur'an and does not only reflect the Islamic concept of 'beneficial knowledge'. The civilisation of Muslims today—for better or worse—is necessarily very much a part of modern global civilisation and technology. Of course, Islamic civilisation was always 'global' in the sense that Muslims spread all over the known world, traded with everyone and exchanged knowledge with everyone, but now Muslims are part of a 'global' civilisation that is not—primarily at least—of their making.

ISLAM AS A RELIGION

In perhaps the most famous and important of all his sayings, the Prophet Muhammad ﷺ defined Islam as a religion to the Archangel Gabriel himself ﷽. This *hadith* is known as '*Hadith Jibril*', 'the saying of Gabriel ﷽'. It was related by the second caliph of Islam, the great 'Umar ibn al-Khattab ﷺ, as follows:

> One day when we were sitting [in Medina] with the messenger of God there came to us a man whose clothes were exceedingly white and whose hair was exceedingly black. There were no signs of travel upon him, but none of us knew him. He sat down knee upon knee opposite the Prophet and placed the palms of his hands on his thighs, saying: 'O Muhammad, tell me what is *Islam*.' The messenger of God answered him saying: 'Islam is to testify that there is no god but God and that Muhammad is God's messenger; to perform the prayer; pay the tithe; fast Ramadan; and make, if you can, the pilgrimage to the Holy House.' He said: 'You have spoken truly,' and we were amazed that having questioned him he should corroborate him. Then he said: 'Tell me what is *Iman* (faith).' He answered: 'To believe in God, and His angels, and His books, and His messengers and the Last Day and to believe that no good or evil comes except by His Providence.' He said: 'You have spoken truly.' Then he said: 'Tell me what is *Ihsan* (excellence; virtue).' He answered: 'To worship God as if you saw Him, for even if you do not see Him, yet He sees you.' He said: 'You have spoken truly'. . . . Then the stranger went away, and I stayed a while after he had gone. The Prophet said to me: 'O 'Umar, do you know the questioner, who he was?' I said: 'God and His messenger know best.' He said: 'It was Gabriel. He came unto you to teach you your religion (*din*).' (*Sahih al-Bukhari*; *Sahih Muslim*)

In short, the whole religion of *Islam* has three 'levels' or 'degrees'—*Islam*; *Iman* (safety, faith—defined by religious scholars as 'acquiescence of the heart'); and *Ihsan* (excellence, virtue, and hence also beautiful behaviour)—but the practice of *Islam* as such has only five 'fundamental pillars'. The Prophet Muhammad ﷺ said:

> Islam was constructed on five [things]: bearing witness that there is no god but God, and that Muhammad is His messenger; maintaining the

prayers; giving tithe (*zakat*); pilgrimage [to Mecca] (*hajj*), and fasting the month of Ramadan. (*Bukhari*)

The only pillar that is unconditional is the Two Testimonies of Faith: to bear witness that '*La ilaha illa Allah, Muhammad rasul Allah*' ('There is no god but God, Muhammad is the messenger of God'). It is *the sine qua non* of Islam. All the other pillars are necessary but depend upon having the health or wealth to be able to carry them out (albeit that the prayer can be performed without moving, if someone is incapacitated). Although there are a lot of rules in Islamic law (*shari'ah*), the Qur'an and the custom (*sunnah*) of the Prophet Muhammad 靊, the Five Pillars of Islam are a sufficient minimum for people as individuals in circumstances of necessity (and especially if someone is sincere and virtuous). The following is related about the Prophet Muhammad 靊:

A man from Najd with unkempt hair came to God's messenger. We heard his loud voice but could not understand what he was saying, until he came near. Then we came to know that he was asking about Islam. God's messenger said: 'You have to offer prayers perfectly five times in a day and night (24 hours).' The man asked: 'Is there any more (praying)?' God's messenger replied, 'No, but if you want to offer the *nawafil* (voluntary) prayers (you can).' God's messenger further said to him: 'You have to observe fasts during the month of Ramadan.' The man asked: 'Is there any more fasting?' God's messenger replied: 'No, but if you want to observe the *nawafil* fasts (you can).' Then God's messenger further said to him: 'You have to pay the *zakat* (tithe).' The man asked: 'Is there anything other than the *zakat* for me to pay?' God's messenger replied: 'No, unless you want to give alms of your own.' And then that man went away saying: 'By God! I will neither do less nor more than this.' God's messenger said, 'If what he says is true, then he will be successful (i.e. he will be granted paradise).' (*Bukhari*)

Iman (faith) has six tenets, (sincerely) believing in: (1) God; (2) angels; (3) revealed scripture; (4) God's messengers; (5) the Day of Judgement; and (6) Divine Providence. *Iman* differs from *Islam* in that whereas *Islam* involves the practice of actions, *Iman* involves a state of believing, and so a state of being. God says:

The Arabs of the desert say: 'We believe (amanna).' Say you [Muhammad]:
'You believe not', but say rather 'we submit (aslamna)', for faith has not yet
entered your hearts. Yet if you obey God and His messenger, He will not with-
hold from you any reward that your deeds deserve. Truly God is Forgiving,
Merciful. (Al-Hujurat, 49:14)

Ihsan means 'virtue' or 'excellence'. Actually, there is no exact English word
for the term. The closest in a European language is perhaps the Ancient
Greek word *aretē*. The triliteral root of the word *'ihsan'* is *h-s-n* which
means 'beauty'. But in Arabic there are two words for beauty: *'jamal'* and
'husn'. *Jamal* is used when there is one beauty or kind of beauty, and *husn*
is used when there is more than one kind of beauty. So *Ihsan* means many
(internal) kinds of beauty and hence, the virtues also of beautiful worship.
Indeed, inner beauty is virtue, excellence and goodness. This necessarily
also includes beautiful treatment of others. Indeed, God loves those who
treat others with goodness—i.e. as well as possible. God says:

And spend in the way of God; and do not cast yourselves by your own hands into
destruction; and do what is good (ahsinu); God loves the virtuous (muhsinin).
(Al-Baqarah, 2:195)

THE INNER MEANING OF THE RITES OF ISLAM

The rites and requirements of *Islam*, *Iman* and *Ihsan* are not random and
they are not arbitrary. They each have a unique inner meaning and they are
all perfectly complementary to each other. They are providentially designed
to engage every part of human beings. Through doing this—through
practising them—human beings are gradually spiritually transformed.

In the Qur'an every person is seen to have a body, an individual soul
(which has an ego and a conscience) and a spirit which God blew into
Adam ﷺ (*Al-Sajdah*, 32:9). Also, the soul has certain obvious faculties
such as intelligence, will, sentiment, speech, imagination and a memory.
In addition to the physical heart that pumps blood around the body,
human beings also have a 'spiritual' heart through which they 'see' or
know spiritual realities. God says: *Have they not travelled through the land*
with hearts to comprehend, or ears to hear? Indeed it is not eyes that are blind,
but the hearts within the breasts (Al-Hajj, 22:46).

So: (1) The inner meaning of the Two Testimonies of Faith is acknowledgement of God. They engage the will and the intelligence and direct them to God. The Prophet Muhammad ﷺ said: 'I bear witness that there is no god but God, and that I am His messenger. No servant [of God] who meets God with these two [testimonies], having no doubt about them, is barred from paradise' (*Muslim*).

(2) The inner meaning of the five daily prayers is attachment to God. They engage the body (through movement) and speech, the imagination and the memory (particularly through reciting the Qur'an in prayer) and direct them to God. The Prophet Muhammad ﷺ said: 'Prayer is the basis of religion. Whoever leaves it has indeed destroyed his religion' (*Bukhari*; *Muslim*). An indivisible part of prayers are 'ablutions' (ritual washing, beforehand). These engage the individual limbs by 'purifying' them. This is meant to detach a person from his (or her) ego and previous sins, and also to engage his (or her) conscience and direct it to God. The Prophet Muhammad ﷺ said: 'Purification is half of faith' (*Muslim*).

(3) The inner meaning of the tithe (obligatory alms) is detachment from the world, and it engages the faculty of sentiment. The Prophet Muhammad ﷺ said: 'Save yourselves from hell by giving even half a date' (*Bukhari*).

(4) The inner meaning of fasting the month of *Ramadan* annually is detachment, and it engages the body and the ego. God says in a 'holy *hadith*' ('*hadith qudsi*'—a *hadith* in which God Himself is the Speaker, but which is transmitted by the Prophet ﷺ): 'All the deeds of a human being are for himself [or herself], but fasting is solely for Me, and I shall reward him [or her] for it' (*Bukhari*; *Muslim*).

(5) The inner meaning of pilgrimage to the Ka'bah in Mecca is the return to one's own (spiritual) heart and to God. The Ka'bah is the mysterious black-shrouded cubic structure at the centre of Mecca. It is called 'the house of God' ('*bayt Allah*') in the *hadith* (*Muslim*). It was the first house of prayer on earth (Qur'an, *Aal 'Imran*, 3:96) and the Angels and then Adam ﷺ had performed pilgrimage to it (Bayhaqi, *Sunan al-Kubra*). It was later built up higher by Abraham ﷺ and Ishmael ﷺ (Qur'an, *Al-Baqarah*, 2:127). It is an outward and macrocosmic symbol of the (spiritual) heart. Perhaps this explains why the Prophet Muhammad ﷺ said: 'Sound *hajj* has no reward except paradise' (*Bukhari*; *Muslim*).

As regards faith (*Iman*), its seat is in the heart. We cited God's words: *... for faith has not yet entered your hearts ...* (*Al-Hujurat*, 49:14). It involves a change of the soul for the better. The Prophet Muhammad ﷺ said: '*The believer is likeable, and there is no good in someone who likes no one and who no one likes*' (*Ahmad*).

Also, in more than fifty passages in the Qur'an, the phrase 'those who believe' ('*alladhina amanu*') is immediately followed by the phrase 'do good works' ('*amilu al-salihat*'). In other words, when the soul is changed by faith, this should lead to good works. That is its inner meaning. Indeed, Prophet Muhammad ﷺ tied the definition of the (true) belief (*Iman*) to the linguistic root of the word '*Iman*' as 'safety', saying: '*The believer is he [or she] whom [all] people trust with their lives and their property*' (*Nasa'i; Ahmad; Ibn Majah; Al-Mustadrak li 'l-Hakim*).

Finally, the inner meaning of *Ihsan* (excellence; virtue) — 'To worship God as if you saw Him' — is clearly complete spiritual transformation. God says in the Qur'an:

> *And who is better (ahsan) in religion than he who submits his purpose to God and is virtuous (muhsin)?...* (*Al-Nisa'*, 4:125)

In summary, each of the rites and requirements of *Islam, Iman* and *Ihsan* is like a carefully-constructed piece of a jigsaw puzzle, which has its own unique place. When it is assembled properly it reflects a complete picture of human beings, body, soul and spirit, as they should be when they are morally and spiritually transformed.

Islam is made for human beings as they are in themselves as individuals. It is based simply on people's primordial nature. That is why it is not bound by time or place. That is also why it has no clergy and no castes, and is not restricted to particular countries, nations or races. It seeks to make people better, wherever they are, and whatever time they have been born into.

∼

In the Qur'an, God speaks to Moses ﷺ in the sacred valley of *Tuwa*, saying:

> *Truly I am God — there is no god except Me. So worship Me and establish prayer to make remembrance of Me.* (*Ta Ha*, 20:14)

In fact, these words represent the essence of Islam. They summarize the rites and requirements of *Islam*, *Iman* and *Ihsan* perfectly:

'*There is no god except Me*': the Unity of God, as we will see later, is the essential doctrine of Islam. So these words, said to God's messenger Moses 🕮, exactly prefigure the Two Testimonies of Faith: that *there is no god but God, and Muhammad is the messenger of God*.

'*Truly I am God*': the emphasis on '*truly*' implies the necessity of real faith (*Iman*) in God. They are words of the Qur'an — echoing the Bible — so this implies faith in God's messengers, revealed scriptures, and the angels who brought them. It is interesting to note also that only God can truly say 'I am' in an absolute sense, since human beings and other creatures did not always exist, are always changing, and will not exist forever. This implies faith in the Last Day and also in Divine Providence.

'*So worship Me*': this implies the four other pillars of Islam (prayer, tithe, fasting and pilgrimage), for they are all acts of 'worship' in the larger sense of the word.

'*And establish prayer to make remembrance of Me*': this clearly implies *Ihsan* (excellence; virtue), 'To worship God as if you saw Him'. It also emphasizes prayer, the second pillar of Islam.

In this way, the whole of *Islam*, *Iman* and *Ihsan* are wonderfully summarized in a single short verse in the Qur'an. This shows the unity and simplicity of the religion of Islam.

∼

This verse, spoken to Moses 🕮, brings up another essential point. This point is that Islam is not fundamentally a new religion, and does not claim to be. God says to the Prophet Muhammad 🕮 in the Qur'an: *Say: 'I am not a novelty among the messengers. . .'* (*Al-Ahqaf*, 46:9). Monotheism was the religion of all God's messengers. God says in the Qur'an: *And We did not send any messenger before you but We revealed to him that, 'There is no god except Me, so worship Me'.* (*Al-Anbiya'*, 21:25). Islam is merely a restatement of Abrahamic monotheism, and Abraham 🕮 was someone who submitted himself totally to the One God (as were the other prophets). This is precisely the true meaning of the term '*Muslim*'. God says in the Qur'an: *No; Abraham in truth was not a Jew, neither a Christian, but he was an upright Muslim, and he was never of the idolaters. (Aal 'Imran, 3:67).* Consequently, Muslims believe in all God's revealed books in their original form. God says:

> *Say, 'We believe in God, and that which has been revealed to us, and that which has been revealed to Abraham and Ishmael, and Isaac and Jacob, and the Tribes; and in that which was given to Moses and Jesus, and the prophets, from their Lord; we make no division between any of them; and to Him we submit.' | Whoever desires a religion other than Islam, it shall not be accepted from him and in the Hereafter he shall be among the losers. (Aal 'Imran, 3:84–85)*

In one sense, Islam is exclusive, because it is religion as such. God says: *Indeed, religion with God is Islam (Aal 'Imran, 3:19).* In another sense—and also because it is religion as such—Islam is inclusive, and those who practice it with faith will have their reward, no matter what other people say. God says:

> *It is not [according to] your hopes, nor the hopes of the People of the Scripture. Whoever does evil will be requited for it; and he will not find apart from God any friend or helper. | And whoever does good deeds, whether male or female, and is a believer will enter into paradise, and not be wronged, as much as the dint in a date-stone. (Al-Nisa', 4:123–4)*

∽

WHY IS IT IMPORTANT TO KNOW ALL THIS?

It is important to know all of this for a number of different, but very important, reasons.

1. This is what Islam actually *is*, in principle. The point of this book is to explain what Islam is, and everyone in the world should know what the religion of a quarter of the world is.

2. Islam is not a nation state; it is not a group of countries; it is not a region of the world; it is not a tribe or a group of tribes, and it is not a race. In fact, Muslims are arguably the only people in the history of the world—until the twentieth century—who have not discriminated on the basis of race. This is because God says in the Qur'an:

O humankind! We have indeed created you from a male and a female, and made you nations and tribes that you may come to know one another. Truly the noblest of you in the sight of God is the most God-fearing among you. Truly God is Knower, Aware. (Al-Hujurat, 49:13)

Moreover, the Prophet Muhammad ﷺ said (and this was perhaps the first time in history that anyone made such a statement and laid down this principle so clearly):

O People, verily your Lord is One, and your father [Adam ﷺ] is one. No Arab is superior to a non-Arab, and no non-Arab is superior to an Arab—and no white person is superior to a black person, and no black person is superior to a white person—except through piety. (*Ahmad*)

So Islam is a universal religion that does not distinguish between colour, race, nation or region. It is not limited by space and not outdated by time. It is not contradicted by science, and not made obsolete by technology. It is here to stay, everywhere.

3. Islam is intelligible. Anyone can understand it. It is not a random collection of artificial rituals from seventh-century Arabia. Rather, it is a complete, holistic and interlocking programme for human beings, bodily, morally and spiritually. It appeals to everyone as they are, and tries to guide them to everything they can be, in their souls and in their hearts, before God, right here, right now.

4. Islam is an offer for forgiveness and a plan for salvation. The Prophet Muhammad ﷺ said: 'God has forbidden hell to whoever says: *"La ilaha illa Allah"* (*there is no god but God*) desiring God's Countenance' (*Bukhari*). This seems to imply that people can just say these words with a vague good will, and then every bad thing they have done—or will do—will not come back to them at some point. It seems to imply that agreeing mentally to a logical or theological truth is all that is required, and that we can carry on being ourselves and doing whatever we please, no matter what effect it has on others or on ourselves. In fact, this is not the case at all, at least not for immediate salvation after death. There is no concept of purgatory as such in Islam, but there is a concept of believers having to face their own unatoned-for major sins—and suffering for them—before they are ultimately forgiven by God. Moreover, the stipulation 'Desiring

God's Countenance' means that people have to be utterly sincere. Being utterly sincere means that they have to do certain things. These things bring about moral and spiritual transformation. And that is the key point here: being *Muslim* requires *a change of soul*. The soul has to change for the better—or spend its life trying. In the Qur'an, Moses 🙏 says: *'I will not give up until I reach the place where the two seas meet, even if I spend ages'* (*Al-Kahf*, 18:61).

~

Chapter 3

'WHO IS YOUR LORD?'

He said, 'So who is your Lord, O Moses?' | He said,
'Our Lord is He Who gave to everything its [particular]
creation and then guided [it]'. (Ta Ha, 20:49–50)

In a verbal confrontation with the Prophet Moses 🕊 in the Qur'an,
Pharaoh asks:

. . . So who is your Lord, O Moses? (Ta Ha, 20:49)

That is to say, 'Who is God?'—the greatest question of all. It is a challenge—and a trap—for Moses 🕊. Of course, the question is meant by
Pharaoh as a trick question. By saying *'who'*, Pharaoh assumes that God
is a person. But God is not a person. He is in Himself Transcendent, and
thus unlike and totally different from any *thing* or person in existence.
God says about Himself: *. . . There is nothing like Him . . . (Al-Shura, 42:11).*

But God also has 'Names'. He describes these Names through revela-
tion. Immediately before this story in the Qur'an, God says: *God—there
is no god save Him. To Him belong the Most Beautiful Names (Ta Ha, 20:8).*
These Names tell people something about His qualities. The Prophet
Muhammad 🕊 mentioned two slightly different collections of 99 of these
Names in two famous sayings (in *Tirmidhi* and in *Ibn Majah*), but in the
Qur'an there are a total of around 150 of these Names, in various forms.

There are also another 70 Names mentioned by the Prophet Muhammad ﷺ, but not mentioned in the Qur'an (making a total of 220 Divine Names in the Qur'an and the sayings of the Prophet ﷺ). They include such Names as: 'the Forgiving'—'*Al-Ghafūr*', 'the All-Knowing'—'*Al-'Alīm*', and 'the Mighty'—'*Al-'Azīz*'. They say something about what sort of God He is, and what He does. So Pharaoh's question was also daring Moses ﷺ to show that he had received a real revelation. He was daring Moses ﷺ to prove that he really knew God's qualities. Moses ﷺ answers as follows:

> He said, '*Our Lord is He Who gave to everything its [particular] creation and then guided [it].*' (*Ta Ha*, 20:50)

This short answer is unexpected, and unusual. Yet it is one of the most perfect and profound theological truths ever spoken. It points to mercy and love as the 'most essential' qualities of God. And it defines what mercy and love are. It even contains the secret of existence.

How exactly does it define mercy and love? What are mercy and love, actually? We will discuss this in what follows.

MERCY

The Arabic name for God is simply '*Allāh*'. But in the Qur'an, this Name is equivalent to another of His Names, '*Al-Raḥmān*', which means 'the All-Merciful' or 'the Compassionate'. God says: *Say: 'Invoke God or invoke the Compassionate One; whichever you invoke, to Him belong the Most Beautiful Names'. . .* (*Al-Isra'*, 17:110). This means that Mercy is of God's Essence. God actually says: . . . *Your Lord has inscribed mercy on His Self . . .* (*Al-An'am*, 6:54). The Prophet Muhammad ﷺ said: 'When God created creation, He wrote in a place with Himself above His throne, "Truly, My mercy is greater than My anger." ' (*Bukhari*; *Muslim*).

God's mercy encompasses everything. He says: . . . *My mercy embraces all things . . .* (*Al-A'raf*, 7:156). It underlies God's gifts to all things. God says: *To each do We bestow—both these and those—the gift of your Lord; and the gift of your Lord is not restricted* (*Al-Isra'*, 17:20). It underlies creation itself. God created human beings *out of* His mercy. He says: *The Compassionate One | has taught the Qur'an. | He created man, | teaching him [coherent] speech.* (*Al-Raḥmān*, 55:1–4).

Mercy underlies the Qur'an. One hundred and thirteen of the 114 chapters of the Qur'an begin with the phrase *'In the Name of God, the Compassionate, the Merciful'* (*'Bism Illah al-Rahman al-Rahim'*). From this it could be inferred that the Qur'an (and Islam) is over 99% about mercy and less than 1% about retributive justice (though this too is really a mercy). The exception is the ninth chapter of the Qur'an (*Surat al-Tawbah*) which describes fighting and just war, but even this 'missing' phrase 'reappears' later in (*Surat al-Naml*, 27:30) being, as it were, 'delayed', but not withheld.

Mercy can be delayed, but it is not restricted or withheld. Mercy means to give something out of compassion and goodness. The Prophet Muhammad's 🕊 'premier saying' in terms of importance (*'al-hadith al-awwal'*), traditionally transmitted to the students of Islamic studies first is:

> The merciful ones receive mercy from the Merciful One. Show mercy to all on earth, and you shall be shown mercy from the One in the heavens. (*Tirmidhi*)

LOVE

Mercy is a kind of love, but love is a special kind of mercy. The Loving (*Al-Wadud*) is also one of the Names of God in the Qur'an: *And He is the Forgiving, the Loving. | Possessor of the Throne, the Glorious.* (*Al-Buruj*, 85:14–15). God's 'throne' is all of creation, and *His footstool embraces the heavens and the earth . . .* (*Al-Baqarah*, 2:255). So whereas God gives His mercy to 'things', He gives His love to totalities, that is, 'wholes'—to creation as a whole. Mercy means a partial gift. Love means a total gift. Mercy means a gift of something. Love means a gift of oneself. As William Blake wrote (in his *Songs of Experience* in 1794):

> Love seeketh not itself to please,
>   Nor for itself hath any care,
> But for another gives its ease,
>   And builds a heaven in hell's despair.

Or as Jalal al-Din Rumi (d. 672/1273) wrote (*Mathnawi*, I, l. 2246):

> To give their wealth is fitting for the rich
>   the lover's gift's to give the soul itself.

Accordingly, when people are merciful, they are kind to each other, or to animals or even plants. But when they truly love someone or something, they give their time; they give everything they have and they give all of themselves. Falling in love with another person romantically can also lead to this kind of love. Christina Rossetti (d. 1894) eloquently witnesses this kind of love precisely (in her sonnet, 'I loved you first: but afterwards your love'):

> For verily love knows not 'mine' or 'thine';
>> With separate 'I' and 'thou' free love has done,
> For one is both and both are one in love:
>> Rich love knows nought of 'thine that is not mine';
> Both have the strength and both the length thereof,
>> Both of us, of the love which makes us one.

So romantic love can become an extremely powerful kind of love, and can even be spiritually beneficial. Nur al-Din Jami (817–897 /1414–1492) wrote:

> You may try a hundred things, but [ultimately] only love will release you from your ego. So never flee from love — not even love in an earthly guise — for it prepares you for love of the Real. (*Yusuf and Zulaikhah*, Prologue)

Nevertheless, whilst people's love for each other can be extremely powerful, it is not the greatest kind of love. The greatest love human beings can have is for God, not for each other. God says in the Qur'an:

> *Yet there be people who take to themselves rivals besides God, loving them as God is loved; but those who believe love God more ardently . . . . (Al-Baqarah, 2:165)*

Many people feel love for others very intensely. Few people know love for God that is as intense as the one described above. So how can we understand it? To understand it, we have to know what love *is*, not merely what love *does*.

Love is a sentiment and so there is something about it that is beyond words. But Prophet Muhammad ﷺ said: 'God is Beautiful, and He loves beauty' (*Muslim*). This means that true love is love of beauty. And the function of beauty is precisely to attract its lover towards it, with ease.

God says in the Qur'an: *As for him who gives and fears [God], | and affirms beauty (al-husna) | We will surely smooth towards ease* (*Al-Layl*, 92: 5–7).

Now there are two kinds of beauty: outer beauty and inner beauty. Outer beauty is beauty of form. Inner beauty is beauty of soul. The Prophet Muhammad ﷺ also said: 'God does not look at your forms and possessions, but He looks at your hearts and your deeds' (*Muslim*). This means that inner beauty is far more important than outer beauty, which is always changing anyway. This explains why, in the Qur'an, there are eight categories of 'inwardly beautiful' people whom God says that He loves (especially).

These eight categories consist of different kinds of virtues, which is to say then that virtue is nothing other than inner beauty and beauty of the soul. Specifically, they are: (1) 'Those who rely' (on God) ('*al-mutaw-akkilin*' or '*al-mutawakkilun*') (*Aal 'Imran*, 3:159); (2) 'Those who cleanse themselves' ('*al-mutatahhirin*') or 'purify themselves' ('*al-muttahhirin*') (*Al-Baqarah*, 2:222; *Al-Tawbah*, 9:108); (3) 'Those who repent' ('*al-tawwabin*') (*Al-Baqarah*, 2:222); (4) The just' ('*al-muqsitin*') (*Al-Ma'idah*, 5:42; *Al-Hujurat*, 49:9; *Al-Mumtahanah*, 60:8); (5) 'Those who fight for His cause in ranks, as if they were a solid structure' ('*al-ladhina yuqati-luna fi sabilihi saffan ka'annahum bunyanun marsus*') (*Al-Saff*, 61:4); (6) 'The patient' ('*al-sabirin*') (*Aal 'Imran*, 3:146); (7) 'The God-fearing' ('*al-muttaqin*') (*Aal 'Imran*, 3:76; *Al-Tawbah*, 9:4; *Al-Tawbah*, 9:7); and (8) 'The virtuous' ('*al-muhsinin*') (*Al-Baqarah*, 2:195; *Aal 'Imran*, 3:134; *Aal 'Imran*, 3:148; *Al-Ma'idah*, 5:13; *Al-Ma'idah*, 5:93).

All of these eight groups are categories of inner beauty, because it is inner beauty that God loves in particular. Love can thus be understood as *love of beauty* (of various kinds), exactly as the Prophet Muhammad ﷺ said, remembering that love also means *a gift of self* towards that beauty.

With romantic and conjugal love, people love other people for their outer and their inner beauty taken together. They love them, body and soul. Outer beauty is the most immediately attractive, but without a lovely personality there will only be lust and not love, or at least love will not endure. This is natural and normal. But both outer beauty and even human virtue are limited in the end. However, God's Beauty is not limited. God's Beauty is infinite, and his Qualities are perfect and beautiful. Gods says: *And to God belong the Most Beautiful Names—so invoke Him by them. . . . (Al-A'raf,* 7:180). So God's Beauty is incomparably greater than human beauty. This is what explains why: *those who believe love God more ardently . . . . (Al-Baqarah,* 2:165).

~

Hatred can also be a powerful human emotion. It can consume people entirely, and sometimes it does. Robert Frost (d. 1963) wrote (in his poem 'Fire and Ice'):

> Some say the world will end in fire,
>   Some say in ice.
> From what I've tasted of desire
>   I hold with those who favor fire.
> But if it had to perish twice,
>   I think I know enough of hate
> To say that for destruction ice
>   Is also great
> And would suffice.

But hatred can never be as powerful as love. This is because hatred is not a Divine Quality. Nowhere in the Qur'an does it say that God hates anyone. Nowhere in the Qur'an or the sayings of the Prophet ﷺ is hatred a Quality belonging to God. It is true that God says in the Qur'an that *'the evil of'* certain acts is odious to Him *(Al-Isra',* 17:38), and that He 'does not love' *('la yuhibb')* certain kinds of evil-doers and sinners (see my book, *Love in the Holy Qur'an,* Islamic Texts Society, Cambridge). But He never says that He hates anyone as such. To 'not love' is not the same as 'to hate'. 'To hate' is negative; to 'not love' is merely neutral. Besides, God only says that He 'does not love' certain people *in so far as* they are evil-doers of various kinds, but not *in themselves,* as individuals, or as people. Perhaps there is a great lesson here: that people must hate evil acts and not the people that do them. They must hate 'the sin' and not 'the sinner'. God says:

> *It may be that God will bring about between you and those of them with whom you are at enmity, affection. For God is Powerful, and God is Forgiving,*

*Merciful. | God does not forbid you in regard to those who did not wage war
against you on account of religion and did not expel you from your homes, that
you should treat them kindly and deal with them justly. Assuredly God loves
the just.* (*Al-Mumtahanah*, 60:7–8)

~

When Moses 🌸 said: '*Our Lord is He Who gave to everything its [particular]
creation and then guided [it]*' (*Ta Ha*, 20:50), he was identifying God by
His Mercy and His Love. People did not create themselves. God created
them. So they are in need of Him: *O mankind! You are the ones who are in
need of God. And God, He is the Self-Sufficient, the Praised* (*Fatir*, 35:15). God
gave them their existence and being, their *[particular] creation.* That was
His first great gift to them: He gave them their own 'selves'. It was a free
gift of mercy. Then He guided them to Him, and made Himself known
to them. That was God's second great gift to them. It was a gift of love.
That is what Moses 🌸 was saying to Pharaoh, in answer to his question
'*who is your Lord?*': that God is known by two essential qualities: mercy
and love. Moses 🌸 was answering Pharaoh that God is not a 'who', but
His mercy and His love reveal Him most.

~

WHY IS IT IMPORTANT TO KNOW ALL THIS?

First, this is important to know because it is deeply reassuring. As we will
later see, it explains why God created the world. It also means that love
and mercy are the most essential of all qualities. They are the principles
of all things. They are the true purpose of God's actions and they should
be the true purpose of human actions. They are the reason for religion,
particularly Islam. God says: . . . *Now there has come unto you a clear proof
from your Lord, a guidance and a mercy . . . .* (*Al-An'am*, 6:157). Knowing
that love and mercy are the purpose and essence of all things reassures us
that the world is not senseless, and that the truth is beautiful.

Second, it is important to know that love and mercy are the most
essential of all qualities because this gives us love and mercy as the crite-

ria by which we know whether things are right or wrong—or if they are true. That is what Moses ﷺ was telling Pharaoh. And that is what the Qur'an is telling us.

~

It seems that this was not enough for Pharaoh. He also asks the question: *'And what is "the Lord of the Worlds?"'* He and Moses ﷺ have the following exchange:

> *Pharaoh said, 'And what is "the Lord of the Worlds?"' | He said, 'The Lord of the heavens and the earth and all that is between them—if you have certainty'. | He said to those who were around him, 'Did you not hear?!' | He said, 'Your Lord and the Lord of your forefathers'. | He said, 'Truly this messenger of yours sent to you is a madman!' | He said, 'The Lord of the east and the west and all that is between them—if you comprehend'. (Al-Shu'ara, 26:23–28)*

This question is also wrong. The word 'what' does not apply to God. God is not a 'thing'. But since Pharaoh's question implies a 'thing', Moses ﷺ answers on the basis of every 'thing'. Created things are God's acts. Creation is an act of God. God's Names and Qualities are manifested in His acts. God says: *So behold the effects of God's mercy, how He revives the earth after it has died. . . . (Al-Rum, 30:50).* For some people, God's acts are revealed through created things. For others, they are veiled by them. This is what Moses ﷺ tells Pharaoh.

First, Moses ﷺ says: *The Lord of the heavens and the earth and all that is between them.* In other words, God's existence is shown by the existence of things—*if you have certainty.* And their infinite variety comes from and reflects His infinitude. Then Moses ﷺ says: *Your Lord and the Lord of your forefathers.* In other words, the transience of time itself shows God's eternity, and the form of transient people reveals an eternal Lord and Creator. Finally, Moses ﷺ says: *The Lord of the east and the west and all that is between them.* In other words, space shows God's limitlessness. So we have 'things' and people, time and space, and all of them 'point to' God. They comprise every 'thing' and so *everything* 'points to' God. Two are 'contents', and two are 'containers'. The contents are things, made of matter and form—and people. The containers are time and space. Matter reveals God's existence. Form reveals God's infinitude. People reveal a Creator and Lord. Time reveals God's eternity. Space reveals God's limitlessness—*if you comprehend*. This time Moses ﷺ gives Pharaoh a perfect philosophical and metaphysical answer to his question. It is a perfect philosophical answer because it in fact contains all of what would later be known as the 'classical proofs of God' (the 'cosmological', 'teleological' and 'ontological' proofs of God). More importantly, it is a perfect metaphysical answer because through it Moses ﷺ is trying to get Pharaoh to contemplate and intuit something of the Reality of God from the metaphysical 'transparency' of things. But still Pharaoh does not get it. He says Moses ﷺ is *a madman,* but in reality he is the real madman. Everything in creation reflects God's Qualities. By reflecting God's Existence through their existence, they proclaim His glory. By reflecting God's mercy and love, they praise Him, because to praise something is to show its goodness. God says:

> *The seven heavens and the earth and all that is therein proclaim His glory. And there is not a thing, but glorifies Him in praise; but you do not understand their glorification. Lo! He is Forbearing, Forgiving. (Al-Isra', 17:44)*

~

We have seen that all of this is beneficial—and indeed, beautiful—to know. But what do all Muslims *have to know* about God? What is the minimum they need to know? We have already mentioned the tenets of *Islam* and the articles of *Iman* (faith). These are what are *necessary* for salvation in Islam. But what is the minimum of doctrine (*'aqidah*) they have to know about God? Do they have to know any theology and philosophy?

There are a number of formulations that Muslim scholars have written as summaries of doctrine. One of the earliest is Imam Abu Hanifah's (d. 150/767) *Al-Fiqh al-Akbar.* The definitive formulations of orthodox (Qur'an-derived) Sunni theology (as opposed to what is called Mu'tazili theology and rationalism) were set out by Abul Hasan al-Ash'ari (d. 324/935) and Abu Mansur al-Maturidi (d. 333/944). Perhaps the best known and widely-read short summaries of Islamic theology are Imam Abu Ja'far al-Tahawi's (d. 321/933) *'Aqida Tahawiyyah* (*'Tahawi's Creed'*) and Burhan al-Din al-Laqani's (d. 1041/1631) didactic poem *Jawharat al-Tawhid* ('*The Jewel of Monotheism*'). Typically they lay out theological doctrines like:

> God Most High is One, not in terms of number but in that He has no partner. He neither begets nor is begotten. There is none that is equal or comparable to Him. He is not like anything in His creation and nothing in His creation is like Him. . . . (Abu Hanifah, *Al-Fiqh al-Akbar*, 1.)

The first generations of Muslims obviously did not all have these formulations. Rather they became necessary through contact with other religions—particularly Christianity—which challenged Muslims with theological questions. Two statements initially served as doctrine. One is a negation. The other is an affirmation. The negation is simply the first and greatest creed of Islam. It is bearing witness (*Shahadah*) that there is *no god but God* ('*la ilaha illa Allah*'). God says: *Know, then, that there is no god except God* (*Muhammad*, 47:19). The second is one of the shortest chapters ('*surahs*') in the Qur'an. It is simply: *Say: He, God, is One. | God, the Eternally Sufficient unto Himself | He did not beget, nor was He begotten. | And none is like unto Him.* (*Al-Ikhlas*, 112:1–4). These are what the first Muslims regarded as their doctrine. And in fact, together they make up a perfect summary of Islamic doctrine. They contain the essence and principles of Islamic theology and philosophy. They contain the minimum that every Muslim needs to know about God. Islam explains the greatest complexities for those who seek to understand them fully, but also makes the most profound and complex truths easy to understand, and accessible to everyone. All human beings need to know the Truth, so Islam makes the Truth simple.

~

Chapter 4

WHY DID GOD CREATE PEOPLE?

*Except those on whom your Lord has mercy; and
for this He created them.... (Hud, 11:119)*

Why did God create people? That is the next great question. It contains
the secret of existence. As we saw earlier, God created people *out of* His
Mercy. Did He create them *for* His Mercy as well?

We mentioned that almost every chapter in the Qur'an begins with
the phrase: *In the Name of God, the Compassionate, the Merciful* ('*Bism Illah
al-Rahman al-Rahim*'). What is the difference between the Divine Name
'*the Compassionate*' ('*Al-Rahman*'), and the Divine Name '*the Merciful*'
('*Al-Rahim*')? Some Islamic scholars have said that '*the Compassionate*'
refers to God as He is in Himself. They say that '*the Merciful*' refers to God
as He is towards people and living things. This implies that God created
people and living things so that He would be '*the Merciful*' towards them.

The verse cited above seems to say the same thing. Together with the
verse before it, it says:

> *Had your Lord willed, He would have made mankind one community, but
> they continue to differ, / except those on whom your Lord has mercy; and for
> this He created them.... (Hud, 11:118–119)*

Islamic scholars say that the word '*this*' refers to '*mercy*'. That was the opinion of the Prophet's ﷺ cousin Ibn 'Abbas ؓ. In other words, God created people for His Mercy.

This corresponds with God's words elsewhere in the Qur'an: *And I did not create the jinn and mankind except that they may worship Me* (*Al-Dhariyat*, 51:56). Referring to this verse, Ibn 'Abbas ؓ said: 'Worshipping God' means 'knowing Him'. 'Worshipping God', however, is more inclusive than 'knowing God' because it includes those with blind faith but little knowledge of God. It also means that God created us to love Him: how can anyone worship God without loving Him? Or for that matter, how can anyone know God without loving Him? And loving God means also being loved by Him. God promises: . . . *God will assuredly bring a people whom He loves and who love Him* . . . (*Al-Ma'idah*, 5:54).

In other words, God created us to worship Him and to love Him, so that He could be merciful to us and love us. For love—as discussed in Chapter 3—is a special kind of mercy. Indeed, over the course of Islamic history, countless Muslims have loved God beyond words. And countless others have tried to express their love with words, such as Abu Firas al-Hamadani's (d. 357/968) poem:

> If You be sweet, let life run bitterly;
>> If You be pleased, let men be wroth with me;
> If all things are well between me and Thee,
>> Let all between me and the world ruins be.
> If I have love from Thee, all is easy
>> All things on the earth, are just earth to me.

Other scholars say that the word '*this*' (in *Hud*, 11:119, as cited above) refers to the word '*differ*'. In other words, that God created people to be free to 'differ'. That is to say then that God created people to be free. Now spiritual freedom is freedom from the ego and its desires, not freedom to follow the ego and its desires. But spiritual freedom also requires freedom to make a moral choice, and that means freedom to make the wrong choice.

Both opinions are true. That is the opinion of the majority of Islamic scholars. God created people *for* His Mercy (and Love). That is our purpose in life, and that is the *secret of existence*. But God also created people free. They are free even to reject His Mercy (and Love). They are free to reject goodness. They are free to be evil. For freedom to exist, evil has to be possible. Evil can be an unfortunate by-product of freedom.

KINDNESS TO OTHERS

Worshipping God necessarily means love of other people as well. God says:

> Truly the Compassionate One will give love to those who believe and do righteous deeds. (*Maryam*, 19:96)

And the Prophet Muhammad ﷺ said:

> By Him in whose hand is my soul, you shall not enter paradise until you have faith, and you will not have faith until you love each other. (*Muslim*)

So worshipping God is not just prayer. People were not created to live in isolation, praying and fasting. There is no bitter isolationism in Islam. People were created to be kind to others as part of their love for God. Indeed, God says:

> It is not piety that you turn your faces to the East and to the West [in prayer]. True piety is [that of] the one who believes in God and the Last Day and the angels and the Book and the prophets, and who gives of his wealth, for the love of Him, to kinsmen and orphans and the needy and the traveller and beggars, and for slaves, and who observes prayer and pays the alms, and those who fulfil their covenant when they have engaged in a covenant, those who endure with fortitude misfortune, hardship, and peril are the ones who are truthful, and these are the ones who are God-fearing. (*Al-Baqarah*, 2:177)

In other words, people cannot spend their whole time praying and fasting and yet be unkind or impatient towards others. There is no real piety without kindness towards others. On the contrary, true piety *necessarily involves* virtue and kindness towards others—all others—because kindness is the fruit and result of love. The Prophet Muhammad ﷺ said: 'God is Kind, and God loves kindness ('*rifq*') in all things.' (*Bukhari*; *Muslim*). We were also created to be kind to each other. We were created to be kind to our neighbours, no matter who they are or what their faith. That is also part of the secret of existence.

~

WHY IS IT IMPORTANT TO KNOW ALL THIS?

It is important to know that God created us for Mercy, because it reassures and helps us to love God and place our hopes in Him. It helps us to trust God, and this in itself helps us to be content with our lives. It also leads to many of our problems being resolved with unforeseen help from God. God says:

> . . . *And whoever fears God, He will make a way out for him; | and He will provide for him from whence he never expected. And whoever puts his trust in God, He will suffice him. Indeed God fulfils His command. Indeed God has ordained for everything a measure.* (Al-Talaq, 65:2–3)

It is also important to know that God created us for mercy, because it reminds us to practise mercy. Without practising mercy we cannot expect to receive mercy, neither from God nor from other people. The Prophet Muhammad ﷺ said: 'God does not have mercy on someone who is not merciful towards other people' (*Bukhari*; *Muslim*). Similarly, it is important to know that God created us for love, so that we may love others. And it is important to know that love necessarily means kindness to others, so that others may benefit from our love and so that it does not just remain an abstract emotion.

Finally, it is important to know that God created us for mercy, so that we take things easy on ourselves — and others — particularly in matters of religion. Many religious people — and even some scholars — make religion unnecessarily difficult. They adopt a Pharisaic attitude and overemphasize endless details and religious rules. They make things more complicated than they need to be. Sometimes they make things practically impossible. They give the impression that God is 'out to get us', just waiting for people to make a mistake so that He can punish them. They seem to believe that the more severe and extreme people are in their religious attitudes, the more pious they are. They even look down on people who look for the easiest valid way in religion, and privately consider themselves better than them. But God created us for Mercy, and this means that He wants us to make things easy for us. God actually says: . . . *God desires ease for you and does not desire difficulty for you* . . . (*Al-Baqarah*, 2:185). Similarly, the Prophet Muhammad ﷺ said: 'Make things easy; do not make things difficult; give good news; do not drive people away.' (*Bukhari*; *Muslim*). And it is recorded that the Prophet ﷺ himself 'always took the easiest of two options, as long as it was not sinful' (*Bukhari*; *Muslim*).

~

Chapter 5

WHAT ARE HEAVEN AND HELL?

'Read your book! This day your soul suffices as
your own reckoner'. (Al-Isra', 17:14)

Human life as such arose from a juncture of God's spirit with the human body. The body is originally from clay, but then reproduces via seminal fluids. God says that He is the One,

> *Who perfected everything that He created. And He began the creation of man from clay, | then He made his progeny from an extract of a base fluid, | then He proportioned him, and breathed into him of His spirit. And He made for you hearing, and sight and hearts. Little thanks do you give. (Al-Sajdah, 32:7–9)*

But then, through death, God separates our souls from our bodies and from the world, and returns us to the spirit, and to Him:

> *. . . As He brought you into being, so you will return. (Al-A'raf, 7:29)*

The various stages of the afterlife, and heaven and hell, are what happens during this return, after death. There are many descriptions of heaven and hell in the Qur'an. How they feel is described. Heaven is beautiful and wonderful. Hell is terrifying and painful. But what are they?

Heaven and hell are true. They are objective realities. God says:

The day it comes, no soul shall speak except by His permission. Some of them will be wretched, and some happy. | The wretched ones will be in the fire, sighing and groaning. | Remaining there as long as the heavens and the earth endure, unless your Lord wills. Your Lord does what He wills. | And as for those who are happy they shall be in paradise, remaining there for as long as the heavens and the earth endure, unless your Lord wills — uninterrupted giving. (Hud, 11:105-108)

But they are subjective realities as well. People judge themselves in the afterlife. God says:

And We have fastened every person's destiny on to his neck and We shall bring forth for him, on the Day of Resurrection, a book which he will find wide open. | 'Read your book! This day your soul suffices as your own reckoner.' (Al-Isra', 17:13-14)

So heaven and hell are both objective and subjective. The Day of Judgement is real and objective. But there is also self-judgement. There is also an inner judgement. This is the judgement of the conscience. In the Qur'an, the conscience is called the *'self-reproaching soul'*. That is what a conscience does: it reproaches you. God swears by the human conscience and the Day of Judgement together:

Nay! I swear by the Day of Resurrection. | And, nay, I swear by the (self-) reproaching soul. (Al-Qiyamah, 75:1-2)

So heaven and hell are the result not only of God's judgement, but of people's own self-judgement. They are internal and external. Indeed, as suggested by these two verses, there is a certain correspondence between the Day of Resurrection and its various events, and the human soul and its various faculties (and its individual state), the Day of Resurrection perhaps being a kind of universal conscience, and the human conscience perhaps being a kind of individual Day of Resurrection. The Prophet Muhammad's ﷺ son-in-law and first cousin, 'Ali ؑ bin Abi Talib said (in his collected *Diwan* of poems):

Your medicine is inside you — but you are not patient
    Your medicine is inside you — but you cannot feel it.

Do you think you are just a small body?
    Within you the larger world is enfolded.

However, in the next life, what is inside of us becomes external. God says:

So whoever does an atom's weight of good shall see it, | and whoever does an atom's weight of evil shall see it. (Al-Zalzalah, 99:7-8)

In fact, in the Qur'an, God never says that He will reward or punish people with *the equivalent ('mithl')* of what they have done. He always says that He will reward or punish them *with ('bi')* what they have done, or simply 'what they have done' will punish them. For example, God says:

And every soul will be paid in full what it did, and He is best aware of what they do. (Al-Zumar, 39:70)

Our deeds—whose record is contained inside of us—*themselves* come back to us. All that we have done in our lives—good or bad—returns to us and brings us happiness or misery. For these deeds have become part of us. So all that we have done to others we will experience ourselves. God says: . . . *And they shall find all that they did present. . . (Al-Kahf, 18:49)*. So in fact, all that we do to other people we actually are doing to ourselves, even though we may not see it that way yet, or fully understand it now. God says:

And fear a day wherein you shall be returned to God, and every soul shall be paid in full what it has earned; and they shall not be wronged. (Al-Baqarah, 2:281)

~

When we judge ourselves during our lifetimes, we tend to let ourselves off the hook. We take it easy on ourselves. We know when we have done something wrong, but we make excuses for ourselves. God says:

Truly man has insight into his [own] soul, | despite all the excuses he may put forward. (Al-Qiyamah, 75:14-15)

Sometimes we behave as if we do not really believe in an afterlife. And when we think of the afterlife, we tell ourselves: 'Don't worry; it will be fine'. In the Qur'an, there is the story of a man who thinks to himself:

Moreover, I do not think that the Hour will ever come; and even if I am indeed returned to my Lord, I will find something even better there'. (*Al-Kahf*, 18:36)

But in fact we do not judge ourselves like that in the next life. Since death is the separation of the soul from the body and from the world, in the next life the distractions of the body and the world are removed. Then everyone sees with spiritual insight. That inner sight is piercing:

You were indeed oblivious of this: So [now] We have removed from you your covering, and so your sight on this day is sharp. (*Qaf*, 50:22)

The truth will come out in the end. The afterlife is true. And the afterlife is the world of truth. God says:

They will ask you, 'Is it true?' Say, Aye, by my Lord, it is true, and you cannot escape it. (*Yunus*, 10:53)

~

Having said all this, it is important in Islam not to despair, but to remember that God created people for His Mercy. This means He forgives—and loves to forgive—people's innumerable sins, when they repent of them. God says:

Say [that God declares]: 'O My servants who have harmed their souls by their own excess, do not despair of God's mercy. Truly God forgives all sins. Truly He is the Forgiving, the Merciful. | And turn to your Lord and submit to Him, before the punishment overtakes you, and you can no longer be helped'. (*Al-Zumar*, 39:53–54)

So God can erase all the things people regret, and He—and only He—can free people of all the wrong things they have done. The following poem was said to have been found under the pillow of the great Islamic scholar Abu Hamid al-Ghazali (d. 505/1111) after he died:

Say to my brothers when they see me dead,
  And weep for me, lamenting me in sadness:

'Think you I am this corpse you are to bury?
 I swear to God, this dead one is not I.
I am in the Spirit, and this my body
 Was my dwelling, my garment for a time.
I am a treasure: hidden I was beneath
 This talisman of dust, wherein I suffered.
I am a pearl; a shell imprisoned me,
 But leaving it, all trials I have left.
I am a bird, and this was once my cage;
 But I have flown, leave it as a token.
I praise God who has set me free, and made
 For me a dwelling in the heavenly heights.
Ere now I was a dead man in your midst,
 But I have come to life, and shed my shroud.'

~

WHY IS IT IMPORTANT TO KNOW ALL THIS?

It is important to know that God wants to forgive us when we sin and that He created us for His Mercy. This is the basis of human hope. Without this knowledge and the hope it brings, human existence—now and in the future—would be a bleak reality with an even bleaker future.

However, it is important to know that judgement is objective, because then we know we cannot change it, cannot talk or plead our way out of it, and cannot escape it. We need to fear it a bit. This kind of fear is positive, not negative. It helps us to not be lazy and to constantly do our best to avoid it. We do our best by doing good deeds, and by always being kind to others. This kind of fear is like pain in the body: it may hurt a bit, but it teaches us how not to damage ourselves, and ultimately, how to save ourselves. That is surely the providential reason for physical pain, and for fear.

Equally, it is important to know that judgement is also subjective, because then we know that we cannot blame God for our own justly-deserved punishment. God created us for Mercy, but He also created us free. Through His Mercy, He warned us and guided us, so we cannot blame

Him for our own freely-chosen evil deeds. We cannot justify our actions by blaming them on God's Omnipotence. Indeed, God says:

> And the idolaters say, 'Had God willed we would not have worshipped anything but Him, nor would our fathers. We would not have declared anything sacred besides Him'. Those before them said the same. But are messengers obliged to do anything other than convey [their message] clearly? (Al-Nahl, 16:35)

It is not God who is responsible for the bad things we have done to others. We have done them freely. And we received fair warning not to do them. So whatever punishment we receive, it is entirely our own fault. We must take responsibility for ourselves. It is us—not God—who have wronged ourselves. God says: *Indeed God does not wrong people in any way, but people wrong themselves* (Yunus, 10:44).

∼

Chapter 6

WHAT IS THE QUR'AN?

Now We have sent down [as revelation] to you,
a Book in which there is your remembrance.
Will you not understand? (Al-Anbiya', 21:10)

THE QUR'AN AS REVELATION

The Qur'an is the most misunderstood part of Islam—by Muslims and non-Muslims alike, so we have to discuss it in a little detail. What is the Qur'an, precisely? The Qur'an uses around 55 different terms to describe itself (such as: *huda* [guidance]; *rahmah* [mercy]; *bushra* [good tidings]; *nur* [light], and *dhikr* [remembrance]). But in essence it is a direct revelation in Arabic from God to the Prophet Muhammad ﷺ, or from God through the Archangel Gabriel ﷺ to the Prophet Muhammad ﷺ. As will later be seen, it was transmitted, without doubt or uncertainty, via 'massive testimony', and written (in Arabic, of course) in book-form (the *'Mushaf'*). Its origin, purpose, form and reception are eloquently summarized in the following verses:

> *A revelation from the Compassionate, the Merciful. | A Book whose signs have been set out in detail as an Arabic Qur'an for a people who have knowledge, | [containing] good tidings and a warning. But most of them turn away so that they do not hear. (Fussilat, 41:2–4)*

But it is not God's only revelation in history. God says in the Qur'an:

He has revealed to you the Book, by the truth, confirming what was before it, and He revealed the Torah and the Gospel. (Aal 'Imran, 3:3)

This means that Islam acknowledges and respects previous revelations and the religions they brought. Perhaps that is why God calls the Qur'an 'a protector' of previous revelations:

And We have revealed to you the Book with the truth confirming the Book that was before it and as a protector over it. So judge between them, according to what God has revealed, and do not follow their whims away from the truth that has come to you. To every one of you, We have appointed a [divine] law and a way. If God had willed, He would have made you one community, but that He may try you in what He has given to you. So vie with one another in good works; to God you shall all return, and He will then inform you of that in which you differed. (Al-Ma'idah, 5:49)

THE ARABIC LANGUAGE

Before turning to the Qur'an itself, it is important to clarify a few things about the language in which it was revealed: Classical Arabic. Indeed, its being 'a protector' of previous revelations was in a sense only possible because the Arabic language itself was 'protected'. Contrary to what most people think, ancient languages tend to be more precise and complex than modern languages. They reflect times when the full energy and genius of human thought were poured into oral culture. Plato suggests (in his *Cratylus*) that the roots and meanings of words in Ancient Greek mysteriously *are* one with the things named, and reflect them exactly in their sound, form and behaviour.

This is certainly true for Classical Arabic. They are not—as, Ferdinand de Saussure (1857–1913) argued with reference to modern languages—arbitrary conventions, momentary 'fixes' of 'the signifier and the signified'. Rather, each of the 28 letters of the Arabic language, through its own sound, nature, way of pronunciation with the breath, and even its written form, is associated with one of the 28 lunar mansions, and so also with all that is 'sublunary': that is, everything in the world. These in turn reflect a specific set of archetypal meanings, and ultimately one or more of the Divine Names (the Qur'an's use of certain 'isolated letters' at the beginning of certain chapters may have something to do with this idea). Individual letters bring their meanings to the words they make up. So for example (amongst other meanings in each case), *alif* brings the idea of transcendence, of activity, of primacy, of masculinity to a word; *ba* brings passivity, receptivity; *ha* brings breath or the idea of air; *ra* brings movement; *qaf* brings power; *kaf* brings weakness or thinness; *mim* brings an end, death, and so on. Words then have definite meanings intelligibly constructed from archetypal sounds. This also means that words with the same root letters in different orders often have similar meanings, or that the change of one letter brings an appropriate change in meaning. For example, *'ka-la-ma'* is the triliteral root of the word *'kalimah'* meaning 'word'. When the *'ka'* is changed to a (heavier) *'qaf'*, we get *'qa-la-ma'*, the root of the word for 'pen' (*'qalam'*). A pen writes words down, making them 'heavier' and more permanent, and this is precisely in accordance with the nature of the letter *qaf*. In short, in Arabic (and perhaps in other ancient languages) words are mysteriously mirrors of the things named, not random and ever-changing two-sided tags, and these meanings come from the sound and nature of the letters of their alphabets.

Now there are traditionally said to be two kinds of Arabs: the 'Arabized Arabs' (*al-'Arab al-musta'riba*) who were Arabs of the Northern part of the Arabian Peninsula, and the 'Pure Arabs' (*al-'Arab al-'ariba*) who were Arabs of the Southern part of the Arabian Peninsula. The 'Arabized Arabs' trace their lineage back to Ishmael (*'Isma'il'* in Arabic) ﷺ the son of Abraham ﷺ (c. 2100 BCE), while the 'Pure Arabs' trace their lineage back to an even earlier ancestry, that of Qahtan. In the Book of Genesis, Qahtan is called 'Joktan', and he is the son of Eber, the son of Salah, the son of Arphaxad, the son of Shem, the son of Noah (Nuh ﷺ) (Genesis 10:21-30). Likewise according to the Book of Genesis, Abraham's ﷺ great grandfather's grandfather, Peleg, was the brother of Joktan.

The first person to speak Arabic, according to Al-Tabari's monumental *History*, was 'Ya'rub' (*Jobab* in Genesis) the son of Qahtan (the son of Eber, the son of Salah, the son of Arphaxad, the son of Shem). This seems to be confirmed in the Book of Genesis (10:31) which states that at the time of Joktan's sons: *'These were the sons of Shem, according to their families, according to their languages, in their lands, according to their nations'.*

Arabic is of the same family of Semitic languages as ancient Akkadian, Aramaic and Hebrew. And since Arabic is at least three generations older than Abraham ﷺ himself, Muslim scholars have argued that it is the oldest of all extant languages. The immemorial age of Arabic is seen in its retention of very ancient forms like the dual, irregular plurals, the double plural (as for example in: man [*rajul*]; men [*rijal*]; groups of men [*rijalat*]) and the 'energetic' form. Even other ancient languages like Hebrew have lost most of these forms. There is also historical evidence for this: there are Arabic inscriptions in Hasa (in the Eastern Arabian Desert) that date back to 800 BCE, and there are written Akkadian accounts of Arabs going back to at least 853 BCE. Further back, there are even etchings of Arabic proto-scripts found in the Sinai Desert (on display in the Cairo Museum) written by Arab workers working in the Pharaonic turquoise mines in the Sinai dating back to 1850 BCE (see: T.A. Ismail, *Classical Arabic as the Ancestor of Indo-European Languages*). There is no reason to suppose that Arabic is not around the same age as arguably the oldest known language, Akkadian (which goes back to at least 2500 BCE). Indeed, according to the Book of Genesis (10:1-10), the city of 'Accad' was founded by Nimrod, the son of Cush, the son of Ham, the son of Noah ﷺ, who was therefore Joktan's second cousin and so also, presumably, his contemporary (at least according to the Bible's genealogy—albeit that the *Midrash Rabbah* and the Qur'anic Commentary tradition have Nimrod living until the time of Abraham ﷺ).

The preservation of the Arabic language is historically explained by the fact that for millennia, the Bedouin speakers of Arabic were isolated from other more powerful civilisations in the virtually impregnable deserts of Arabia, as if on an island. There, they jealously and proudly guarded their oral culture and so guarded the purity of the Arabic language. Indeed, the Arabs prided themselves on the nobility and inner wealth of meaning of the Arabic language. This can easily be seen in the beautiful but complex language and enormous vocabulary of pre-Islamic *Jahiliyyah* poetry, especially the famous *Mu'allaqat* poems. These were poems which were awarded annual prizes for being the finest displays of Arabic in Arabia and then granted the supreme honour of being hung on the Ka'bah in Mecca (hence the name *'mu'allaqat'* which literally means 'hung' or 'suspended'). Now the Prophet Muhammad 🕮 was, as mentioned, a direct descendant of Ishmael 🕮, but being from Mecca, where the poetry competitions were held, it is easy to see how he 🕮 and his tribe, the Quraysh, spoke the finest and purest Arabic in Arabia.

It remains to be said that the Qur'an tells us that the original language of human beings was originally a Revelation—or at least an inspiration— from God to Adam 🕮. God says in the Qur'an:

And He taught Adam the names, all of them; then He presented them to the angels and said, 'Now tell Me the names of these if you speak truly'. | They said, 'Glory be to You! We know not except what You have taught us. Surely You are the Knower, Wise'. | He said, 'Adam, tell them their names'; And when he had told them their names He said, 'Did I not tell you that I know the Unseen in the heavens and the earth?, And I know what you reveal and what you were hiding. (Al-Baqarah, 2:31-33)

From this, we may assume that Arabic—and perhaps other ancient languages—were inspired languages. How else can its words 'be one' with what they name, in their 'sound, form and behaviour'? And how else could Arabic be the receptacle of a Revelation? After all, God says:

Had We sent down this Qur'an upon a mountain, you would have surely seen it humbled, rent asunder by the fear of God. And such similitudes do We strike for mankind, that perhaps they may reflect. (Al-Hadid, 59:21)

THE ARABIC LANGUAGE OF THE QUR'AN

It is difficult to describe the Arabic of the Qur'an in another language because it is so unique. It is unique even in its use of Arabic, and differs not only from pre-Islamic poetry (of which there is a large corpus of least 20,000 verses extant) but also from the Arabic in *hadith* literature. The Arabic of the Qur'an also predates Arabic translations of the Bible (the first of these dating back to the ninth century CE) and differs greatly from all Biblical languages and translations. Nevertheless, a few things can be conveyed about it.

The first is that the Arabic of the Qur'an is not pronounced or read in the same way that colloquial Arabic is. To start with, Arabic has 28 letters (with three minor vowels which are not written as letters), and each of these must emerge from 17 different points of the throat, mouth, tongue, teeth, lips and nose. There is a whole science dedicated to this (*Makharij al-huruf*) which even children are taught, and it is this science that keeps the classical language pronounced the same way everywhere despite the passage of time.

Qur'anic Arabic is also read differently from standard written Arabic; there are special rules of pronunciation for different letters and different combinations of letters and words. This way of reading (*tajwid* or *tartil*) is ordained in the very first revelations of the Qur'an (see: *Al-Muzammil*, 73:4), and was the practice of the Prophet ﷺ and his Companions. The rules are too complicated to explain here so it suffices to say that their effect is to allow continuity in the reading of the text so that the words flow together more mellifluously, to avoid jarring clashes of sound, and to emphasize the more sonorous and majestic syllables. Though there are natural variations in the speed of verses, every letter and every word is pronounced relatively slowly, and completely distinctly. There are also deliberate periodic pauses whose silence not only allow the reciter to breathe (independently from the recitation), but also allow for penetration into the depths of the listener's or reader's heart. Finally, there is the mandatory prolongation of the long vowels following certain letter combinations or positions—particularly the *alif* (the 'a' sound)—which infuses the sound of the Qur'an with, as it were, constant cries for transcendence. Consequently, the overall effect of Qur'anic recitation is said to be one of melancholy (*huzn*), but not out of melancholy from the loss of a worldly thing. Rather, it is out of longing for God, for His Beautiful Attributes, for the sacred and for paradise. Moreover, the sound of the language in itself is not only beautiful, but also majestic. It has splendour with dignity and gravity. It is full of poetic flow, cadence and rhythm without artifice, jingle or levity. It is calm but with immense power. For these reasons perhaps, just listening to the language of the Qur'an, *without even understanding the words*—and 80% of Muslims cannot speak Arabic—is said to be one of the four purposes of its revelation (the other three being to purify people's souls, to teach them scripture and to teach them wisdom). God says in the Qur'an:

Truly God was gracious to the believers when He sent to them a messenger
from among their own to recite to them His verses, and to purify them, and
to teach them the Book, and wisdom, though before, they were in clear error.
(Aal 'Imran, 3:164)

The second thing to be said about the language of the Qur'an is that it
is filled with natural imagery—particularly desert, mountain, sky and sea
imagery—and indeed seems to contain and recapture their beauty within
its very words and in the magnificent sweeps of certain of its verses and
chapters. But then, after being lyrical, it constantly comes back to simple
and practical subjects and language. Ultimately, it uses the mundane and
worldly as a bridge to the sublime and heavenly, and this too induces
longing and yearning.

Third, there is a lot of variety in the forms of the language of the
Qur'an, despite the relatively easy vocabulary (it contains only 1810 root
words out of a total possible 70,000 Arabic root words). Some verses are
extremely short (the shortest composed of words—55:1—being one word
long; and the shortest composed of 'isolated letters'—20:1 and 36:1; and
40:1; 41:1; 42:1; 43:1; 44:1; 45:1 and 46:1—being two letters long), and
some are very long (the longest—2:282—being a whole page of fifteen
lines long). Equally, some chapters are very short (the shortest are three
verses, or two lines, long); some are very long (the longest, *Al-Baqarah*,
is almost 50 pages long). The verses of some chapters are all more or less
the same length. In other cases they differ considerably in length. Some
chapters end with the same rhyme and letter in every single verse (for
example, the fifty-fourth chapter, *Surat al-Qamar*, which has 55 verses all
ending with the letter 'r' preceded by a consonant). Other chapters use
many different rhymes. Some verses flow lyrically, and others are more
measured and staccato. And it is full of bewildering shifts between the two,
each of which has its secret meaning and deliberate effect. Despite these
shifts, however, there is always a clear consistency of tone and texture, so
that it is unmistakably all part of the same, one 'book'.

Moreover, whilst the whole Qur'an is clearly a unity, each chapter
('*surah*') often contains words and linguistic constructs that are unique to
it and not found in any other chapter in the Qur'an. Indeed, the word
'*surah*' is related to the Arabic word '*sur*' meaning 'wall', which suggests

a unique and particular identity to each chapter of the Qur'an. This can even be seen at the level of individual verses (*'ayat'*). The name for an individual Qur'anic verse is *'aya'* (meaning 'miracle'). This suggests that each verse is a miracle in itself. For although there are some verses that are repeated in the Qur'an, these actually mean, or refer to, different things in their different contexts. On the other hand, there are verses which are clearly unique and miraculous, in language and content, each in their own way. For example, the famous Throne Verse, *Ayat al-Kursi*, (*Al-Baqarah*, 2:255)—the 'greatest verse' in the Qur'an according to a *hadith* in *Muslim*—is a completely unique and systematic verse about God's Attributes. Equally, the Verse of Light, *Ayat al-Nur*, (*Al-Nur*, 24:35) is a unique parable about God's Light. In a different way, the Verse of Debt, *Ayat al-Dayn*, (*Al-Baqarah*, 2:282) is a uniquely long but complete instruction, in practical language, on how to record debts harmoniously. There are many other examples like this.

Fourth, the language itself is *in a clear Arabic tongue* (*Al-Shu'ara*, 26:195). Despite its internal variety of form, it uses a relatively small number of different words that are not complicated (even if they do not mean exactly the same thing as in modern colloquial Arabic). Moreover, the Qur'an is *easy to remember* (*Al-Qamar*, 54: 17; 22; 32 and 40)—the proof of this being the millions of Muslims who have memorized it. It has simple, powerful rhetoric, all the more powerful because it is so naturally and effortlessly compelling. It contains neologisms (i.e. new Arabic words—like the different names for heaven and hell) and new verbal forms as well as many new linguistic constructs (a number of which are mentioned only once in the whole Qur'an), but which are immediately intelligible and made totally clear by their contexts. It is pithily eloquent: it does not use more terms than necessary to say something, so that there is no redundancy. It has near-synonyms that reveal important distinctions without tautology. In other words, when the Qur'an seems to be repeating the same thing with slightly different words, it is actually not. Rather, it is making some subtle but precise distinctions. This is made stunningly clear in books like Al-Hakim al-Tirmidhi's (d. 320/932) *The Book of Impossibility of Tautology* (*Kitab Man'a al-Taraduff*) and his *The Book of Explaining the Differences* (*Kitab Bayan al-Farq*), and Al-Raghib al-Isfahani's (d. 502/1109) *Lexicon of Qur'anic Terms* (*Mu'jam Mufradat Alfazh al-Qur'an*).

Fifth, as regards the clarity of the language of the Qur'an, it will be noted that the Qur'an occasionally—but impeccably—uses the language of reason and even logical induction, particularly as regards proofs of God's existence (e.g. 27:60-5; 29:61; 52:35-37; 10:31-36) or His Unity (e.g. 17:40-43; 23:84-91), but this language flows naturally and is never belaboured like that of formal logic and syllogism, so that unless the reader or listener is a trained logician, he or she will never be aware that rigorous logical proofs are being used in the Qur'an.

Finally, the language of the Qur'an itself echoes the truth of its content. For example, the parables, similes, and metaphors it uses are perfect not only because they correspond exactly to what they name and bring its real essence to light, but because they usually correspond to something within human beings as well. The profoundness, nobility and consistency of its content are also maintained in the depth, dignity and harmony of its tone. On the other hand, its dramatic shifts and sudden turnarounds in style and in the length of its verses reflect the bewildering complexity of the truth and provoke shock and contemplation. Much more could be said here, but it is enough to say that there is something about the language and structure of the Qur'an that reflects the texture and the deep structure of the primordial human soul, or more precisely, spirit. This is necessarily so because the soul is the receptacle of the individual human spirit, and the Qur'an is the expression of the Universal Spirit in the Arabic language. This, incidentally, is the most profound reason why scholars and Qur'anic reciters have traditionally instinctively completely refused to let Qur'anic recitation turn into musical tones and melodies: music affects the soul and its sentiments, whereas the Qur'an aims to awaken the spirit.

All of this explains the direct challenge in the Qur'an—which has never been met—that no one can produce another book like it (17:88; 28:49); or even 10 chapters like it (11:13-14); or ultimately even a single chapter like it (2:23-24; 10:37-38). For the Qur'an is truly unique, not merely in its content—which ... *has been revealed by Him Who knows the secret of the heavens and the earth* ... (*Al-Furqan*, 25:6)—but also in its language. Anyone who really knows Arabic can see this.

It remains to be said that millions of intelligent people willingly and lovingly spend—and over the course of history, have spent—their entire lives learning, reading, reciting and contemplating the Qur'an. Some people read it in its entirety once every three days, and can do this for a hundred years starting in childhood (making it possible to read the Qur'an 10,000 times in a lifetime). Most literate practising Muslims complete it once a month, meaning they read it some 500–700 times in their lifetimes (if they live 70 years or so). If all we have said above were not true, then surely Muslims would get bored with it, but they simply do not. Rather, they find new meaning in it every time they read it, and fall more and more in love with it. This is perhaps the most the unique thing about the Qur'an, and indeed the Prophet Muhammad ﷺ said: 'Those who know cannot get enough of it . . . despite constant repetition, and its wonders never cease' (*Tirmidhi*).

THE OBSTACLES IN READING THE QUR'AN

In addition to the language of the Qur'an, the form of the Qur'an is unique. It differs somewhat from previous revelations—and not just because it is in Arabic. When people (even Muslims) who have never read the Qur'an in their lives, start to read it with concentration, their first reaction is often one of surprise and even confusion. Some people cannot seem to make sense of it at all. This is because there are obstacles to overcome in reading the Qur'an. These obstacles are not difficult to overcome, but it helps to be aware of them.

In fact there are three kinds of obstacles that prevent people from understanding the Qur'an. These are: (1) obstacles in the act of reading; (2) obstacles in the reader; and (3) obstacles in the Qur'anic text itself.

As regards **(1) obstacles in the act of reading**, we should briefly consider the following:

(a) The Qur'an is in Classical Arabic in the dialect of the tribe of Quraysh (notwithstanding a few well-known words of non-Arabic origin). It is not the same as colloquial or Modern Standard Arabic. Because of its linguistic richness it cannot be translated properly (its 'translations' are all only 'interpretations'). Qur'anic Arabic has to be learnt anew even by native Arabic speakers. Nevertheless, this is usually a question of a limited number of Arabic words.

(b) The Qur'an was an oral revelation, set in an oral culture. Without hearing it read aloud according to its own rules of recitation, the reader misses not only the melody of the verses, but also the power and resonance of the words—as well as their inner connections with each other.

(c) Modern education leads people to expect to read simple, short texts which immediately offer up all their information and which are nothing more than they appear. Usually these also have even simpler executive summaries of their important points. But the Qur'an must be read slowly and in depth because the Author is Omniscient and so all the different linguistic possible meanings of the words are pre-intended by the Author. Also it is full of symbols, similes, metaphors, allegories, hints, leads, allusions and internal references. This is perhaps because certain truths cannot be fully conveyed by the surfaces of words alone. Moreover, it is not a short text—600 pages in most Arabic editions—and needs time and patience to even begin to contemplate it. Indeed, most devout Muslims learn it in childhood (anywhere between one to 10 million Muslims know the Qur'an by heart) and spend between 30 minutes and an hour every day of their lives reading it.

(d) The Qur'an is not a 'chronological' or a 'linear' text. The Bible is basically a historical, chronologically-arranged text. It starts with the beginning (the Book of Genesis) and goes right through to the end of the Hebrew Prophets—notwithstanding an interlude of timeless 'wisdom books' (such as the Psalms). Then the New Testament tells the story of Jesus 🕮, then his disciples, and it ends with the Book of Revelation, looking 'forward', as it were. But the Qur'an is not arranged in the order it was revealed and does not refer to events chronologically. It does not seek to tell a history—even a sacred one. Rather, it is atemporal, or at least achronological. So it often returns to the same themes, again and again. Equally, it is not a systematic exposition of philosophy (like Plato's dialogues); nor of morality and theology (like Plotinus's *Enneads*); nor finally of cosmology and logic (like Aristotle's *Metaphysics* and his *Organon*). Rather, it contains different kinds of wisdom scattered throughout, and the reader has to piece them together.

(e) The Qur'an is an *operative* text, not a *speculative* text. Reading it is meant to be *transformative* and *informative*. It has to be approached like a student begging for knowledge, not a film critic passing judgement on a pastime. Without this attitude and intention—different from when reading a normal book—the Qur'an does not transform, or even really, inform. It merely confirms the reader's prejudices. God says: *And indeed We have explained things in various ways in this Qur'an, so that they may remember, but it only increases them in aversion.* (*Al-Isra'*, 17:41)

As regards (2) **obstacles in the reader**, these come from:

(a) The difference in time, place, culture, circumstance, experience and context between the reader and the Qur'anic revelation.

(b) Distraction, 'scatteredness', lack of concentration, wandering imagination, interruption by bodily functions and needs, lack of patience, improper intentions, lack of openness, lack of humility and blindness to spiritual truths, all of which lead to an inability to contemplate the Qur'an and an inability to meditate upon it. Now God calls upon people to 'contemplate' (*'tafakkur fi'*, see: 16:43–44; 59:21; 13:3; 3:190-192) His signs (*'ayat'*) in the Qur'an and 'meditate' upon the Qur'an (*'tadabbur'*, see: 4:82; 23:68; 38:29; 47:24; see also 50:37). The difference between the two is that 'contemplation' (*'tafakkur fi'*) is active (it requires having 'an image in the mind' according to Raghib al-Isfahani's *Mu'jam Mufradat Alfazh al-Qur'an*) whereas as 'meditation' (*'tadabbur'*) is more passive but more profound (*'dubur'* literally means 'the bottom' of something, and therefore *'tadabbur'* means to 'turn one's back', but also to 'get to the back of something'). Nevertheless, both can set off in the heart of the listener either a rainfall of startling and luminous intuitions, or even a kind of internal silent flash of understanding so that he or she instantly understands dozens of things at once with their multiple connections. God says in the Qur'an:

> *Is he whose breast God has opened to Islam, so that he follows a light from his Lord [like he who disbelieves]? So woe to those whose hearts have been hardened against the remembrance of God. Such are in manifest error. | God has revealed the most beautiful of teachings, a Scripture that is consistent and draws comparisons; that causes the skins of those who fear their Lord to quiver; then their skins and their hearts soften to the remembrance of God. That is God's guidance, by which He guides whomever He wishes; and whomever God leads astray, for him there is no guide.* (*Al-Zumar*, 39:22–23)

(c) The demands that the Qur'an makes upon people: the Qur'an urges not only laws but also ethical principles and they can be quite demanding.

So there is bound to be something in the soul that shrinks from these. This is because the ego does not want to be told what to do or leave its 'comfort zone', much less to have to change its ways completely.

Finally, as regards **(3) obstacles in the Qur'anic text itself**, there are providentially a number of these and they take some getting used to. They include:

(a) The constant shifts (in Arabic called '*iltifat*'), not only of subject but also of narrative tone. Even the pronominal narrative voice changes: God sometimes refers to Himself as 'He'; sometimes as 'I'; sometimes as 'We', and sometimes by His Divine Names. God clearly cannot be limited or contained by pronouns or by a single point of view, and each of these shifts contains a secret and a meaning. Sometimes the Qur'an also shifts whom it is talking to: sometimes it is the Prophet, sometimes it is believers, sometimes disbelievers, and sometimes everybody. Each of these shifts draws attention to something new. In so doing it shocks the reader (or listener) out of his or her mental habits in order to show them something about themselves.

(b) The Qur'an at first seems to contain a number of apparent obscurities, repetitions, interrupted sentences, abridgements and ellipses. These too each have certain secrets and meanings that have to be penetrated. They force people to stop and think deeply, and that is perhaps part of the reason they are there. They are like geodes—rocks that look plain from the outside, but once they are cracked open, reveal a pattern of unexpected and beautiful crystals.

(c) There are also a number of things that can seem strange and unlikely to the modern reader. Some of these we have already mentioned (such as the explicit descriptions of the afterlife), and some will be discussed later (such as *shari'ah*, *jihad* and 'the heart'). Some of them seem to reflect the context of seventh century CE Arabia (such as descriptions of the natural desert environment, tales of ancient Arabian and Biblical prophets and even business imagery). The important thing to bear in mind is that the Qur'an seeks to address every possible human mentality, motif and level of education and sophistication—not to mention every spiritually-relevant subject. So it contains something that speaks to every kind of person.

THE SUBJECTS OF THE QUR'AN

What is the Qur'an about? What are the subjects of the Qur'an? According to Abu Hamid al-Ghazali's (d. 505/1111) book *The Jewels of the Qur'an*, the Qur'an's 6,236 verses all deal with one (and some more than one) of only six basic subjects. These six subjects are: (1) God and His Names and Acts (including His creation); (2) spiritual wisdom and the path towards God (especially through remembrance of God); (3) descriptions of the afterlife and the next world; (4) stories of the pre-Islamic prophets, messengers and sages—as well as disbelievers and sinners; (5) arguments for belief and refutations of disbelief; and (6) laws, commandments, prohibitions and prescriptions for life. In fact it is difficult, if not impossible, to find a single verse in the Qur'an that does not go back to one of these subjects. The reason for this, Ghazali says, is that:

> The secret of the Qur'an . . . and its ultimate aim consist in calling people to God. . . . For this reason the *surahs* of the Qur'an and its verses are limited to six types. (Ghazali, *The Jewels of the Qur'an*, 3)

In other words, the Qur'an is focused only on things that are useful to people—whether they understand them or not—in their religion, and also therefore in their spiritual, moral and social lives. Hence its subjects are (1) God; (2) the path to God and its inner reality; (3) the return to God; (4) those who have and those who have not taken the path to God and what happened to them; (5) arguments for the truth of the path to God and refutations of arguments against it, and (6) the outward rules of the path to God. The Qur'an does not provide spiritually useless information. It does not contain useless facts or trivia. It does not stray from its aim. It is always consistent. God says in the Qur'an: *If it had been from other than God surely they would have found therein much inconsistency* (*Al-Nisa'*, 4:82).

THE QUR'AN AS MIRROR

The Qur'an contains an image of human virtue, and so of human spiritual potential. But it also contains and reflects an image of human souls as they generally are. So it reflects their constantly shifting inner states, emotions and internal chatter. It shows people what they cannot see about themselves. This is one of the meanings of the Qur'anic verse:

Now We have sent down [as revelation] to you, a Book in which there is your remembrance. Will you not understand? (Al-Anbiya', 21:10)

According to the great commentary (*Mafatih al-Ghayb*) of Fakhr al-Din al-Razi (d. 606/1209), *'your remembrance'* can mean not only 'your remembrance of God', but also 'your likeness'. In other words, the Qur'an is like a miraculous mirror that shows people what they are; what they can be, and how they can be it. To see clearly in this mirror, the mind and the soul must be still, and ultimately—as will be discussed in Chapter 8—the heart must be pure. God says in the Qur'an: *And to Him belongs all that rests by night or by day . . . . (Al-An'am, 6:13).* Only when people are internally at rest can they meditate upon and understand the Qur'an (as described earlier)—and themselves through the Qur'an—properly. Actually, this is not a new idea. In Psalms 46:10, it is written: *Be still and know that I am God. . . .* Rumi summarizes all of this beautifully as follows (*Mathnawi*, I, l.s 1538–1544):

The Qur'an is (a description of) the states of the prophets,
  (who are) the fishes of the holy sea of (Divine) Majesty.
And if you read and do not accept the Book,
  do you suppose you have (really) seen the prophets and the saints?

But if you are open when you read the stories,
  the bird—your soul—will be distressed in its cage.
The bird that is a prisoner in a cage,
  and does not seek to escape—that is ignorance. . . .

From outside, the voice comes to them, from the spirit,
  saying, 'This is the way of escape for you'.
And so we have escaped from this narrow cage:
  there is no other way of escape from this cage.

THE IMPORTANCE OF THE QUR'AN

It is impossible to overstate the importance of the Qur'an to Muslims and to Islam. Muslims recite the *Fatihah* (the first chapter of the Qur'an) and some other verses from the Qur'an in every single prayer, five times a day, in addition to reading it daily as mentioned. Until the Reformation, Christian laypeople were not allowed to read the Bible directly, and the Bible contains about 807,000 words (623,000 approx. in the Old Testament and 184,000 in the New Testament). The Qur'an is only about 78,000 words or 375,000 characters long (332,795 letters on modern computers). It has only 114 chapters and 6,236 verses, and out of the around 70,000 verbal roots in Classical Arabic it uses only about 1,800 (which makes it easier to read and memorize). Bearing these facts in mind, it will quickly be obvious that the Qur'an is the most read book in history. The Qur'an is also definitely the most memorized book in history: today there are well over a million people who know the Qur'an by heart perfectly and perhaps another 10 million who have learnt it at one point in their lives and know it by heart almost perfectly. In the past, an even higher percentage of Muslims (though there were fewer Muslims in total than there are today) learnt it by heart, as it was the basis of all education and literacy.

Finally, no book in history has had as many serious commentaries as the Qur'an. There are tens of thousands of full length commentaries or explanations of the Qur'an. They look at the Qur'an from different standpoints including: linguistic, legal, historical, theological, philosophical, spiritual, and even scientific (or a mix thereof). Many of these are thousands of pages long. Arguably the most influential and best known Sunni commentaries over the course of history are: (1) *Jami' al-Bayan fi Ta'wil al-Qur'an* (historical) by Muhammad ibn Jarir al-Tabari (d. 310/922); (2) *Ahkam al-Qur'an li 'l-Shafi'i* (legal) by Abu Bakr al-Bayhaqi (d. 458/1066); (3) *Mafatih al-Ghayb* (theological and philosophical) by Fakhr al-Din al-Razi (d. 606/1209); (4) *Tafsir al-Kashshaf* (linguistic) by Mahmud al-Zamakhshari (d. 538/1143); (5) *Al-Jami' li-Ahkam al-Qur'an* (legal) by Muhammad al-Qurtubi (d. 671/1272); and (6) the one-volume 'ready reference' *Tafsir al-Jalalayn* by Jalal al-Din al-Mahalli (d. 864/1459) and Jalal al-Din al-Suyuti (d. 911/1505). As will later be discussed, the two largest branches of Islam are Sunnism and Shi'ism. Probably the most influential Shi'i classical *tafsirs* are (1) the *Tafsir* by 'Ali al-Qummi (d. 307/980); (2) *Al-Tibbyan fi Tafsir al-Qur'an* by Muhammad al-Tusi (d. 459/1067) and (3) *Majma' al-Bayan* by Fadl al-Tabarsi (d. 459/1067). However, there are dozens of others—both Sunni and Shi'i—almost as influential and authoritative as the ones mentioned here. Even in our day, commentaries are still being written. There are even commentaries on

72

the commentaries, and further commentaries on those as well. All this is to say then that no book in history—Divine or human—has been read, recited, thought about, written about, contemplated or memorized as much as the Qur'an. So in these respects, it is the single most important book, not just for Muslims, but in human history in general.

THE INFLUENCE OF THE QUR'AN
ON ISLAMIC THOUGHT

It should already be clear even from this book that the Qur'an determines Muslims' worldview (their 'Weltanschauung'). Equally, it should be evident that the Qur'an says something about everything. God says this in the Qur'an:

> *There is no animal on the earth and no bird that flies with its wings, but they are communities like you. We have neglected nothing in the Book. . . .* (*Al-An'am*, 6:38)

Now the Qur'an is obviously the basis of all the Islamic religious sciences (such as doctrine, theology, sacred law and spiritual practices and ethics). It is also—as already mentioned—the basis of all the Arabic language's linguistic sciences (including—as already mentioned—semantics, etymology, hermeneutics, rhetoric, logic, grammar, vocalization, phonetics, melody, harmony, recitation, writing, calligraphy, manuscript and book-making, and painting and colouring). But what is not so well known is that it is the basis of all Islamic philosophical sciences (such as: psychology, anthropology, sociology, epistemology, cosmology, metaphysics, oneirology, numerology, love, time, logic, cognition and so on). Some people in the modern world even try to relate it to the physical sciences, but this is controversial because scientific knowledge is always developing and changing. So if science is equated with specific interpretations of verses in the Qur'an, and then it changes, this creates a big problem. Finally— as already mentioned—the Qur'an is the basis of Islamic Art, especially calligraphy and architecture. What we have not yet mentioned is that the proper melodious recitation of the Qur'an is a sublime auditory art. It is not music as such, but many people listen to it for the unique beauty of its sound. In fact, in any traffic jam in any Islamic city in the world the likelihood is that you will overhear someone listening to a drawn-out recitation (*'tajwid'*) of the Qur'an by one of the twentieth century's great Egyptian reciters of the Qur'an (such as 'Abd al-Basit 'Abd al-Samad or Mahmoud Hosari or Muhammad Tablawi).

The Qur'an also determines the everyday outlook and attitudes of Muslims. It is the ultimate reference for every axiom, the final word in every discussion, and the channel for every emotion. Indeed, almost every aspect of a Muslim's life is woven with Qur'anic phrases, and so, influenced by it. Muslims use Qur'anic phrases all day every day to an extent that these phrases have become second nature, even for non-Arabic speakers. We have touched on the Qur'anic greeting *'Al-Salamu 'alaykum'*. We should mention also the following ubiquitous Qur'anic sayings in Islamic culture (which are actually also all invocations):

- *'Bism Illah'* (or *'Bism Illah al-Rahman al-Rahim'*)—meaning: 'In the Name of God (or 'In the Name of God, the Compassionate, the Merciful')—said at the beginning of anything.
- *'Al-Hamdulillah'* (or *'Al-HamduLillah Rabb al-'Alamin'*)—meaning: 'Praise be to God' (or 'Praise be to God, Lord of the worlds')—said at the end of anything, and with every joyous thing.
- *'In sha Allah'*—meaning: 'if God wills [it]'—said whenever talking about something in the future tense.
- *'Ma sha Allah'*—meaning: '[this is] what God wills'—said whenever talking about something beautiful.
- *'La quwwata illa Billah'* (or *'la hawla wa la quwata illa Billah'*)—meaning: 'there is no strength save through God' ('there is no power nor strength save through God')—said during moments of powerlessness.
- *'Tawakkalna 'ala Allah'*—meaning: 'we trust in God'—said before going anywhere.
- *'Hasbi Allah'* (or *'Hasbuna Allah wa ni'm al-Wakil'*)—meaning: 'God suffices me' (or 'God suffices us and how fine a Patron')—said to show patience and contentment, or when facing great challenges and odds.
- *'Subhan Allah'*—meaning: 'Glory be to God'—said whenever talking about something astonishing.
- *'Allah Akbar'*—meaning: 'God is [the] Greatest'—said during moments of victory (or when trying to overcome or understand something).

- *'Tabarak Allah'* — meaning; 'God bless', or 'God has blessed' or *'Exalted is God'* (as in Qur'an 25:1 and 67:1 et al.) — said particularly in North Africa to mean that God is the Source of every blessing and good thing.
- *'Inna Lillah wa inna ilayhi raji'un'* — meaning: 'We are God's and we will return to Him' — said in times of calamity or death.
- *'Ya Latif'* — meaning: 'O Gentle One' — said in times of extreme pain or hurt.
- *'A'udhu Billah* (or *'A'udhu Billah min al-shaytan al-rajim'*) — meaning 'I seek refuge in God' (or 'I seek refuge in God from the accursed devil') — said when confronted with something evil or foul.
- *'Allahumma salli 'ala sayyidina Muhammad'* — meaning: 'O God, bless our master Muhammad' — said when trying to calm down (e.g. during anger) or when trying to remember something.
- *'La ilaha illa Allah'* — meaning: 'There is no god but God' — said before death.

In short, the Qur'an is the direct basis of Islamic spiritual life, ethics, knowledge, sciences, language, outlook, social interaction, art and culture.

THE INTERPRETATION OF THE QUR'AN

It is possible to misinterpret any long text in a number of different ways. Through misinterpretation, a text can be made to appear to say the opposite of what it intends to say. For example, let us take William Shakespeare's (d. 1616) longest play, *Hamlet* (which is only half the length of the Qur'an). In it, Hamlet says to Ophelia the important lines: 'Virtue cannot so inoculate our old stock, but we shall relish of it'. Taken out of context — as we have just done — it seems to be saying: 'a leopard cannot change its spots', and so also: 'virtue is an illusion'. What it is actually saying — and in a certain sense it summarizes the whole play — is: 'we need a total change in nature to reverse our original sinfulness'. This is the opposite of what it seems to mean, but it is only clear if we understand its context and the greater scheme of the play.

Let us take another example, this time from the Gospels (the four Gospels together are shorter than the Qur'an). Their overall message of love, peace and otherworldliness is very clear. Nevertheless, someone can easily 'cherry-pick' Jesus's 🕮 words: *I did not come to bring peace but a sword . . .* (Matthew 10:34); *Compel them to come in* (Luke 14:23); and *But bring here those enemies of mine, who did not want me to reign over them, and slay them before me* (Luke 19:27). From these words only, one could conclude that Jesus 🕮 authorized war on the whole world in order to force people into Christianity or else be killed.

The same danger exists with the interpretation of the Qur'an. Let us take what is sometimes called the 'sword verse':

> *Then, when the sacred months have passed, kill the idolaters wherever you find them, and take them, and confine them, and lie in wait for them at every place of ambush. But if they repent, and establish prayer and pay the alms, then leave their way free. God is Forgiving, Merciful. (Al-Tawbah, 9:5)*

This verse gives very clear instructions to kill idolaters in all-out war, after a certain period of warning time has elapsed. However, if one completes the Qur'anic passage in which this verse occurs, then one reads the following verse:

> *Will you not fight a people who broke their oaths and intended to expel the messenger—initiating against you first? Are you afraid of them? God is more worthy of your fear if you are believers. (Al-Tawbah, 9:13)*

This verse makes it clear that the war in question was a defensive war. It was initiated by the idolaters against the Muslims. The idolaters then treacherously broke a truce with the Muslims. Legally and morally speaking, this is a completely different situation. Moreover, the verse refers to a particular case and context and to generalize and extend it beyond its time and context to a different time and context is wrong. So one cannot 'cherry-pick' a verse from a passage, and one has to consider a situation in its full context.

Let us consider an even simpler example to make the point absolutely clear. The Qur'an contains the phrase: *O you who believe, do not come anywhere near to prayer. . . (Al-Nisa', 4:43).* Someone hearing this phrase alone might well conclude: 'Prayers are cancelled; no need to pray!'—a very strange idea for any religion. But actually the phrase is a part of a gradual prohibition on drinking alcohol. The verse goes on to say: *O you who believe, do not come anywhere near to prayer whilst you are drunk, until you know what you are saying. . . . (Al-Nisa', 4:43).* So quoting from the Qur'an arbitrarily or incompletely can lead to completely misunderstanding it.

Happily, the Qur'an itself clearly explains the rules for its own interpretation. God actually promises in the Qur'an: *It is for Us to explain it (Al-Qiyamah, 75:19).* We will not go into these rules in too much detail here, save to say they include the following:

1. As just seen, when looking at any issue, one has to take into consideration *everything* that is said about it in the Qur'an (and in the *hadith*), and not merely 'cherry-pick' the verses we prefer. God says in the Qur'an: '. . . *What, do you believe in part of the Book, and disbelieve in part? . . .' (Al-Baqarah, 2:85).* Elsewhere He warns against '. . . *those who divided the Qur'an into fragments' (Al-Hijr, 15:91).*

2. As we have also seen, the context and the historical causes or 'occasions' for individual revelations (*'asbab al-nuzul'*) must be taken into consideration if applicable. In the Qur'an, God clearly condemns those who take things out of context: '. . . *they pervert words from their contexts; and they have forgotten a portion of what they were reminded of. . .' (Al-Ma'idah, 5:13).*

3. Even before the questions of completeness and context, there is the question of Arabic language. Anyone interpreting the Qur'an must obviously know Classical Arabic as well as the few words of non-Arabic origin that are used in the Qur'an. One must know exactly what Classical Arabic words actually mean, and that some words have more than one meaning, more than one of which (but not necessarily all of which) may be applicable in a given context. God says in the Qur'an: *Ha Mim. | A revelation from the Compassionate, the Merciful. | A Book whose signs have been set out in detail as an Arabic Qur'an for a people who have knowledge (Fussilat, 41:1–3).* One must also know grammar, rhetoric, word tropes (such as: hyperbole, ellipsis, metaphor, metonymy, synecdoche and the like), syntax and, most important, *semantics* (the meaning of the connotations of words—this is known by studying pre-Islamic Arabic poetry) and *etymology* (the study of the origin and root meanings of Arabic words). God says: *He created man | teaching him [clear] communication (Al-Rahman, 55:3–4).*

4. Only about five per cent of the Qur'an's verses pertain to legal rulings. These verses are generally quite clear in meaning. The rest pertain to reality, virtue, wisdom, guidance, earlier prophets, disbelievers, the afterlife and

77

the like. Many of these other verses are ambiguous and can be allegorical or symbolic. God says in the Qur'an: *He it is Who revealed to you the Book. Some verses are clear—they are the cornerstone of the scripture—and others are ambiguous...* (*Aal 'Imran*, 3:7). So obviously anyone interpreting the Qur'an must know exactly which verses are legal ones and why. Moreover, some legal verses are qualified, some are absolute. Some are universal or general, some are particular.

5. Whilst all the legal verses are clear (and the vast majority of these are linguistically literal as well, albeit that some—like 4:103—do use metaphorical language), some 'ambiguous' verses are literal and some are not. For example, the following verse refers to 'insight'—not sight—and clearly does *not* mean that all blind people are damned: *Those who were blind in this life will be blind in the hereafter, and even further off the path* (*Al-Isra'*, 17:72).

6. It is legitimate to interpret ambiguous verses symbolically, allegorically or even analogically so long as the interpretation holds true linguistically, does not contradict doctrine or *shari'ah*, and is not definitively confined to only one meaning or teaching. The Prophet ﷺ said: 'Every verse has an exterior and an interior meaning' (*Sahih Ibn Hibban*). One commentator said the following about this *hadith*:

> Its remit is that it does not overstep the Book or the Prophetic *Sunnah*, and it should not be stated categorically that this inward meaning of the verse is the only meaning intended and nothing else, for there is a clear difference between such an interpretation and that of the Esotericists (*Batiniyyah*)... An example of this is the saying of Ibn Abbas ﷺ regarding the saying of God ﷻ, *He sends down water out of heaven, and the valleys flow each according to its measure...* (*Al-Ra'd*, 13:17): 'water in this verse means knowledge, while valleys mean the hearts.' ('Abd al-Rahman al-'Aydarus, *The Fragrant Scent*, 1)

Indeed, it is helpful to know this so that whilst reading the Qur'an, people see that the unbelievers in the Qur'an have their equivalents inside of themselves; that their arguments are reflected in their own psychic chatter; that the Prophets and their warnings are mirrored by their consciences (*al-nafs al-lawwamah*); that the cities to which they come are their own hearts, and that virtues and vices represented in the Qur'an are so many spiritual and worldly attitudes that constantly occur in their own souls. This is another way in which the Qur'an is 'like a miraculous mirror that shows people what they are; what they can be, and how they can be it', as mentioned earlier, and as implied in the verse cited at the beginning of this chapter: *Now We have sent down [as revelation] to you, a Book in which there is your remembrance. Will you not understand?* (*Al-Anbiya'*, 21:10)

7. Order of revelation: some Qur'anic verses annul or supersede others. Some merely modify others. God says in the Qur'an: *And whatever verse We abrogate or postpone, We replace with a better, or the like of it; do you not know [O Prophet] that God has power over all things?* (*Al-Baqarah*, 2:106). So anyone interpreting the Qur'an has to know the order of revelation of all the legal verses of the Qur'an.

All of this may sound like a lot to take in, but in fact in an elementary medieval or classical education—in the Islamic world *and* in the West— most of these topics were taught to children or adolescents as the basic tools of thought. The 'trivia' of a classical education—that is to say the three topics of grammar, dialectic (including logic) and rhetoric—were considered the mere beginnings of a proper education. They were what enabled a person to learn how to learn and to think straight, and they were considered so elementary that they gave rise to the English word 'trivial' meaning 'minor' or 'insignificant'. So, what (sadly) may seem difficult to understand today as regards interpreting texts, and especially the Qur'an, was in the past considered natural and reasonable.

Nevertheless, there are a number of other things that Qur'anic inter- preters have to know, such as knowing the Prophet's ﷺ own explanations of verses; having studied the classical commentaries; knowing which verses have general applications and which ones have specific applica- tions; knowing the internal references of the Qur'an; understanding that there is no redundancy in the Qur'an; knowing legal theory in general; understanding the laws of logic, and so on. These are laid out clearly in books like Al-Suyuti's (d. 911/1505) *Al-Itqan fi 'Ulum al-Qur'an* (*The Perfect Guide to the Sciences of the Qur'an*). But the point here is this: whilst anyone can read the Qur'an for different kinds of wisdom, very few people are qualified to make rulings based on it, and no one unqualified should try. It is like medicine: anyone can appreciate medicine and benefit from it, but only a few people become qualified doctors. The Qur'an has to be studied for many years under qualified teachers. This is especially true with interpretations that can lead to harming or punishing others. The Prophet Muhammad ﷺ specifically warned of this:

> Whoever speaks about the Qur'an according to his own opinion or according to that of which he [or she] has no knowledge, then let him assume his place in hell. (*Tirmidhi*; *Abu Dawud*; *Ahmad*)

Fortunately, however, there is a practical 'port in the storm'—a 'safety zone'—for anyone with questions about the Qur'an. The Arab world actually has the three oldest universities in the world, and they are all Islamic universities. These are: Al-Zaytunah University in Tunis, Tunisia (founded in 120/737); the Karaouine University in Fez, Morocco (founded in 859 CE by an Arab woman); and the Azhar in Cairo, Egypt (founded in 975 CE—now one of the largest universities in the world as well). The Azhar in particular is considered the greatest and most prestigious bastion of Sunni learning, and is also one of the largest universities in the world (with 4,000 teaching institutes, about half a million university students and over two million students in its feeder schools). So the best thing to do is to refer to these centres of learning; to their scholars; to scholars who have studied there or to scholars of more recent institutes (such as Darul Uloom of Deoband and its affiliates in the Indian Subcontinent) who use their same methodology.

THE PRESERVATION OF THE QUR'AN

Finally, it is perhaps worthwhile saying something about the preservation of the Qur'an, as this seems to be a topic about which some people today are confused. The Qur'an we have in our hands today is the exact same one—to the letter—that was revealed to the Prophet Muhammad ﷺ. This is unique amongst the world's scriptures, and perhaps even among regular books. As every publisher knows, books are usually edited or contain tiny mistakes in transcribing, typesetting or printing, even in our digital age.

The process by which the Qur'an was preserved is well-recorded and historically remarkable. During the Prophet's ﷺ own lifetime, whenever new verses were revealed, his Companions wrote them down on bones, stones, wooden planks, boards, leaves, parchments, vellum and skins and then read them back to him ﷺ (for the Prophet ﷺ could not read). Even the very first revelations were written this way. The Companion (later caliph) 'Umar ibn al-Khattab ؓ converted to Islam in Mecca (in 616 CE—six years before the emigration to Medina, the event which marks the start of the Islamic calendar) after an altercation with his brother-in-law Sa'id bin Zayd ؓ and his sister Fatimah ؓ who were reading the Chapter (*Surah*) of *Ta Ha* from a parchment (Ibn Hisham, *Al-Sirah al-Nabawiyyah*). This shows that the Qur'an was being written down in the very first years of revelation.

Approximately 65 of the Prophet Muhammad's ﷺ Companions functioned at various times as scribes for the revelations. The exact ordering of the verses and the chapters was personally overseen by the Prophet ﷺ during his own lifetime. In his lifetime, the Prophet ﷺ also forbade anything but the Qur'an (including his own sayings) to be written down alongside the Qur'an—in order to avoid any confusion. So the entire Qur'an was available in written form during the Prophet's ﷺ own lifetime.

Because new revelations were being revealed until not long before the Prophet's ﷺ death in 11/632, these revelations were not collected in a single book during his ﷺ own lifetime. And in battles shortly after the death of the Prophet ﷺ, a number of the Companions who had memorized the Qur'an in its entirety were killed. The Companions were a university in the original sense of the word: 'a community of teachers and scholars' ('Universities', *Encyclopaedia Britannica*, 11th ed., 1911). They not only knew and studied the Qur'an but were experts in Classical Arabic, for the Arabic language was the focus and pride of the (oral) culture of the Arabs prior to Islam. So when some of their number started to die, there was concern that the Qur'an would be lost. Therefore the first caliph—the Prophet Muhammad's ﷺ immediate successor—Abu Bakr al-Siddiq ؓ bin Abi Quhafa (r. 11–13/r. 632–634), tasked one of the main scribes of the Qur'an, Zayd bin Thabit ؓ (who himself knew the Qur'an by heart perfectly) to collect all the fragments into a single folio. Zayd ؓ was a relatively young man but was trusted by the Prophet ﷺ, and indeed by the whole early Muslim community. He was also one of the few people who were privileged to attend the sessions of Archangel Gabriel ؈ reciting the whole Qur'an to the Prophet ﷺ during Ramadan.

Zayd ؓ—despite the fact that he knew the Qur'an by heart himself perfectly—set about gathering all the fragments that had been written in the Prophet's ﷺ presence and checked by him, and did not accept any fragment that was not sworn to by two witnesses. Abu Bakr ؓ had issued a general summons to the whole Muslim community inviting any qualified person to participate, and the process was conducted in the Prophet's ﷺ own mosque in Medina. This led to a complete collection of the Qur'an, in proper order, into a single folio, albeit of differing 'page' sizes. It was called the *Suhuf* (meaning 'pages'). After it was completed, it was given to the Prophet's ﷺ widow, the Lady Hafsah ؓ, for safekeeping.

By the time of the third caliph, 'Uthman bin 'Affan ؓ, Islam had spread to many distant places, from Asia to Africa. Reports reached 'Uthman ؓ that the Qur'an was being read in different Arab dialects in different places. So 'Uthman ؓ decided to make the Qur'an into an actual book (*Mushaf*), and keep it, as it was revealed, in the dialect of the Tribe of Quraysh (the Prophet's ﷺ own tribe). 'Uthman ؓ had copies of that book made and sent to major cities. To be absolutely certain of the written text, 'Uthman ؓ independently repeated the whole gathering and testimony process that Abu Bakr ؓ had done, with the Prophet's ﷺ remaining Companions and a committee of twelve knowledgeable Companions (including Zayd bin Thabit ؓ himself), to oversee it. They then checked it against Hafsah's ؓ *Suhuf* and it was exactly the same. 'Uthman ؓ also checked it against the collection of material that was with the Prophet's ﷺ other widow, the Lady 'A'ishah ؓ. 'Uthman ؓ then ordered all other remaining fragments of the Qur'an to be burnt or harmonized with his *Mushaf* (for fear of scribal errors). He then had a number of copies of these *Mushafs* made. They were sent to Kufa, Basra, Syria, Mecca, Bahrain, Egypt, Al-Jazeera (in today's Northern Iraq) and Yemen (and some of these have been preserved until today). He kept one for himself and left the master-copy in Medina. Every generation of Muslims since then has spared no effort to ensure that the Qur'an is unchanged, and that no Qur'an is published that is not 100 per cent correct. Indeed, the Qur'an we have in our hands today is exactly the same as the master-copy of Medina, and there are no regional variations.

Gradually, even the written Arabic script itself was developed to maintain the correct readings of the Qur'anic text, as so many non-Arabs had become Muslim and they needed more aids to help them pronounce the text correctly. Also, Muslims invented a whole science of phonology to make sure that the Qur'an was always read and pronounced the right way (or right ways, since 10 slightly variant readings were remembered and acknowledged). So whereas all other languages submit to local dialects, place and time (e.g. English English, American English, Australian English, French French, Canadian French and so on), Qur'anic Arabic is written and read the same way at every time, in every place, by every race—and this on pain of the wrath of the whole Muslim community everywhere. Moreover, parts of the Qur'an have been read out loud at least three times a day (during three of the five prayers) in every mosque in the world every single day since the Prophet's ﷺ time—in exactly the same way.

In short, no text in history has ever been the object of so much care and exactitude in its preservation. Yet despite this, for the last 200 years, there has been a constant barrage of Orientalists trying to say that there have been changes in the Qur'an. But all their arguments have come to nothing, and have been shown to be jealous incredulity, missionary zeal or even, perhaps, mere spite (see: *The History of Qur'anic Text from Revelation to Compilation* by M.M. Al-Azami). Rather, the Qur'an has been miraculously preserved, and even the story of its preservation has been preserved. Indeed, God precisely promised this in the Qur'an itself fourteen centuries ago—and that is itself one of the proofs of the Qur'an. God says:

> *Verily it is We Who have revealed the Remembrance, and assuredly We will preserve it.* (*Al-Hijr*, 15:9)

~

WHY IS IT IMPORTANT TO KNOW ALL THIS?

All of this is a lot to take in. But it is extremely important that it be clear. There are wars and terrorist acts all over the world waged by extremists claiming the Qur'an as authority for their evil acts and crimes. *One* of the reasons for this is simply ignorance of the Qur'an. Extremists listen to unqualified and ignorant 'shaykhs' who give their own novel and selective interpretations of the Qur'an or of *hadith*, rejecting the consensus of

Muslim scholars down the ages. This situation will not be resolved unless people understand that legitimately interpreting the Qur'an takes a lot of work and a lot of knowledge. God says in the Qur'an: ... *only those who have knowledge among God's servants [truly] fear Him* (*Al-Fatir*, 35:28).

~

The Opening Chapter of the Qur'an (*Al-Fatihah*)

In the Name of God, the Compassionate, the Merciful, | Praise be to God, Lord of the Worlds. | The Compassionate, the Merciful. | Master of the Day of Judgment. | You [alone] we worship, and You [alone] we ask for help. | Guide us to the straight path, | the path of those upon whom You have bestowed Your grace, not [the path] of those against whom there is wrath, nor of those who are astray.

The Chapter of Divine Unity (*Al-Ikhlas*) (from Chapter 3)

Say: He, God, is One. | God, the Eternally Sufficient unto Himself | He did not beget, nor was He begotten. | And none is like unto Him.

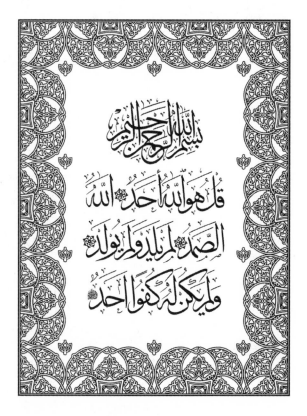

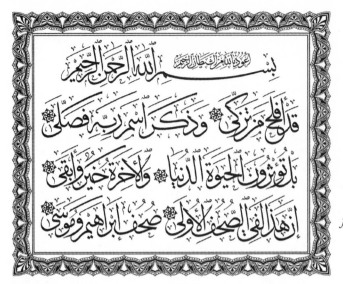

Chapter 1

Successful indeed is he who purifies himself, | and mentions the Name of his Lord and prays. | Nay, but you prefer the life of this world, | whereas the Hereafter is better and more lasting. | Truly this is in the former scrolls, | the scrolls of Abraham and Moses. (Al-A'la, 87:14–19)

Chapter 2

Truly I am God—there is no god except Me. So worship Me and establish prayer to make remembrance of Me. (Ta Ha, 20:14)

Chapter 3

He said, 'So who is your Lord, O Moses?' | He said, 'Our Lord is He Who gave to everything its [particular] creation and then guided [it]'. (Ta Ha, 20:49–50)

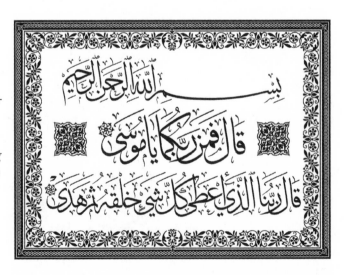

Chapter 4

Had your Lord willed, He would have made mankind one community, but they continue to differ, | except those on whom your Lord has mercy; and for this He created them. And the Word of your Lord has been fulfilled: 'I will surely fill Hell with jinn and mankind together'.
(*Hud*, 11:118–119)

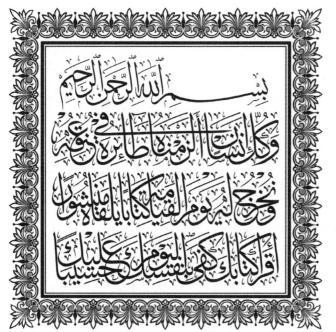

Chapter 5

And We have fastened every person's destiny on to his neck and We shall bring forth for him, on the Day of Resurrection, a book which he will find wide open. | 'Read your book! This day your soul suffices as your own reckoner.'
(*Al-Isra'*, 17:13–14)

Chapter 6

*Now We have sent down [as revelation] to you, a Book in which there
is your remembrance. Will you not understand? (Al-Anbiya', 21:10)*

Chapter 7

*We did not send you except as a mercy to all the worlds.
(Al-Anbiya', 21:107)*

Chapter 8

*Have they not travelled in the land so that they may have hearts with which
to comprehend, or ears with which to hear? Indeed it is not the eyes that turn
blind, but it is the hearts that turn blind within the breasts. (Al-Hajj, 22:46)*

Chapter 9

Bear in mind that the life of this world is merely play, diversion, adornment, mutual boasting and rivalry in wealth and children. It is like plants that spring up after the rain: their growth at first delights the sowers, but then they wither away, and you see them turn yellow; then they become chaff. And in the next life there is severe punishment, and forgiveness from God—and Beatitude. The life of this world is only the pleasure of delusion. (Al-Hadid, 57:20)

Chapter 11

And fight in the way of God with those who fight against you, but aggress not; God loves not the aggressors. (Al-Baqarah, 2:190)

Chapter 10

Then We set you upon a [clear] course (shari'ah) of the commandment; so follow it, and do not follow the desires of those who do not know. (Al-Jathiyah, 45:18)

Chapter 12

Verily, God commands you to restore trusts to their rightful owners. And when you judge between people, that you judge with justice. Excellent is the instruction God gives you. God is ever Hearer, Seer. (Al-Nisa', 4:58)

Chapter 7

WHO IS THE
PROPHET MUHAMMAD ?

*We did not send you except as a mercy to
all the worlds. (Al-Anbiya', 21:107)*

WHO *IS* THE PROPHET
MUHAMMAD TO MUSLIMS?

Not who *was* he ?—we have touched on that already. Who *is* he ?
Who *is* he still, to Muslims, as a role model? And who is he , in his
eternal spiritual reality?

People who do not understand the Prophet —non-Muslims and even
Muslims—tend to ask only who the Prophet *was*, and this is missing
the whole point. The answer to that leads to historical facts, and to details
which can be misinterpreted when dubious motives are projected back
on to them, or when the context or the circumstance is not understood.

Muslims see the Prophet as the personification of human virtue and
spiritual perfection. That is who he *is* for them.

HUMAN VIRTUE

The Prophet Muhammad was born in the small Arabian desert-town
of Mecca—originally called 'Becca' (see: Qur'an, 3:96; Psalm 84:5–6)—in

around 570 CE. The Prophet 🕌 was from the Bani Hashim clan of the tribe of Quraysh, whose ancestor Ishmael 🕌 had first settled in the desert (see Genesis, 21:21; 25:18). The Prophet 🕌 had no brothers or sisters. His 🕌 father died before he was born and then his mother died whilst he 🕌 was still a young child. He was thus an orphan, brought up first by his paternal grandfather, 'Abd al-Muttalib, and then by his paternal uncle, Abu Talib, when his grandfather also died. Although like most Arabs of his time he 🕌 did not learn to read and write, he 🕌 grew up and became a merchant, travelling long and difficult desert routes on camelback on behalf of other people in order to make a living. He 🕌 was naturally honest, so much so that people in Mecca came to call him 'al-amin' — 'the trustworthy'. Until the age of 40 he 🕌 lived a quiet life. At the age of 40, whilst in solitary retreat (as was his custom), he 🕌 began to receive visions from God and revelations (these comprise the Qur'an). These revelations then compelled the Prophet Muhammad 🕌 to call on Meccan society to reform its evil practices. In particular, they compelled him to call on the Meccans to stop worshipping stone idols and to worship instead the One-and-Only God (whose Name in Arabic is 'Allah'), to stop killing their infant daughters, to care for orphans, treat women fairly, give alms to the poor and the weak, and to set their slaves free as a virtuous act. The Meccan chiefs reacted with hostility to his message for they perceived it would not only change their way of life, but also their social and economic privileges. They sent him a delegation with the following offer:

> If the aim of all you are doing is to gain much money . . . we shall gather enough and give it to you so that you will be the richest among us. . . . If you seek to be king, we shall make you our king. If what is happening is a type of obsessive vision that you cannot stop by yourself, we shall seek your cure sparing no money until you are fully recovered. (Ibn Hisham, *Al-Sirah al-Nabawiyyah*)

Still he 🕌 persisted. The Meccan chiefs then reacted with abuse and violence against him and his followers. Many of those who listened to him were humiliated, boycotted, spurned, abused verbally and physically, and finally tortured or killed. After about 12 years of patiently enduring such attacks (including 13 assassination attempts on his own life), in the year 622 CE he 🕌 left to a town 300 miles north of Mecca (now known as

'Medina') whose leaders had invited him ﷺ and his followers to come and settle. There he ﷺ organized his followers into a community and, for the first time—and after receiving a revelation (*Al-Hajj*, 22:39–40) instructing him to do so—into armed resistance. The Meccans were now waging full-on war on him ﷺ and his community and inciting others to do so as well.

Within eight years the Prophet ﷺ was the most powerful leader in Arabia. He ﷺ did not always win battles, but he ﷺ constantly won hearts. Converts to Islam steadily streamed into Medina from everywhere. The Prophet ﷺ then led his followers to free Mecca. Despite the unnecessary cruelty, bloodshed and bitterness inflicted upon him and his followers, he ﷺ did not shed a drop of blood nor take any revenge. He ﷺ refused even to verbally reproach the Meccans in his moment of victory. He ﷺ said to them: 'I say to you what my brother Joseph said: "There will be no reproach today". Go. You are all free!' (Al-Bayhaqi, *Al-Sunan al-Kubra*).

The Prophet ﷺ lived for another two years or so until 632 CE. Even after victory, he ﷺ spent his life as he always had: in prayer and devotion, hunger (he ﷺ used to tie a stone against his belly to suppress hunger), and combating sleep in the watches of the night in order to pray. He ﷺ gave away almost all his possessions (except for a few personal items) and kept only one change of clothes. He ﷺ loved purity and so also cleanliness, and always kept himself immaculately clean. He ﷺ had three beloved sons, all of whom died in infancy, and four beloved daughters, three of whom died in his lifetime leaving no offspring. Until the age of 50 or so he ﷺ had one wife, the Lady Khadijah, who was 15 years older than him. They had married when he ﷺ was 25 and she was 40, and they shared a harmonious marriage for 25 years until her death. After her death, he ﷺ married several times, mostly to cement tribal alliances (or, as in the case of his ﷺ second wife, the Lady Sawdah ﷺ, to support a widow). He ﷺ said: 'The best of you is he who is best to his family' (*Tirmidhi*).

The Prophet ﷺ loved people in general. Indeed, he ﷺ was always kind, merciful and quick to forgive, even in war. At times he ﷺ felt anger, but never raised his voice or lost his temper. He ﷺ was easy-going, kind, friendly, courteous, modest, and moderate in all things. He advised: 'The thing that most enables people to enter paradise is being mindful (*taqwa*) of God and having a beautiful character' (*Tirmidhi*). He ﷺ would jest sometimes with those around him, but never compromised his dignity.

When Umm Ayman Barakah ﷺ, a lady who had been a treasured member of his household since he was a child, came to him asking for an adult camel as a mount, he ﷺ replied 'I will not let you mount save on the child of a she-camel' (*Ahmad*; Ibn Sa'd, *Kitab al-Tabaqat al-Kabir*). She protested until he ﷺ smiled and she realized that every camel is the child of a she-camel. Even in jest, he ﷺ never told a lie. He ﷺ said: 'The worst of all cardinal sins are idolatry, murder, abuse of one's parents and false testimony' (*Bukhari*). He ﷺ also said: 'Whoever defrauds us is not one of us; deception and guile are hellish' (*Abu Dawud*). He ﷺ never claimed to be more than a mortal man. God instructed him in the Qur'an to: *Say: 'I am only a human being like you to whom it has been revealed that your God is One God. So whoever hopes to meet his Lord, let him do good deeds and not associate anyone in the worship of his Lord'* (*Al-Kahf*, 18:110). And he ﷺ loved goodness. He ﷺ said: 'By Him in whose Hand is my life, none of you believes until he [or she] loves for their neighbour what they love for themselves' (*Muslim*).

These details give a very brief sketch of the very human virtues Muslims know him for—who he ﷺ *is* for them. In the last century, the great Hindu leader Mahatma Gandhi explained it as follows:

> I wanted to know the best of the life of one who holds today an undisputed sway over the hearts of millions of mankind. . . . I became more than ever convinced that it was not the sword that won a place for Islam in those days in the scheme of life. It was the rigid simplicity, the utter self-effacement of the Prophet, the scrupulous regard for pledges, his intense devotion to his friends and followers, his intrepidity, his fearlessness, his absolute trust in God and in his own mission. These and not the sword carried everything before them and surmounted every obstacle. (*My Jail Experiences*, Vol. 29)

SPIRITUAL PERFECTION

It remains to be said that everything the Prophet Muhammad ﷺ said and did had only one motive: it was done for the sake of God. God says to him: *Say: 'My prayer and my rituals, and my living, and my dying, are all for God, the Lord of the Worlds'* (*Al-An'am*, 6:162). Love of God was the basis of the Prophet's ﷺ devotion. When you are in love with someone, you are always thinking about them or talking about them, or trying to be with them. Love of God is similar. The Lady 'A'ishah ؆, wife of the Prophet ﷺ, said of him that: 'The Prophet used to remember God at all times' (*Muslim*). His life was marked by constant remembrance of God. He ﷺ never forgot or betrayed God, whatever the pressure or circumstance. That is spiritual perfection, and that is who the Prophet Muhammad ﷺ *is* in his spiritual reality. Hence God says in the Qur'an:

> *Truly there is for you a good example in the messenger of God for whoever hopes for [the encounter with] God and the Last Day, and remembers God often.* (*Al-Ahzab*, 33:21)

THE MISSION OF THE PROPHET

The religion of Islam is the last universal religion. That is to say it is the last religion that any human being—regardless of the caste, race or nation he or she was born into—can choose (and is invited) to join. In the Qur'an, the Prophet's ﷺ mission is described as the fulfilment of Biblical prophecies:

> *Those who follow the messenger, the unlettered Prophet, whom they will find described in the Torah and the Gospel which are with them. He will enjoin on them that which is right and forbid them that which is wrong. He will make lawful for them good things and make bad things unlawful; and he will relieve them of their burden and the fetters that were on them. Then those who believe in him, and honour him, and help him, and follow the light which is sent down with him will be successful.* (*Al-A'raf*, 7:157)

What precisely are these descriptions in the Torah and the Gospel?

1. Muslim scholars argue that one is Deuteronomy 18:15: *The Lord your God will raise up for you a Prophet like me from your midst, from your brethren. Him you shall hear.* Clearly the Prophet mentioned here could not be Jesus Christ ؆ because Jesus Christ ؆ was not from the *brethren* of the Children of Israel (i.e. the descendants of Ishmael ؆, the brother of Isaac ؆) but an actual descendant of Israel through his blessed mother. This same Prophet is alluded to in John 1:21 and 1:25 when John ؆ is asked '*Are you the Prophet?*' (who is not the Messiah ؆, and not Elijah ؆

either), and he 🕮 replies that he 🕮 is not. The same is true for all of the other Biblical prophets between Jesus 🕮 and Moses 🕮 (as they were all Jews as well). Besides, Jesus 🕮 was not like Moses 🕮. God says in the Qur'an: . . . *The Messiah, Jesus the son of Mary, was only the messenger of God, and His Word which He cast to Mary, and a spirit from Him. . .* (*Al-Nisa',* 4:171). Moses 🕮, on the other hand, was born in the normal way, married, had children, received revelation, led his people, fought armed battles and died in the normal way, and the Prophet Muhammad 🕮 was more like Moses 🕮 in all these respects.

2. Muslim scholars see Jacob's deathbed prophecy about 'Shiloh' (in Genesis 49:10; see also the allusion to it in the Qur'an, *Al-Baqarah,* 2:133) as referring to the Prophet Muhammad 🕮: *The sceptre shall not depart from Judah, nor a lawgiver from between his feet, until Shiloh comes; And to Him shall be the obedience of the people.* The Hebrew prophets and kings from David 🕮 to Jesus Christ 🕮 were from 'between the feet' (i.e. from the loins) of Judah, and after them the sceptre (symbolizing temporal power) and the lawgiver (of revealed law) have only come to one man in history: the Prophet Muhammad 🕮, and it is to him that there has been 'the obedience of the people' where this prophecy was made — in Palestine or Egypt.

3. Muslim scholars argue that there are many other clear references to Prophet Muhammad 🕮 in the Bible (including many passages in the Psalms; Deuteronomy 33:2; the 'rider on the camel' in Isaiah, 21:7; 13–16; Isaiah 29:12; Isaiah 42:11–17, and his name is even specifically mentioned in Hebrew in Song of Solomon 5:16 and in Habakkuk 3:3).

4. Finally, Muslim scholars see the Qur'an and the Prophet Muhammad 🕮 as being the 'Spirit of Truth' ('Paraclete', literally the 'helper' or 'intercessor') referred to in Jesus' 🕮 words in the Gospel: *I still have many things to say to you, but you cannot bear them now. / However, when he, the spirit of truth, has come, he will guide you into all truth; for he will not speak on his own authority, but whatever he hears he will speak. . .* (John 16:12–13). This is because there is an allusion in the Qur'an to this verse:

> *And when Jesus son of Mary said, 'O Children of Israel I am indeed God's messenger to you, confirming what is before me of the Torah and bringing good tidings of a messenger who will come after me, whose name is Ahmad'. . . .* (*Al-Saff,* 61:4)

'Ahmad' is then the Qur'anic name for the Prophet Muhammad ﷺ on the Day of Judgement when he is the 'helper' or 'intercessor' (with God) for people. Moreover, Jesus' ﷺ prediction *for he will not speak on his own authority, but whatever he hears he will speak* is also fulfilled by the coming of the Prophet Muhammad ﷺ, since that is exactly how the Prophet Muhammad ﷺ received and transmitted the Qur'an. This is described in the Qur'an itself as follows:

> *Nor does he speak out of [his own] desire. | It is but a revelation that is revealed, | taught to him by one of awesome power. (Al-Najm, 53:3–5)*

All this is to explain then why the Prophet Muhammad ﷺ is called *the Seal of the Prophets. . . (Al-Ahzab, 33:40)*: 'seal' ('*khatim*') means 'last' but also 'culmination'. It also explains why Islam is the last universal religion and consequently why Muslims believe Islam has superseded all other religions: clearly, the final Prophet means the final religion (since only true prophets bring genuine religions). This was the mission of the Prophet Muhammad ﷺ. God says to him in the Qur'an:

> *O Prophet! Indeed We have sent you as a witness, and as a bearer of good tidings, | and as a warner, and as a summoner to God by His leave, and as an illuminating lamp. (Al-Ahzab, 33:45–46)*

LOVE FOR THE PROPHET MUHAMMAD ﷺ

Muslims love the Prophet Muhammad ﷺ as part of their faith. God says: *The Prophet is closer to the believers than their [own] souls . . . (Al-Ahzab, 33:6)*. This love is not merely because of the importance of his mission. Rather, it is because of the way he ﷺ carried it out; because of his love for them, and also because of God's love for him ﷺ. This is a vast topic in Islamic devotional literature, and over the course of history (and until today) there have been thousands, if not millions, of beautiful poems and litanies written by Muslims out of love of the Prophet ﷺ. Perhaps the best known poem is the *Burdah* by the Berber poet Sharaf al-Din al-Busiri (608–693/1211–1294), and perhaps the best known litany is the *Dala'il al-Khayrat* by Muhammad al-Jazuli (807–870/1404–1465). Howbeit, it is enough here to quote God's words:

Indeed, there has come to you a messenger from among yourselves for whom it
is grievous that you should suffer; who is full of concern for you, to the believers
full of pity, merciful. (Al-Tawbah, 9:128)

The love will continue after death until the Day of Judgement, and
Muslims believe that on the Day of Judgement the Prophet ﷺ will pray
for them to be forgiven their sins. So the Prophet ﷺ is a mercy to Muslims,
not just in this world, but in the next as well. Consequently, Muslims are
constantly invoking blessings and prayers on their Prophet ﷺ, and indeed
are instructed to do so in the Qur'an (33:56). This, combined with the
Prophet's merciful teachings to all sentient beings and—very topically
now—to the whole natural (and spiritual) environment, explains God's
words: *We did not send you except as a mercy to all the worlds (Al-Anbiya',*
21:107). And these words providentially provide the golden principle
against which anything attributed to the Prophet ﷺ—or to the religion
of Islam in general—can be measured.

THE SAYINGS OF THE PROPHET MUHAMMAD ﷺ

After the Qur'an, the words (*hadith*; plural: *ahadith*) and instructions of
the Prophet Muhammad ﷺ are the most important source of Islamic law
(*shari'ah*). This is because God says in the Qur'an, . . . *And whatever the*
messenger gives you, take it; and whatever he forbids you, abstain [from it]. . .
(*Al-Hashr*, 57:7). *Ahadith* are an important source of guidance on the details
of Islamic practice, moral guidance, doctrine, culture and knowledge in
general. Consequently, the study of *hadith* is central to Islamic studies,
and the religion of Islam cannot be properly understood without taking
the *ahadith* into consideration. We have cited a number of them already;
it remains to be said that they are generally masterpieces of eloquence,
and many of them are perfect aphorisms of wisdom, moral clarity and
spiritual guidance. We cite only the following as an example (typical in
its emphasis on moral action and goodness):

> Whoever rescues a believer from a worldly calamity, God shall rescue
> him [or her] from a calamity on the Day of Arising. Whoever is kind to
> the bankrupt, God shall be kind to him [or her] in this world and the
> next. Whoever conceals the fault of a Muslim, God shall conceal his [or

her] faults in this world and in the next. God helps His servant as long as His servant helps his [or her] brother [or sister]. Whoever treads a path to seek knowledge, God shall make his [or her] path to paradise easy. Whenever a group of people gather in a house of God to recite His book, and study it among themselves, God's peace descends on them; the angels surround them; mercy covers them, and He mentions them in His Presence. Whoever lags behind in doing good works, his [or her] [noble] lineage will not advance him [or her]. (*Muslim*)

Nevertheless, *hadith* studies themselves are perhaps the most complex, contested—and as will later be seen, potentially dangerous—part of Islamic studies. This is because there were over 500,000 texts of sayings attributed to the Prophet ﷺ, many of which are clearly not genuine. Over 200,000—Al-Suyuti was said to have memorized 200,000 *ahadith*—are taken seriously enough by Islamic scholars to merit further examination, but the majority of these (over two thirds perhaps) are the same *ahadith* related with different chains of transmission or with different wordings. This leaves some 40,000–60,000 completely distinct *ahadith*. Determining which *ahadith* are genuine is an important, complex and ongoing science in Islam. Scholars have divided the *ahadith* into many subtly different categories, ranging from the clearly fake to the completely certain. It is a *specialist* topic that involves logical, linguistic, biographical, historical, psychological and ethical judgements and debates. It involves not only knowing the texts ('*matn*') of the *ahadith*, but also knowing the chains of transmission ('*isnad*'). There are around 20,000 different men and women whose names appear in the chains of transmission, and *hadith* scholars have studied each of them individually—when they lived, where they travelled, whom they met and studied with, whether they ever lied, and if they had good memories—in order to know if they could be trusted. The great *hadith* critic 'Ali Daraqutni (d. 385/995) was reported to have said that if all 20,000 transmitters were miraculously to appear before him on a hill, he could call on every one of them individually by their names, by their fathers' names, by their tribes, and say if they were reliable or not.

Generally speaking, there is a pool of over 50 collections of *ahadith* or books in which *ahadith* are cited that Sunni scholars regularly fall back on, and another 200 or more that have been written. The historically last collection containing previously undocumented *ahadith* is generally thought to be that of Abu Bakr al-Bayhaqi (d. 458/1066). Among the 50 regularly-used collections, there are nine books or so (*Sahih al-Bukhari*; *Sahih Muslim*; *Sunan Abu Dawud*; *Sunan al-Nasa'i*; *Jami' al-Tirmidhi*; *Sunan Ibn Majah*; *Sunan al-Darimi*; *Musnad Ahmad*; and the *Muwatta'* of Malik) that scholars rely on most often (containing some 50,000 different *ahadith*). From the nine books, two collections in particular are generally — with a well-known handful of exceptions — taken as genuine. These two are the *Sahih* ('true') collections of Muhammad al-Bukhari (d. 256/870) and his student Muslim ibn al-Hajjaj (d. 261/875). *Sahih al-Bukhari* contains around 7,397 *ahadith*, some 2,602 of which are unique, and *Sahih Muslim* contains around 12,000 *ahadith*, some 4,000 of which are unique. Extensive commentaries have been written on both books, the most famous being perhaps Ibn Hajar al-'Asqalani's (d. 852/1449) encyclopaedic commentary on *Sahih al-Bukhari*, *Fath al-Bari*, and Yahya al-Nawawi's (d. 676/1277) commentary on *Sahih Muslim*. The overlap between the two collections is around 2,326 *ahadith,* and these are obviously regarded as even more certain. They are called '*muttafaq 'alayhi*', which means 'agreed upon' in Arabic. However, perhaps the most certain of all — and some of the *ahadith* in Bukhari and Muslim also fit into this category — are those *ahadith* (selected from the entire *ahadith* corpus) that are related from 10 or more completely different, but reliable, chains of transmission. These are called '*mutawatir*' meaning 'massively transmitted'. These are obviously all but impossible to forge, so they are used for doctrine, but there are not many of them. (Al-Suyuti relates only 111 of them in his book *Qatf al-Azhar al-Mutanathirah fi 'l-Akhbar al-Mutawatirah.*)

Finally, it should be noted that, unlike Qur'anic verses which were recited verbatim by thousands of Muslims from the moment they were revealed and therefore 'collectively memorized', *ahadith* were generally remembered privately by individuals. Therefore, not all of the *ahadith* — even the *mutawatir ahadith* — were remembered verbatim. Rather, their *meanings* were remembered. Scholars always took this into consideration, since the Companions could have understood *ahadith* differently from each other, or could have mistaken the context, or even misunderstood how the words were meant. The Lady 'A'ishah , the wife of the Prophet

Muhammad , famously once criticized some senior Companions for misunderstanding (and so, *misrepresenting*) an important *hadith* about the status of women—showing precisely how important this issue can be.

IMITATION OF THE PROPHET MUHAMMAD

In addition to legal prescriptions, the books of *hadith* form the basis of the *'sunnah'*, the custom of the Prophet Muhammad . As we have seen, the Prophet Muhammad is taken as the perfect role model for human beings—the exemplar of human virtue and spiritual perfection. As an anonymous Arab poet wrote:

Muhammad was human
   Unlike other humans,
He was like a ruby,
   And people are like stones.

So voluntarily following his custom, particularly in matters of worship and devotion, is taken as the best way to become virtuous (*Ihsan*). In Chapter 2, we saw that 'the virtuous' (*'muhsinin'*) are loved by God. Therefore, sincerely following the *sunnah* is synonymous with *Ihsan* and even being loved 'more' by God. God confirms this in the Qur'an as follows:

> Say: 'If you love God, follow me, and God will love you more [yuhbibkum], and forgive you your sins; God is Forgiving, Merciful.' (*Aal 'Imran*, 3:31)

This explains why Muslims try to emulate the Prophet Muhammad in everything he did. It also explains why they regard this behaviour as the epitome of virtue and spiritual perfection, or at least the way towards it par excellence: sincerely practising virtue is the best way to learn it and to be changed by it.

~

WHY IS IT IMPORTANT TO KNOW ALL THIS?

It is important to know all this for a number of reasons. First, and most obviously, no one can understand the religion of Islam without understanding something about the Prophet Muhammad 🕊. The religion of Islam is epitomized not just by the first Testimony of Faith, *'La ilaha illa Allah'* ('There is no god but God'), but by the second Testimony of Faith—*'Muhammad rasul Allah'* (Muhammad is God's messenger)— together *with* the First Testimony of Faith. There is an eighth century (CE) gold coin, minted—presumably for trading purposes—by King Offa of Mercia (r. 757–796 CE in what is now England) that is preserved in the British Museum that bears the inscription (in Arabic) *'La ilaha illa Allah'*. This illustrates the difference between Islam and all other religions. Other religions might believe, and some do, that 'There is no god but God', but Muslims are unique in believing that 'Muhammad 🕊 is His messenger'. So no one can really understand anything about Islam without knowing something about the Prophet Muhammad 🕊.

Second, starting with St John of Damascus (d. 749) and right up until the right-wing Islamophobes of today, there has been a sustained misunderstanding—if not active negative polemic—from certain Christian and Jewish Orientalist writers about the Prophet 🕊, his actions and his motives. These misunderstandings and misrepresentations have seeped deep into the culture, media and psyche of the West. They are well detailed as far back as 1960 in Norman Daniel's excellent study *Islam and the West: The Making of an Image*. So it is important to know that when Muslims think about the Prophet Muhammad 🕊, they are generally seeing a completely different person from the effigy that non-Muslims have constructed or are seeing. God says in the Qur'an: *And some of them look at you: but can you guide the blind, if they will not see?* (*Yunus*, 10:43). If non-Muslims saw the same person as Muslims see, they would no doubt have a completely different view of the Prophet 🕊. It is rather similar to the case of some followers of pre-Christian religions, who can harbour stereotypes about Jesus Christ 🕊 that Christians themselves cannot recognise at all.

Third, Muslims take great offense at insulting 🕊 depictions of the Prophet Muhammad 🕊. Of course the Prophet 🕊 himself in his spiritual reality cannot be affected by this, so the reason for taking offence is the love that Muslims feel for the Prophet 🕊, which, as we have seen, is part of their faith. At the same time, Muslims know well that when their exemplar is insulted, every single Muslim on earth who believes in the religion that he brought is being targeted, deliberately insulted and dehumanized. Indeed, the genocide of over 100,000 innocent Bosnian Muslims during the years 1991–1995 (according to the *Bosnian Book of the Dead*) was preceded by precisely this kind of religious vilification and dehumanization.

∼

Chapter 8

WHAT IS 'THE HEART'?

Have they not travelled in the land so that they
may have hearts with which to comprehend, or ears
with which to hear? Indeed it is not the eyes that
turn blind, but it is the hearts that turn blind
within the breasts. (*Al-Hajj*, 22:46)

WHAT ARE HUMAN BEINGS?

Earlier on we said that in the Qur'an every human being is seen to have a body, an individual soul (which has an ego and a conscience) and a spirit (which God first blew into Adam 🙵). We said that the soul has certain obvious faculties such as intelligence, will, sentiment (scholars like Ghazali sometimes equate these three with the 'capacities' for 'intelligence', 'anger' and 'desire' respectively), speech, imagination and memory. The body is clear enough, and its faculties obviously include the five senses (sight, hearing, smell, taste and touch). It is mortal, death being the separation of the body from the soul. The soul is the individual personal core of the human being, and it is immortal. In the Qur'an, the soul is seen to have three major parts—or perhaps three 'modes' (since the soul remains one). These are: 'the soul which incites to evil' (*Yusuf*, 12:53); 'the self-reproaching soul' (*Al-Qiyamah*, 75:2); and 'the soul at peace' (*Al-Fajr*, 89:27). In other words, the soul has an ego, a conscience and a state which is beyond the ego. The spirit is beyond the whole individual personality, and so little can be said about it in words. God says in the Qur'an: *And they will question you concerning the Spirit. Say: 'The Spirit is of the command of my Lord. And of knowledge you have not been given except a little'* (*Al-Isra'*, 17:85). The soul is said to be the individual 'inner witness' of the body, and 'the captain of its ship'. The spirit is said to be the supra-individual 'inner witness' of the body and the soul taken together, and the wind and life in their sails. In the Qur'an there are two paradises for each of the blessed (see: *Al-Rahman*, 55:46), and some commentators take this as the paradises of the soul and spirit respectively. In other words, there is a state of perfect happiness for each of the human subjectivities: the soul and the spirit.

WHAT IS 'THE HEART'?

We mentioned also that in addition to the physical heart that pumps blood around the body, human beings also have a non-physical, 'spiritual' heart that corresponds to the physical heart, but on a higher level of reality. This 'spiritual heart' is actually the 'doorway' or 'bridge' between the soul and the spirit. In the Qur'an, it has four 'degrees': (in 'ascending' order) the 'breast' ('*sadr*'); the 'heart' ('*qalb*'); the 'inner heart' ('*fuad*'), and the 'core' ('*lubb*'—sometimes thought of as the inner heart and intellect together). The 'breast' is identified with the soul, and the 'core' is identified with the spirit. Consequently, this is the heart that God 'looks at'. As cited earlier, the Prophet Muhammad ﷺ said: 'God does not look at your appearances and wealth, but rather He looks at your hearts and your deeds' (*Muslim*). It is therefore the part people need to get right!

In addition to God's looking at this heart, it is through this same heart that people 'see' and know spiritual realities. God says in the Qur'an:

> *Have they not travelled in the land so that they may have hearts with which to comprehend, or ears with which to hear? Indeed it is not the eyes that turn blind, but it is the hearts that turn blind within the breasts.* (*Al-Hajj*, 22:46)

This is even more true of the 'inner heart', for whereas the heart 'comprehends' (or, conversely, turns 'blind'), the 'inner heart', actually sees ('spiritually'). God says, referring to the Prophet Muhammad ﷺ, in the Qur'an:

'The inner heart did not distort what it saw.' (*Al-Najm*, 53:11). Throughout history, innumerable Muslim scholars and mystics have also attested to the reality of the 'spiritual heart'. For example, Sahl al-Tustari (d. 283/896), one of the earliest commentators on the Qur'an, wrote (in a poem):

> The hearts of knowers have eyes
> > That see what 'lookers' see not,
>
> And tongues with discourses of secrets
> > Beyond what the recording angels know,
>
> And wings that fly without feathers
> > To the kingdom of the Lord of the worlds.
>
> We have inherited a drink of the knowledge of the unseen
> > Rarer than the ancients' knowledge.

~

Ever since the German philosopher Immanuel Kant published his *Critique of Pure Reason* in 1781, this kind of 'metaphysical knowledge' has not been taken seriously by Western philosophers and academia. Before that, however, spiritual or 'inner' vision was a well-known religious doctrine. For example, in Plato's *Republic* we find Socrates saying:

> By pursuing [certain philosophical studies] a certain organ in every student's soul is cleansed and rekindled, which has been blinded and destroyed by his other pursuits. Yet it is more worth saving than a thousand eyes, for by this organ alone is the truth perceived.' (527e)

Equally, in the Gospel of Matthew, Jesus ﷺ says: *Blessed are the pure in heart, for they will see God* (Matthew 5:8). However, in the Qur'an it is clear that God cannot be seen (at least in this life), although spiritual realities and truths from God can be seen through inner vision. God says:

> *Vision cannot attain Him, but He attains [all] vision. And He is the Subtle, the Aware. | Now clear proofs have come to you from your Lord; whoever sees (absara), then it is for his own good; and whoever is blind, then it will be to his own hurt. . . (Al-An'am, 6:103–4)*

SELF-KNOWLEDGE

It should be noted also that the heart's vision is as much *self-knowledge* as it is knowledge of 'external' spiritual truths and realities. We said earlier (in Chapter 4) that God created people to know Him. Later (in Chapter 6) we said that the Qur'an helps people to know themselves. It remains to be said that it is precisely self-knowledge that leads to knowledge of God and of spiritual realities. In fact, God created souls with innate knowledge of Him as a testimony arising from their own self-knowledge:

> And when your Lord took from the Children of Adam, from their loins their seed and made them testify against themselves, 'Am I not your Lord?' They said, 'Yes, indeed we testify', lest you should say on the Day of Resurrection, 'Truly, of this we were unaware.' (Al-A'raf, 7:172)

And God requires people to maintain this testimony and self-knowledge in this life. God says:

> O you who believe, uphold justice and bear witness to God even if it is against yourselves. . . . (Al-Nisa', 4:136)

Moreover, God says:

> Vision cannot attain Him, but He attains [all] vision. And He is the Subtle, the Aware. | Clear proofs have come to you from your Lord; whoever perceives, then it is for his own good; and whoever is blind, then it will be to his own loss. . . (Al-An'am, 6:103–104)

Perhaps this is why the famous oracle at Delphi in ancient Greece bore the inscription '*Know thyself*'. At any rate, God promises that through contemplating the world and self-knowledge, people will know the Truth: *We shall show them Our signs in the horizons and in their own souls until it becomes clear to them that it is the Truth. Is it not sufficient that your Lord is witness to all things?* (Fussilat, 41:53)

RUST ON THE HEART

Not every heart 'sees'. The heart's ability to 'see' depends on a person's deeds. The Prophet Muhammad ﷺ said:

> If a servant [of God] commits a sin, a black spot forms on his heart, and if he changes, repents and asks for forgiveness, his heart is cleansed. But if he [the servant] relapses, it returns until it dominates the heart. This is the rust that God mentioned: *'No indeed! Rather that which they have earned is rust upon their hearts.'* (*Al-Mutaffifin*, 83:14) (*Tirmidhi*)

In other words, the heart only 'sees' when it is sufficiently pure. Spiritual vision, then, is a matter of virtue and constant repentance. Conversely spiritual blindness is the result of sin and egotism, or at least complacence, like a total eclipse of the sun. And since the heart is also the seat of faith, spiritual knowledge increases faith and vice versa. God says in the Qur'an:

> *He it is Who sent down the Sakinah [great peace] into the hearts of the believers, that they might add faith to their faith. . . . (Al-Fath, 48:4)*

POLISHING THE RUST OFF THE HEART

How can a person polish his or her heart to remove the rust that accumulates over the course of life? The Prophet ﷺ said: 'There is for everything a polish that takes away rust; and the polish for the heart is the remembrance of God.' (*Bukhari*). In the previous chapter, we quoted God's words about the Prophet Muhammad ﷺ:

> *Truly there is for you a good example in the messenger of God for whoever hopes for [the encounter with] God and the Last Day, and remembers God often. (Al-Ahzab, 33:21)*

This is the only description in the Qur'an of the Prophet ﷺ that specifically uses the words *a good example*. It describes a state and an act. These are part of the *sunnah* (custom) of the Prophet ﷺ—if not their essence. The state is one of love: hoping *for [the encounter with] God and the Last Day* necessarily implies love. The act is remembering God often. So following the example of the Prophet ﷺ means remembering God often: essentially, as much as one can, with love. Indeed, the cardinal spiritual commandment in the Qur'an seems to be to remember or glorify God in some way (with the right intention), including through reciting the Qur'an itself, as we have seen. Equally, most of the *sunnah* itself consists of either invocations or supplications to be said before or after almost every imaginable legitimate and necessary action or vital function. These include everything from the moment of birth to the moment of death; from marking the beginning of each day of the week to marking its end; from waking up in the morning to going to bed at night; from hearing a rooster crow in the morning to seeing the moon at night; from putting on one's clothes to taking them off; from eating and drinking to going to the bathroom; from (against) being angry to making love; from coughing to sneezing to laughing to yawning; from leaving one's home to entering it; from greeting someone to saying goodbye to them; from before starting one's prayers to after finishing them; from before starting a conversation to after finishing one, and so on. As already noted, the Lady 'A'ishah ☙, the wife of the Prophet ☙, said of him that: 'The Prophet used to remember God at all times' (*Muslim*). And the Prophet ☙ himself said: 'Keep your tongue moist with the remembrance of God' (*Tirmidhi*).

This explains the Prophet Muhammad's ☙ definition of '*Ihsan*' ('excellence' or 'virtue')—corroborated by the Archangel Gabriel ☙ himself—as seen in Chapter 2. The Prophet ☙ defined *Ihsan* as: 'To worship God as if you saw Him, for even if you do not see Him, yet He sees you' (*Bukhari*). Worshipping God as if one saw Him necessarily means remembering Him at all times (or as often as possible) with love, even outside of the formal prayers. Hence *Ihsan* or virtue means to invoke God as much as possible (if not constantly), and this is precisely the *sunnah*. It also explains why the main practice of Islamic mystics (sometimes called 'Sufis') is the constant remembrance of God: the aim of traditional Sufism is precisely *Ihsan*, to 'worship God as if you saw Him'. Indeed, it is fair to say that no one over the course of the history of Islam has put more energy into trying to constantly invoke God and attain *Ihsan* than Sufis. So, in a sense the Sufis are the 'specialists' of *Ihsan*, just as the theologians are the 'specialists' of *Iman* and the jurists are the 'specialists' of *Islam*. Any study of the great mainstream Sufi orders (*turuq*) (such as the Qadiriyyah, the Shadhiliyyah, the Naqshbandiyyah, the Ba 'Alawiyyah, the Tijaniyyah and so on) or their writings clearly shows this.

Remembering God is a relief. When there is no remembrance in the soul, the ego is always there whispering nasty thoughts. God says in the Qur'an: *And verily we created man, and We know what his self [ego] whispers to him. And We are closer to him than his jugular vein.* (*Qaf*, 50:16). It whispers evil things about other people—or even about God Himself—and tries to get you to do foul things, hence its name, *the soul that incites to evil* (*Yusuf*, 12:53), as mentioned above. Failing that, it selfishly whines about itself: about how unjustly it has been treated; how great it really is, puffing itself up like a toad (though toads are nicer than egos), and gloating over its little 'victories'. Anyone who watches his or her thoughts with detachment for long enough will witness this. So God warns: *And whoever turns away from the Remembrance of the Compassionate One, We assign for him a devil (qarin) and he becomes his companion* (*Al-Zukhruf*, 43:36). But when there is remembrance present in the heart, the flow of internal chatter—the ego's 'stream of consciousness'—dries up, and the heart finally gets some peace and rest. God says: *Those who believe and whose hearts are reassured by God's remembrance. Truly by God's remembrance are hearts made serene* (*Al-Ra'd*, 13:28). Instead of being with your own petty self, you are with God, at least in thought. God says: *Remember Me, I will remember you . . .* (*Al-Baqarah*, 2:152). And over time, frequent remembrance heals the heart and makes it sound. For most people, this is what really counts in the end, when they leave their bodies and world behind. God says: *The day when neither wealth nor children will avail, / except him who comes to God with a heart that is sound* (*Al-Shu'ara*, 26:88–89). But beyond that, for some people, constant remembrance can lead to true spiritual vision and inspiration. God says in a 'holy *hadith*' ('*hadith qudsi*'):

> . . . *Nothing is more beloved to Me, as a means for My servant to draw near to Me, than the worship which I have made binding upon him; and My servant ceases not to draw near unto Me with added voluntary devotions of his own free will until I love him; and when I love him I am the hearing with which he hears and the sight wherewith he sees and the hand with which he grasps and the foot with which he walks. . . .* (*Bukhari*)

~

WHY IS IT IMPORTANT TO KNOW ALL THIS?

It is important to know about the heart for a number of reasons:

1. It is important to know about the heart because it allows human beings to understand that they *must* purify their souls (*tazkiyat al-nafs*),

and overcome their own egos and their pettiness. God says: . . .*those who are saved from their own meanness—these are the successful* (*Al-Taghabun*, 64:16). It is in the heart that human greatness really lies—and everything that human beings do they do first in the heart (through having the right intention). The heart is the most sublime aspect of human beings. And it requires constant spiritual work, particularly invocation. As Henry Wadsworth Longfellow wrote (in 'A Psalm for Life', in 1838):

Tell me not, in mournful numbers,
    Life is but an empty dream!
For the soul is dead that slumbers,
    And things are not what they seem.

Life is real! Life is earnest!
    And the grave is not its goal;
Dust thou art, to dust returnest,
    Was not spoken of the soul.

Not enjoyment, and not sorrow,
    Is our destined end or way;
But to act, that each to-morrow
    Find us farther than to-day. . . .

Trust no Future, howe'er pleasant!
    Let the dead Past bury its dead!
Act,—act in the living Present!
    Heart within, and God o'erhead! . . .

2. It is important to know about the heart because it explains the apparent paradoxes of faith and intelligence, and of faith and evil. The first paradox is that there are geniuses with no faith, and apparently unintelligent people with a lot of faith. The second paradox is that there are good people who do good works and have no faith, and, conversely, very evil people who have faith, or who are apparently very religious. Knowing about the heart makes it clear first that faith is not a matter of mental genius—and does not depend on mental 'intelligence'—but rather on active goodness. So being very clever—or not very clever—has little bearing on faith. Second, it makes it clear that those people who do

evil and have faith are, in fact, gradually losing it, through their actions. Conversely, people who do good—for altruistic and not merely egotistical reasons—are gradually gaining it. They are polishing their own hearts.

3. More mundanely, it is important to know about the heart because most people today are educated to believe that they are essentially only their own 'mind' with a body attached to it. The 'mind' is thought of as merely 'programming' plus 'cumulative experiences'. These are believed to be physically inside neural pathways in their physical brains within their skulls, just as a computer is essentially comprised of a microchip within a PC or a mobile phone. So when the 'computer' is permanently turned off or broken, you die. This seems to have the weight of medical evidence behind it, since all body parts except the brain (including the physical heart) seem to be surgically replaceable, and since brain damage is associated with memory loss. So basically, whether we say so or not, we tend to subconsciously believe that we are moving, organic computers. This means that our whole interaction with objective 'reality' is confined by our bodies and mediated by our five senses.

And yet all of us—or perhaps many of us—have experiences that do not fit into this model of ourselves. For example, many people often seem to know in advance who is calling them on the phone, even if they do not ever call at that time, or were not expected to call then. And many times, the person receiving the call says: 'Oh I was just thinking about you.' This seems particularly true for people with genuine affection for each other. Often also, one will have a 'feeling' about something and then it happens or proves to be true. A lot of times the feeling turns out to be wrong or wishful thinking, but often it is correct. And it is astounding how even pets seem to develop a 'sixth sense' about their owners to the extent of knowing when they are returning home: scientific studies have actually been done on this (see, for example, *Dogs that Know when their Owners are Coming Home* and *The Sense of Being Stared At* by Rupert Sheldrake). Then there are 'déjà vus' and, more powerfully, premonition dreams or visions: sometimes you see the thing that is going to happen in a dream; sometimes you see a symbol of it. Most often perhaps, you feel misgivings or ominous unease about something for no apparent reason. Sometimes you *sense* a danger coming. Now psychologists and statisticians have some very good 'scientific' explanations for a lot of these phenomena, but not all of them. And many people begin to recognize from their own trials-and-errors which of their different kinds of intuitions they should take seriously, and which should be ignored. Knowing about the heart is important because it gives you a model that helps look at intuitions more openly and objectively. This is particularly important with strong intuitions about impending danger. In short, knowing about the heart helps you to use your own 'gut feeling'.

~

Chapter 9

WHAT IS WORLDLY LIFE?

Bear in mind that the life of this world is merely play, diversion, adornment, mutual boasting and rivalry in wealth and children. It is like plants that spring up after the rain: their growth at first delights the sowers, but then they wither away, and you see them turn yellow; then they become chaff. And in the next life there is severe punishment, and forgiveness from God—and Beatitude. The life of this world is only the pleasure of delusion. (Al-Hadid, 57:20)

Worldly life is the exact opposite of the life of the heart. This is because the heart is 'inner', and worldly life is 'outer': obviously, 'inwardness' and 'outwardness' are opposites. By 'worldly life' we do not mean 'life in the world'—which is obviously immeasurably precious, and which includes the life 'of the heart'—but life *of* the world: life that is too *worldly*. In the verse cited above, God warns of the futility of worldly life, and defines it as having five (progressively worse) levels: (1) *play*; (2) *diversion*; (3) *adornment*; (4) *mutual boasting*; and (5) *rivalry in wealth and children*. These can be understood as follows:

1. 'Play' is necessary, natural and neutral. It is how children learn, and

how adults relax. But when it interferes with something important and serious, it can become an obstacle.

2. 'Diversion' is a momentary lapse in focus and concentration; it is a kind of unintended dereliction of duty.

3. 'Adornment' implies a misplaced passion for something: loving something you should not really be loving or loving something for a wrong or superficial reason. In other words, it implies a 'lust' for external beauty and for worldly life at the expense of loving internal beauty (which is virtue and goodness of heart). Elsewhere in the Qur'an, God says:

> Adorned for mankind is love of lusts—of women, children, stored-up heaps of gold and silver, horses of mark, cattle, and tillage. That is the pleasure of the life of this world; but God—with Him is the most excellent abode. (Aal 'Imran, 3:14)

4. If 'adornment' means misplaced passion, 'mutual boasting' means misplaced pride. Whereas passion is love for something external, pride is love for something internal. Passion— as just discussed—is good to the extent that its object is good, and bad to the extent that its object is bad. The same is true for pride. When pride is love for the heart and inwardness, it becomes dignity. When, on the other hand, it is love for the ego, it becomes egoism. This kind of pride is at the root of all sin and even all nastiness. In the Qur'an, it is what caused Satan to fall from grace by refusing to bow to Adam ﷺ. Satan says to God: . . . I am better than him. You created me from fire, and You created him from clay (Sad, 38:76). So pride is worse than passion because whereas passion merely runs away from the heart, pride is the ego actually rising up to oppose the heart.

5. 'Rivalry in wealth and children': 'wealth and children' here can be taken to include all worldly goods. 'Rivalry' (the Arabic word 'takathur' translated as 'rivalry' here also indicates 'greed' and 'wanting to acquire ever more') in this context does not mean 'healthy competition'. It means greed, jealousy, ill will, hatred and finally, aggression. It is the evil fruit of pride, and it eventually leads to all kinds of violence.

So in this one verse, we have a remarkable description of the entire gamut of what worldliness means (psychologically speaking), starting with the relatively innocent and ending with the completely corrupt. It explains why worldly life is seen as negative and futile in so many passages of the Qur'an. The Prophet Muhammad ﷺ said: 'Abandon desire for the world and God will love you; abandon desire for what other people have, and people will love you' (*Ibn Majah*).

∽

This one verse also remarkably sums up the sequential phases of lives and ages of human beings, through their activities or faults. *'Play'* is the activity of little children. *'Diversion'* is the activity of older children, naturally averse to concentration and duty. *'Adornment'* is the activity of teenagers after puberty and of young adults, as their interest in the opposite sex increases and peaks, and they want to look attractive. *'Mutual boasting'* is the fault of settled, confident people, people making their own living, and people rising in the world. *'Rivalry in wealth and children'* are the two faults of middle-aged people and then of old people who have become physically frail (and can no longer be physically competitive), or who have become so old they have grandchildren ('children' here includes grandchildren) for whose sake they are competitive. In Shakespeare's *As You Like It* (Act II, Scene VII), a character named 'Jaques' famously and brilliantly summarizes the 'seven ages of man' (according to the habits of his age and the symbolism of the seven traditional 'planets', namely: Mercury, the moon, Venus, the sun, Mars, Jupiter, Saturn respectively) as follows :

> All the world's a stage,
>   And all the men and women merely players;
> They have their exits and their entrances,
>   And one man in his time plays many parts,
> His acts being seven ages. At first the infant,
>   Mewling and puking in the nurse's arms;
> And then the whining schoolboy, with his satchel
>   And shining morning face, creeping like snail
> Unwillingly to school. And then the lover,
>   Sighing like furnace, with a woeful ballad
> Made to his mistress' eyebrow. Then a soldier,
>   Full of strange oaths, and bearded like the pard,
> Jealous in honor, sudden and quick in quarrel,
>   Seeking the bubble reputation

Even in the cannon's mouth. And then the justice,
    In fair round belly with good capon lined,
With eyes severe and beard of formal cut,
    Full of wise saws and modern instances;
And so he plays his part. The sixth age shifts
    Into the lean and slippered pantaloon,
With spectacles on nose and pouch on side;
    His youthful hose, well saved, a world too wide
For his shrunk shank; and his big manly voice,
    Turning again toward childish treble, pipes
And whistles in his sound. Last scene of all,
    That ends this strange eventful history,
Is second childishness and mere oblivion,
    Sans teeth, sans eyes, sans taste, sans everything.

However, the single Qur'anic verse cited above (*Al-Hadid*, 57:20), time-lessly summarises not only the ages of human beings, but the inner conditions and spiritual dangers of each age (not withstanding extreme old age whose frailty is not a sin in Islam)—in addition to all the other meanings discussed earlier.

~

What, then, are people supposed to do? What is the practical 'takeaway' from these teachings? It is, simply: 'Don't waste your time!' Worldly life is like plants which *at first delight the sowers, but then they wither away, and you see them turn yellow; then they become chaff.* In other words, life is very brief, and if it does continue, it becomes frail old age and then ends anyway. The notion that people have time to spare is a mere illusion caused by the thrill of youth and health. The American writer and poet Edgar Allan Poe (d. 1849) wrote (in 'A Dream Within a Dream'):

You are not wrong, who deem
    That my days have been a dream . . .
I stand amid the roar
    Of a surf-tormented shore,

And I hold within my hand
    Grains of the golden sand—
How few! yet how they creep
    Through my fingers to the deep,
While I weep—while I weep!
    O God! can I not grasp
Them with a tighter clasp?
    O God! can I not save
One from the pitiless wave?
    Is all that we see or seem
    But a dream within a dream?

Indeed, in reality, worldly life is ephemeral and there is no time to waste. Death is inextricable and anyway always potentially a heartbeat away. And it is coming for us, getting nearer every moment, no matter what age we are. In the Qur'an, we are reminded: *Closer to you and closer / closer and closer still (Al-Qiyamah, 75:34–35)*. That is the grim truth that we all need to face up to.

Perhaps this is why the very next verse after the one cited above says: *Race for your Lord's forgiveness and a garden the breadth of which is as the breadth of the heaven and the earth. . . (Al-Hadid, 57:21)*. Similarly, another verse says: *And hurry towards your Lord's forgiveness and to a garden as wide as the heavens and the earth. . . (Aal 'Imran, 3:133)*. And again, elsewhere: *So flee unto God. . . (Al-Dhariyat, 51:50)*.

∼

WHY IS IT IMPORTANT TO KNOW ALL THIS?

The average person in many countries—and particularly the average student—now spends more time every day on self-entertainment than at any other period in the history of the world. That is to say, the average person expends up to six hours or more a day—a quarter of their time alive; a third of their time awake—every day on television or movies; online surfing and chatting; social media; video games; pornography and adult entertainment; music videos or pop music or radio. That works out to more than 40 hours a week—which is the length of a full-time working week. It means giving a lifetime's worth of work and consumption to films and television, media and internet giants for free. It is a hidden addiction, and a form of internal slavery to fantasy and triviality. It is worldly life that has gone beyond play and diversion to misplaced passion and pride—and perhaps sown the seeds of social violence. And it is worldly life of the most removed-from-reality kind. It necessarily means making entertainment a religion and religion entertainment.

Islam calls for a paradigm shift as regards the value of life and also the immanence of death. Our usual myopia comes from the unspoken illusion that because we are still alive, and death only seems to happen to other people, it does not concern us individually. But of course it does, and will, soon enough.

Al-Ghazali wrote:

> Your time is your life, and your life is your capital: through it you make your trade, and through it you can reach eternal bliss, and nearness to God, Most High. Every single breath of yours is a priceless jewel, as it is irreplaceable. Once it is gone, it will never come back. Don't be like the fools who rejoice because their money increases while their lives decrease. What good is money when your lifespan is running out? (Abu Hamid al-Ghazali, *The Beginning of Guidance*, 1)

Of course, everyone needs to relax and unwind for an hour or two every day. However, six hours a day, without physical exercise, intellectual growth or meaningful human interaction—to say nothing of religious, family, charitable and social duties and activities—is an unprecedented waste of human time, and indeed, life. It also has profound negative psychological, cultural, sociological, medical, economic and even political consequences. The Prophet Muhammad ﷺ said:

> Make use of five things before five things happen: your youth before old age; your health before illness; your money before poverty; your free time before you are occupied, and your life before you die. (*Hakim*)

∼

Chapter 10

WHAT IS THE *'SHARI'AH'*?

*Then We set you upon a [clear] course (shari'ah) of the
commandment; so follow it, and do not follow the desires
of those who do not know. (Al-Jathiyah, 45:18)*

In 1978, a Christian Arab professor at Columbia University, New York,
wrote a remarkable book called *Orientalism* in which he lamented that
the West had so materially dominated the Islamic World that its negative
stereotypes of it were believed by Arabs and Muslims themselves. In our
day this is true of the *shari'ah* itself. The West has associated the *shari'ah*
with medieval subjugation of women and amputation of limbs to the
extent that anyone now seeking to implement the *shari'ah* starts doing
precisely that—as if that were the true yardstick of the sincerity of their
faith. But the *shari'ah* is actually a vast and plural body of thought, laws
and procedures far different from what it is commonly thought to be. On
any given issue there are likely several different opinions—even within
the same school of jurisprudence—all aiming, as will be discussed, at the
good of the individual and of society. But of course this 'good' is not a
random and subjective notion based on changing cultural assumptions.
It is ultimately based on Islamic revelation and inspiration: the Qur'an
and the *hadith*.

THE MEANING OF THE WORD 'SHARI'AH'

It is extremely instructive to look at the origin of the term 'shari'ah'. It has the same root as the modern Arabic word for road or street ('shari''). Its root refers literally to the path—that over time becomes clear and well-worn—that animals make in nature to go to a watering hole. In the desert, of course, these paths are literally the roads to salvation, water meaning life for all living things. So the acquired meaning of the word 'shari'ah'—law derived from the Divine revelation of the Qur'an and Divine inspiration to the Prophet Muhammad ﷺ—implies a law that is a means for people to attain salvation in this life (and the next) and without which people will wander ignorantly in their own deserts until they perish. This is to say, then, that the word 'shari'ah' itself in Arabic is laden with a beautiful, subtle and powerful meaning.

The word 'shari'ah' and its linguistic derivatives actually occur only five times in the Qur'an: twice as a verb (once positively in *Al-Shura*, 42:13, and once negatively in *Al-Shura*, 42:21); once in a parable referring to the course of swimming fish (*Al-A'raf*, 7:163); once in the form 'shir'ah' (*Al-Ma'idah*, 5:48); and only once as a noun referring to Islamic sacred law as such. This once occurs in the verse cited above: *Then We set you upon a [clear] course (shari'ah) of the commandment (al-amr); so follow it, and do not follow the desires of those who do not know (Al-Jathiyah, 45:18)*. The word 'commandment' is usually taken to mean 'religious commandment', but it literally means 'matter', 'concern' or 'affair'. This is to say then that the *shari'ah* is based on *the nature of things*, in much the same way as religious rites correspond to the nature of human beings (as discussed in the second chapter). So the *shari'ah* is not some arbitrary and tyrannical set of inscrutable rules, but a roadmap providentially corresponding to practical and spiritual needs. Moreover, in the form 'shir'ah' it refers to the Divine laws of other religions as well:

> And We have revealed to you the Book with the truth confirming the Book
> that was before it and watching over it. So judge between them, according to
> what God has revealed, and do not follow their whims away from the truth
> that has come to you. To every one of you, We have appointed a [Divine law]
> ('shir'ah') and a way. If God had willed, He would have made you one com-
> munity, but that He may try you in what He has given to you. So vie with

one another in good works; to God you shall all return, and He will then inform you of that in which you differed. (Al-Ma'idah, 5:48)

So if the *shari'ah* is the sacred law of the religion of Islam in particular, the word also implies that there were other such sacred laws, in other religions, also worthy of respect, and also corresponding to practical and spiritual needs.

SHARI'AH AS MORAL CODE

A legal code is a code accountable to—and punishable by—laws in this world. A moral code (to believers at least) is a code accountable to—and punishable by—God, in the hereafter. The *shari'ah* is a moral code before being a legal code. This means that most of what it considers as offences are not punishable by earthly law according to the *shari'ah*, though God will, or might, punish them in the hereafter. For example, if you lie (not under oath) to a friend you do not get punished for it by law, but God will hold you to account for it, if you do not repent. A large part of the *shari'ah* then is about sin, not crime. Moreover, the rules for prayer, fasting, pilgrimage and so on are part of the *shari'ah*, but would not be considered 'law' in the Western sense. Hence to call *shari'ah* 'Islamic Law' is actually quite misleading.

Moreover, even in those areas where it does function as a legal code, the *shari'ah* deliberately contains relatively few legal injunctions (*qillat al-taklif*); is deliberately silent about most things (meaning they are on principle permissible) and deliberately open to interpretation about many other things. Accordingly, Muslim scholars have classified every action into one of five categories (according to most schools of jurisprudence) according to the *shari'ah*:

1. Obligatory (*'fard'*): that which you get rewarded for doing, and punished for not doing.
2. Disliked (*'makruh'*): that which you get rewarded for not doing, but not punished for doing (some Hanafi scholars add further subdivisions here).
3. Permissible (*'mubah'*): that which you do not get punished or rewarded for doing or not doing (unless you do it for the love of good, in which case you are rewarded). It will be noted that in principle everything is permissible unless there is a sacred text specifically forbidding it.

4. Recommended (*'mustahabb'*): that which you get rewarded for doing, but not punished for not doing.

5. Forbidden (*'haram'*): that which you get punished for doing, and rewarded for not doing.

It will also be noted that according to the *shari'ah*, as the Prophet Muhammad 🕮 said, 'Actions are [judged] according to their intentions' (*Bukhari*; *Muslim*), but that every action is valid or invalid according to whether it has met the criteria that define it. All this is to say, then, that the first thing *shari'ah* aims to do is make things morally crystal clear to Muslims, as a guidebook to life and to the world. God says in the Qur'an: *We have revealed to you the Book as a clarification of all things and as a guidance, and a mercy and good tidings to Muslims (Al-Nahl, 16:89).*

THE PURPOSE OF THE *SHARI'AH*

The ultimate purpose of the legal *shari'ah* is actually laid out in the one verse which positively uses the word *'shara'a'* as a verb, as follows:

> *He has prescribed (shara'a) for you as a religion that which He enjoined upon Noah and that which We have revealed to you, and that which We enjoined upon Abraham, and Moses, and Jesus [declaring], 'Establish religion and do not be divided in it'. . . . (Al-Shura, 42:13)*

From this we can understand that the ultimate purpose of the *shari'ah* is twofold: to establish religious practice and social cohesion. In other words, the goal of religious law is simply spiritual equilibrium and social harmony, these corresponding to the spiritual and earthly well-being and needs of human beings and societies. The great Shafi'i jurist Al-'Izz bin 'Abd al-Salam (d. 660/1262) said: 'All God's rulings are [for] the interests of His servants, so good news to whoever accepts [their] advice, and repents from his sin' (*Qawa'id al-Ahkam*). And Ibn al-Qayyim al-Jawziyyah (d. 750/1350) wrote:

> The bedrock and foundation of the *shari'ah* is wisdom and benefit for people in this life and the next. It is all justice, mercy, benefit and wisdom. Every ruling that leaves justice for injustice, that leaves mercy for its opposite, that leaves benefit for corruption, that leaves wisdom for folly,

is not from the *shari'ah*, even if it is inserted into it through interpretation [of the Qur'an and *hadith*]. (*I'lam al-Muwaqqi'in 'an Rabb al-'Alameen*)

More specifically, Islamic scholars like Al-Ghazali (in his *Mustasfa*) and Ibrahim al-Shatibi (d. 790/1388) have gone through every single commandment in the Qur'an and distilled them into five universal 'aims' of the *shari'ah*: *'maqasid al-shari'ah'*. In practice, these translate into five basic rights for all people. They are: (1) the right to life; (2) the right to religion (some scholars even put this right first); (3) the right to family, procreation and honour (this right is sometimes split into two: family and procreation, and dignity); (4) the right to reason; and (5) the right to property—with all the freedoms and protection that each of these rights imply. The following verse in the Qur'an can be thought of as summarizing them:

Truly God commands justice, excellence and generosity towards relatives, and He forbids what is shameful, censurable and oppressive. He admonishes you, so that perhaps you may remember. (*Al-Nahl*, 16:90)

So:

1. *Justice* is the root of the right to life, and indeed of all the rights;
2. *Excellence* (*Ihsan*—which as discussed is defined as *worshipping God as if you see Him*) implies the right to religion;
3. *Generosity towards relatives* refers to family and procreation;
4. *He forbids what is shameful* refers to the right of honour (which in Islamic societies is closely related to the family);
5. *Censurable* (*munkar*—*'inkar'* is defined as the opposite of knowledge or *'irfan'* [see: Raghib Isfahani, *Mu'jam Mufradat Alfazh al-Qur'an*]) and refers to the right of reason;
6. *Oppressive* refers to the right of property and also, a fortiori, to the right to life.

These 'aims of the *shari'ah*' are important to understand the *'why'* of the *shari'ah*—the 'spirit of the law'—and to make sure that legal rulings reflect this. They are not, as some people today think, used to replace it. They are also the basis of 'human rights' in Islam (as can be seen more or less accurately in the 1990 Cairo Declaration on Human Rights in Islam, adopted by 44 Islamic Countries), only in Islam they are actually unconditional God-given rights not convention-based 'human-given' rights. Finally, it should be clear that *shari'ah* in general—and these rights specifically—are not designed to create hardship for people, but to make things holistically easier for them. God says:

> ... *God desires ease for you, and He does not desire hardship for you.* ...
> (*Al-Baqarah*, 2:185)

THE SCHOOLS OF ISLAMIC JURISPRUDENCE

The English word 'jurisprudence' originally comes from the Latin terms *juris prudentia*, which mean 'the study, knowledge, or science of law'. According to the *Oxford English Dictionary* it means 'the theory or philosophy of law'. In an Islamic context we take it to refer to how *shari'ah* law is derived from its fundamental two sources: the Qur'an and the *hadith*. It is the '*what*' of the law.

After the death of the Prophet Muhammad 靉, direct revelation on earth came to an end forever. God stopped pronouncing directly about anything, and no one could claim Divine authority for his or her opinion. Theocracy on earth ceased to exist, and from then on people had only the Qur'an and reports of *ahadith* to fall back on. This was not so much a problem for the Companions of the Prophet 靉 as they had their own memories of the Prophet 靉 (although they occasionally disagreed about the intention and meaning of things they had all witnessed). But the gradual death of these Companions (the last well-known Companion to die, Anas bin Malik, was born in 612 CE, was brought up in the Prophet's 靉 household from the age of 10, and died in 93/712; the last of all the Companions to die was Abu 'l-Tufayl 'Amir ibn Wathilah, who died in Mecca around 102/721) led to a certain crisis of intellectual authority, even after the *ahadith* were definitively collected. So a number of important questions about the Qur'an and the *ahadith* had to be resolved.

These questions were not to do with the *authority* of the Qur'an and the *hadith*, but rather with *how to understand* them. Nevertheless, the questions were very important. They included the following: what happens when there are apparent contradictions or 'annulments' in the Qur'an, or in the *hadith*, or between the two? What happens when there are different narrations of a hadith that seem to contradict each other? Are logic and 'contradiction' even valid concepts when applied to God's laws? How are the differences and disagreements between the different Companions of the Prophet 🌸 on various points to be understood? What to do about things not mentioned in either the Qur'an or the *hadith*? How do we know if the things mentioned in the Qur'an or *hadith* are specific and contextual or general? What were the contexts of each verse or *hadith,* and how do these bear on the distinct instructions the Prophet 🌸 gave to different people? Which verses of the Qur'an are legislative and which are merely informative? Which are literal and which are allegorical, and how do we know? What happens when the known rhetorical meaning of the Arabic language is different from its literal meaning? What happens when words have more than one meaning, and how do we know which meaning (or meanings) is correct? How do we know that we understand Arabic words in the same way they were understood at the time of the revelation of the Qur'an? Of the Prophet's 🌸 actions, which things are sunnah (and to be followed), and which are merely circumstantial, or even exclusive to him 🌸? How 'certain' or 'strong' does a *hadith* have to be in order for it to be a point of reference in law? Is one *hadith* even enough for a law? To whom exactly do laws apply? Who is fit to interpret these laws? Who is responsible for implementing them; how, and under what conditions? What to do about laws that are apparently unjust—or is 'justice' itself a subjective construct with no meaning outside of God's laws? If so, what about laws which clearly contradict the principles of justice as clearly laid out in the Qur'an and *hadith*? Is there a methodology of interpretation inherent in the Qur'an and the *hadith*? Why are there different interpretations and how should the different interpreters regard each other and each other's opinions? If all the scholars agree on one interpretation does it become binding? What if they agree, and then a later generation disagrees? Or what if they agree and then later disagree?—and so on. Much of Islamic legal and intellectual history has been understandably preoccupied with precisely these weighty questions. And they have led to innumerable disagreements and disputes.

Many different scholars—estimates run from 90 to 130—in the first centuries of Islam developed their own integral methodologies for dealing

with all these questions. These are called a *'madhhab'* (pl. *'madhahib'*)—
which literally means '(point of) departure' and therefore also 'direction'—
and that is a perfect description for them, since they determine how to
proceed based on the Qur'an and the *hadith* (in the Sunni world). When
the Prophet Muhammad ﷺ sent Mu'adh bin Jabal as his envoy to the
Yemen, he ﷺ asked Mu'adh how he would make his decisions. Mu'adh
said he would first judge by the Qur'an, then the *sunnah*, then use his
own interpretation, and the Prophet ﷺ approved this methodology (*Abu
Dawud*; *Tirmidhi*; *Sunan al-Darimi*). So those scholars who developed
their own methodologies of interpretation came to be known as *'mujtahid
imams'* and included such scholars as the great ascetic Hasan al-Basri (d.
110/728); Abd al-Rahman al-Awza'i (d. 157/774); the ascetic Sufyan al-
Thawri (d. 161/778); Al-Layth Ibn Sa'd (d. 175/791); (Shafi'i's student)
Ibrahim Abu Thawr (d. 239/854); Dawud al-Zhahiri (d. c. 270/883)
(whose *madhhab* is still consulted by other *madhahib* to this day); and (Ibn
Hanbal's student) the great Qur'anic commentator, Ibn Jarir al-Tabari
(d. 310/923). Each of these scholars was based in a certain region of the
Islamic world and largely represented the thinking of earlier scholars in
their regions. However, only four *madhahib* came to dominate the Sunni
world (and do so to this day): those of Abu Hanifah Nu'man bin Thabit
(d. 150/767); Malik bin Anas (d. 179/796); Muhammad bin Idris al-Shafi'i
(d. 204/820), and Ahmad bin Hanbal (d. 241/855). Broadly speaking **Abu
Hanifah** and his school prioritized (in order of importance):

(a) The Qur'an,
(b) Sound *ahadith*,
(c) The consensus and/or legal opinions of the Companions of the Prophet
    ﷺ (especially the more learned ones such as Ibn Mas'ud ﷺ),
(d) Legal (analogical) reasoning (*qiyas*), and subtle analogy (*istihsan*), based
    on the Qur'an and the *sunnah*.

Abu Hanifah lived in Iraq. He believed that no matter how many
ahadith there were, scholars should look at how the people who actually
heard them (i.e. the Companions of the Prophet ﷺ) understood them,
because they had direct experience and knowledge of the circumstances,
context and intentions of the *ahadith*. In other words, he accepted that
the Companions were in a far better position to understand *ahadith* than

later generations of Muslims who only had isolated texts, and even these were not all accurately verbatim.

The Hanafi *madhhab* remains the largest of all the Sunni *madhahib* with about 50 per cent of all Sunnis being Hanafi. Basically it is the *madhhab* of all of Sunni Central Asia including the Indian subcontinent. It was the official *madhhab* of the vast Ottoman empire (c. 699-1343/1299-1923) and consequently it is the most developed and plural of all the *madhahib*. Moreover, Islamic law is divided into *'ibadat* (laws about worship) and *mu'amalat* (laws about social interaction), so that even Shafi'i strongholds like Indonesia, Malaysia and Egypt sometimes adopted aspects of Hanafi law for social interactions and personal status laws ('*mu'amalat*'), because it is the easiest to implement.

Malik bin Anas lived more or less his whole life in Medina (where the Prophet 🌸 had settled and died). He prioritized the *practice* of the learned people of Medina because he thought that the practice of the people of Medina of his time—separated as they were only by a few generations from the Prophet 🌸 himself—most accurately reflected the true teachings of the Prophet 🌸. Accordingly he prioritized:

(a) The Qur'an,
(b) The Prophet's 🌸 *sunnah* as understood through *ahadith*, Companion rulings and the practices of the people of Medina,
(c) Consensus,
(d) Legal reasoning (*qiyas*),
(e) Communal needs.

Imam Malik wrote the first systemized handbook of Islamic Law, the *Muwatta'*, and this book is still a fundamental resource for Muslim scholars today. His *madhhab* accounts for some 20 per cent of all Sunnis, mostly those in North and West Africa.

Imam Malik's student **Muhammad bin Idris al-Shafi'i** was from a Meccan tribe related to the Prophet 🌸, but travelled around the Arab world. Shafi'i differed with his erstwhile teacher Malik. He held that *hadith* could never on its own abrogate the Qur'an. *After* the Qur'an, he looked at the texts of *ahadith* themselves, judging their reliability from their chains of transmission and contents. His question-and-answer text *Al-Risalah* is considered to be the first complete exposition of the integral methodology of Islamic jurisprudence, and is the seminal text for all those studying it. In it he says:

> No one at all should [give an opinion] on a specific matter by merely saying, 'it is permitted' or 'prohibited', unless he is certain of [legal] knowledge, and this knowledge must be based on the Qur'an and the *sunnah*, or [derived] from *ijma'* (consensus) and *qiyas* (analogical, legal reasoning). (*Al-Risalah, On Al-Bayan*, v)
>
> [Whenever] a certain *sunnah* was abrogated by another [the Prophet ﷺ] never failed to indicate in the abrogated *sunnah* what he intended to abrogate. . . . The *sunnah* cannot be contradictory to the Book of God, but will always follow the Book of God . . . clarifying the meaning intended by God. (*Al-Risalah, On Hadith*)

Thus in practice his school prioritized:

(a) The Qur'an,
(b) Sound *ahadith*,
(c) Consensus of scholars,
(d) Companions' opinions (in the 'old' Shafi'i school at least),
(e) Analogical reasoning (*qiyas*) based on the Qur'an and *sunnah*,
(f) Presumption of continuity (*istishab al-hal*).

Because of its prioritizing the text of *ahadith* over earlier interpretations of them, the *Shafi'is* called their *madhhab* the '*madhhab al-hadith*' (the jurisprudential school of *hadith*). About one quarter of Sunnis are *Shafi'is*, at least in their '*ibadat*.

The '*hadith*' trend was taken one step further by Shafi'i's persecuted and heroic student **Ahmad bin Hanbal**. Ibn Hanbal thought that even weak *ahadith* were preferable to human reasoning and analogical reasoning. He considered that any reported *hadith* with a chance — however slim — of having been truly said by the Prophet ﷺ (and therefore being inspired and infallible) was better than resorting to human reasoning, which he regarded as inherently fundamentally flawed. Consequently, he and his school (only about five per cent of Sunnis, strictly speaking) prioritized:

(a) The Qur'an,
(b) Sound *ahadith*,

   (c)   Consensus of the early community,

   (d)   Companion opinions,

   (e)   Weak *ahadith*,

   (f)   Analogical reasoning (*qiyas*) based on the Qur'an and *sunnah*.

From all of the above it will be clear that each of the schools of law had their own different—but all intelligent and arguable—assumptions behind their methodologies, and *all* are based on the Qur'an and the hadith. And dozens of brilliant scholars in each generation examined them, thought them through, applied them and developed them. Equally, it will be clear that these different methodologies were bound to lead to differing opinions on various issues. In fact, there was only complete agreement, even within each *madhhab*, on less than 10 per cent of all issues, these issues then being regarded as absolute and indisputable ('*qat'i*'). Scholarly opinions on other issues were then generally regarded as being 'based on opinion' and hence 'speculative' ('*zhanni*'). Although and perhaps as a result of this— there was some historical infighting between the four main Sunni *madhahib*, they all recognized each other as valid, and adopted a pluralistic attitude of respect towards each other. Shafi'i himself said: '[We hold our] *madhhab* to be true, but [acknowledge that] it may be mistaken, and we hold that the *madhahib* of others are wrong but [admit that they] may be correct.' This mutual recognition solidified Sunnism as an internally integrated and *plural* system of thought and law. The derivation of *shari'ah* based on the methodologies of the *madhahib* became known as '*usul al-fiqh*' (literally meaning: '[based upon] foundations or principles of *fiqh*').

The term '*usul*' was coined almost immediately after Al-Shafi'i's *Risalah*, even before Muhammad al-Sarakhsi (d. 490/1096) wrote his famous book *Usul al-Fiqh*. This explains why those who follow the *madhahib* system are sometimes known as '*usulis*'. (The word '*usul*' is sometimes mistranslated into English as 'fundamentalism', which is completely wrong in its connotations: it should be translated as 'principlism'). For a thousand years, from the beginning of the third century of Islam, until the thirteenth century (that is, from about 800 until 1750 CE or so) it is impossible to find a single great and universally-recognized Sunni scholar who did not formally belong to one or other *madhhab* (and therefore was not an '*usuli*').

Usuli Islam is no less than the great intellectual and legal tradition of Sunni Islam over the course of Islamic history.

~

It should be noted that all that has been said above relates to how to derive rulings from the primary sources according to a logical and consistent methodology. It relates to what rulings are, or should be, ideal under circumstances normal in the seventh century. Herein lies another hurdle: circumstances change. Specifically they change in four ways: in time (*zaman*); place (*makan*); people (*ashkhas*); and conditions (*ahwal*). Later scholars realized this, and pointed out that rulings cannot be derived from texts once and for all without taking into considering the *context*s in which they are to be applied, and indeed the context in which they were valid in the first place. This in turn requires truly understanding the contexts of the present time, and the reality of the present. This is where many modern Islamic scholars fall short; they do not really understand the context of people today, and they think they do. They do not know what is really going on. And what is going on relates to the 'how' of the law. If the '*how*' is not understood, applying a one-size-fits-all law will likely lead to a mistake. So, often, whilst their derived rulings are in themselves correct, applying them in our world is incorrect because they have not taken into consideration the natural change of context. Applying a derived ruling *as is* often does not actually achieve the goal of the ruling ('*tahqiq al-manat*'). It is therefore in fact incorrect. It is as if a student presents a cut-and-paste answer from Wikipedia to a question different from the one he was asked. This obviously needs to change, and Islamic scholars need to study subjects like history, philosophy, science, technology and medicine in order that the judgements they give reflect the purpose of the living *shari'ah*, and not merely a book-form of it.

For example—as will be discussed in the next chapter—prior to the formation of the League of Nations (in 1920), the natural state of political relations between nations was hostile competition, if not actual war. Things were openly predatory, and if one nation could expand its territory and seize a bit of someone else's and get away with it, it thought this was an excellent thing, and usually found any pretext to do so. Many did not even bother with pretexts. Endless examples abound. Similarly in the Muslim world, the state of relations between Muslims and non-Muslims was assumed to be *jihad*—since nations were also generally based on religion—unless there was a specific peace treaty between two states. Today, all states are members of the United Nations, and the default condition between them is specifically peace. Universal treaties also regulate many aspects of international behaviour. So *jihad* is not the normal state of affairs, and cannot be considered legitimate behaviour (unless of course Muslim countries are invaded and occupied by outside powers): applying *fatwas* written under the conditions of the Mongol invasions is obviously incorrect and illegitimate.

Finally, it is worth mentioning that *usuli* scholars distilled the principles of operative *shari'ah* into legal maxims. These are general rules of thumb identifying patterns in the *shari'ah* that can be used to assist in making humane practical judgements. The five main ones are (according to Egyptian jurist Taqi al-Din Subki [727-771/1328-1370] in *Al-Ashbah wa 'l-Nazha'ir*):

1. Matters are (judged) according to their objectives.
2. Harm is to be eliminated.
3. Custom is binding.
4. Hardship calls for ease.
5. Certainty is not removed by doubt.

These clearly can be very useful, but ostensibly seem to represent a moving away from direct engagement with the Qur'an and the *hadith*.

IBN TAYMIYYAH AND THE BEGINNING OF THE ANTI-*USUL* SUNNI MOVEMENT

Clearly *usul* had become an intricate and perhaps complicated science over the centuries. More confusing still, it could sometimes reach conclusions that seemed to directly contradict certain reliable *ahadith*. (This could be for a number of reasons: prioritizing the Qur'an or other *ahadith*; regarding the *hadith* as weak or abrogated; viewing it as particular not general, or rhetorical not literal, conditional not unconditional, and so on). Enter Ibn Taymiyyah.

Taqi al-Din Ahmad Ibn Taymiyyah (d. 728/1328) was a brilliant Syrian Hanbali scholar. He lived in turbulent times and spent part of his life fighting the Mongol invasions, as well as the Alawites and Isma'ilis—whom he deemed as heretics. He consequently had particular views on *jihad*. He also inveighed against many practices that he believed had come into Islam through popular mysticism (folk Sufism), and were not part of the *sunnah*. But he also inveighed against orthodox Ash'arite-Maturidi doctrine, and in particular said that the 'anthropomorphic' references in the Qur'an to God's Hand, Eyes, Face, Side and establishing Himself on His Throne (see: 48:10; 2:115; 52:48; 39:56; 57:4 et al.) should be understood literally but without asking *why* or *how*. This, he maintained, was not just his opinion but the one-and-only truth, and was obligatory for scholars (those who preceded him he tended to dismiss as plain wrong) to agree with him about this, without compromise and without allowing for a respectful scholarly pluralism of opinions. Finally, he challenged the very edifice of *usul*. By his day and age each of the *madhahib* (including his own) had created precedents as legal touchstones. The situation was a bit like Tennyson's description in 'You ask me, Why' (1842):

It is the land that freemen till,
    That sober-suited Freedom chose,
The land, where girt with friends or foes
    A man may speak the thing he will;

A land of settled government,
    A land of just and old renown,
Where Freedom slowly broadens down
    From precedent to precedent:

Where faction seldom gathers head,
    But, by degrees to fullness wrought,
The strength of some diffusive thought
    Hath time and space to work and spread.

Yet the accumulated precedents of the *madhahib* meant that certain things appeared to be in direct contradiction with *hadith* texts. Also, certain common religious practices could simply not be traced to the *hadith*-recorded *sunnah*, at least as Ibn Taymiyyah saw it. All these he considered as *'bid'ah'* ('heretical innovation'). So he called for a return to what he believed to have been the norms of the first two or three generations of Muslims, the 'righteous forebears' (*'al-salaf al-salih'* — hence the word *'Salafi'* to describe followers of this movement). Like Shafi'i (in his *Risalah*), Ibn Taymiyyah believed every apparent legislative contradiction in the Qur'an and *sunnah* had been resolved somewhere in the *hadith*. Like Tabari, he limited the interpretation of the Qur'an to what could be found about it in the *hadith* or the statements of the *salaf*, effectively making the Qur'an completely subject to the *hadith* (as stated in his book, *Muqadimmah fi usul al-tafsir*). But unlike Shafi'i and Tabari he did not leave space for the possibility of allowing things not mentioned in the *hadith*. He called for not being bound by the 500 years of Islamic scholarship and thought between the 'righteous forebears' and himself. So strictly speaking, Ibn Taymiyyah founded an 'anti-*usul*' movement, even though it is sometimes called the 'no-*madhhab*' (*'la madhhabiyyah'*) movement, for it not only rejects the individual *madhhabs* but the very principles of their methodologies (their *'usul'*, precisely).

In this sense, Ibn Taymiyyah was a bit like Martin Luther. Luther decried what he saw as the excesses of the medieval Church and wanted to go directly to the scripture according to his own understanding of it, without regard to traditional Catholic exegetic methodology. And like Luther, Ibn Taymiyyah (and his followers) saw this as purifying the religion of new accretions that had crept into it. However, by doing away, on principle, with the methodologies that had resolved the two basic problems of textual traditions — the problem of apparent contradictions, and the problem of apparent silence on issues — all the old questions resurfaced without resolution. Consciously forgetting old solutions simply did not abolish the old dilemmas. In addition to these, and because of them, new problems surfaced. These included over-simplification and decontextual- ization of complex issues, and the incomplete and/or arbitrary selection ('cherry-picking') of scripture without taking into consideration what *all* of the Qur'an and all of the *ahadith* have to say on a given topic. This in turn led to the controversies — at least from an *usuli* point of view — that have since characterized the anti-*usul* movement. These include:

(a) Following individual thinkers (like Ibn Taymiyyah himself) rather than *madhahib*. This is an issue because in Islam no one is infallible after the Prophet ﷺ. It also means not having a methodology to deal with the apparent contradictions and discrepancies in the *hadith*. In effect, this means that Salafism is not merely an objective application of the *hadith*, but rather Ibn Taymiyyah's own *madhhab* based on *hadith*. In other words, it is de facto a fifth *madhhab* with maximalist claims, inimical to other points of view, and effectively regarding its own founder as infallible.

(b) Rejecting theological deliberation and Ash'arite-Maturidi theology itself. This does not take into consideration the question of the purpose of the theological details given in the Qur'an, and as already discussed (in Chapter 6), God calls upon people to 'meditate' upon the Qur'an (*'tadabbur'*, see: 4:82; 23:68; 38:29; 47:24; see also 50:37) and 'contemplate' (*'tafakkur fi'*, see: 16:43–44; 59:21; 13:3; 3:190–192) His signs (*'ayat'*) in the Qur'an.

(c) Making the specialist science of *hadith* a partisan issue for ordinary preachers, and even ordinary Muslims, and making it dominate every science of Islam including Qur'anic exegesis and *shari'ah*. At times the anti-*usul* movement has referred to itself as the *'Ahl al-hadith'* (the people of the *hadith*), implying that other *madhahib* are not *hadith*-based. However, it is difficult to find a *sahih hadith* that does not include a Sufi or an Ash'ari/Maturidi in its chain of transmitters. If they were all heretics and liars—as some later anti-*usulis* have claimed—then there are few authentic *ahadith*, and the whole *Ahl al-hadith* approach is itself null and void.

(d) Rejecting both consensus and pluralism in scholarly opinion.

(e) Condemning all non-*hadith*-recorded practices as *'bid'ah'*. Since the *hadith* is not a perfectly complete or unambiguous record—and does not include non-written transmissions and practices, and does not take into consideration that even in speech there occurs a great deal of non-verbal communication (such as context, physical location, group mood, tone of voice, facial expressions and bodily gestures—this naturally led to anachronistic projections back on to the first century of Islam. Moreover, all Muslim scholars are required to study Arabic grammar, even though the study of grammar is actually technically itself a *'bid'ah'* (something new; an 'innovation') later reconstructed and formalized from the Qur'an, *hadith* and Arabic poetry. So, as *usuli* scholars have argued, there must be two kinds of *bid'ah*: negative *bid'ahs* and positive *bid'ahs*.

(f) Rejecting the corpus of pre-Islamic poetry as a semantic and etymological reference for the Arabic language (on the grounds that it was written by pagans) and substituting it with the understanding of the Companions and the first two generations after them (i.e. the *'al-salaf al-salih'*) of Arabic words. Of course this is conceptually a problem since the Qur'an was revealed *in a clear Arabic language* (*Al-Shu'ara*, 26:195 see also 16:103) handed down and learnt from previous generations, and addressed pagans (in some verses). It leads to a potentially doubtful circular self-referentiality of superimposed meaning on Qur'anic interpretation (Ibn Taymiyyah called this *'tafsir bi 'l-tafsir'*). It means that understanding the Qur'an is not delimited by the science of the origin of words (etymology).

Moreover, Ibn Taymiyyah used this concept to argue that there is no such thing as metaphor (*majaz*) in the Qur'an, and everything is literally true. When words *are* unarguably metaphorical (like *'tasting'* death [*Al-'Ankabut*, 29:57 et al.]) he merely widened the original meaning of words (such as 'tasting') to include the metaphorical ones as well ('physically experiencing'). This was to have unforeseen—and later dangerous—practical consequences for interpreting and understanding the Qur'an and *hadith*.

(g) Judging and declaring someone to be an apostate and thereby 'excommunicating' them—i.e. the *takfir* of other Muslims according to their actions (as opposed to their stated intentions *and* actions. *Takfir* may be a death sentence, so this is a very serious issue. Actually, it is worse than death because it means someone is thereby divorced from their spouse; that their spouse and children cannot inherit from them, and that they cannot be buried in a Muslim cemetery: it means death plus the end of one's family, one's works in life and one's estate. It is such a harsh pronouncement that the Prophet ﷺ warned it means taking one's soul and faith into one's hands. He ﷺ said: 'Anyone who says to his brother "you disbeliever", then it refers back to one of them' (*Bukhari; Muslim*). Consequently, though partisan scholars have occasionally pronounced *takfir* on each other's doctrines, the vast majority of Muslims traditionally avoided it as best they could. Ibn Taymiyyah warned against it and tried to avoid it, but after Ibn Taymiyyah's time, radical elements of Salafi thought led to condemning people en masse, according to their ostensible actions, without even giving them a chance to repent. At times it led to actually attacking and killing them based on *takfir*.

Beyond these, there is one more serious matter that Ibn Taymiyyah took issue with; and that is formal logic.

LOGIC

The detractors of Islam have often argued that Islam ignores human reason and the laws of logic and so is in need of an 'Enlightenment' based on reason. They point to the now defunct Muslim Mu'tazilite sect of the 8th-10th centuries CE which prioritized reason. By contrast, Ibn Taymiyyah—and, to be fair, the whole Hanbalite tradition before him—was distrustful of reason and logic, viewing formal logic as basically alien to Islam and mere Greek sophistry that led to entirely uncertain and subjective human speculation.

Now the laws of logic—sometimes called the laws of thought—are basically three.

According to Bertrand Russell, they are as follows:

1. The law of identity: 'Whatever is, is.'
2. The law of contradiction: 'Nothing can both be and not be.'
3. The law of excluded middle: 'Everything must either be, or not be.'

These three laws are samples of self-evident logical principles, but are not really more fundamental or more self-evident than various other similar principles. (Bertrand Russell, *The Problems of Philosophy*, Ch VII)

Although they are self-evident, all three were first expressed in writing by Plato, and then formalized by his student, Aristotle. Of the first law (the 'law of identity'), Plato writes:

The great Parmenides testified to us, from beginning to end . . .: 'Never shall this be proved—that things that are not, are'. So we have his testimony to this. Our own account (*logos*) itself would make the point especially obvious if we but examined it a little. (Plato, *Sophist*, 237, a-b; see also: Aristotle, *Metaphysics*, Book IV, 1006a-b. In *Theaetetus*, 155, Plato further breaks this law down into three operative principles.)

Of the second law (the 'law of contradiction', strictly speaking, the 'law of non-contradiction'), Plato writes:

> It is clear that the same one thing cannot either act or be acted on in opposite ways, at the same time, in the same respect and in the same context. (Plato, *Republic*, 436b; see also: Aristotle, *Metaphysics*, Book IV, 1005b)

Of the third law (the 'law of excluded middle'), Plato writes:

> Socrates: Are there some people who are healthy?
> Alcibiades: Yes.
> Socrates: And others who are sick?
> Alcibiades: Indeed.
> Socrates: They are not the same people, are they?
> Alcibiades: Of course they aren't.
> Socrates: Are there any other people who are neither one thing nor the other?
> Alcibiades: No.
> Socrates: Because a person has to be either sick, or not sick?
> Alcibiades: That is what I think. . . .
> Socrates: And can one thing have two distinct opposites?
> Alcibiades: No.
> (Plato, *Alcibiades* II; see also: Aristotle, *Metaphysics*, Book IV, 1006b)

Now whilst this may initially sound like something foreign to Islam, as Al-Ghazali points out (in his books *Al-Qistas al-Mustaqim*, *Mihakk al-Nazhar* and *Mi'yar al-'Ilm*, the laws of logic, and logical syllogism are used in the Qur'an, explicitly or implicitly, by God (see, for example, 5:18; 6:91; 17:41; 21:99; 34:24; 62:6–7) and by the Prophets (see: 2:258; 6:77). Furthermore, the laws of logic are misused in the Qur'an (through false initial premises), by Satan (see 38:76).

More specifically, Ghazali identifies what is essentially the 'law of identity' as the 'Greater Balance' (with its three principles); and the 'law of excluded middle' and the 'law of contradiction' as the 'Middle Balance' and 'Lesser Balance' respectively. Of the 'Greater Balance', Ghazali says:

Know that the Greater Balance is that which the Friend (Abraham ﷺ)

used with Nimrod. . . . Abraham ﷺ said: *'God brings the sun from the east; so bring it from the west.' Then the disbeliever was confused; and God guides not the folk who do evil. (Al-Baqarah, 2:258).* . . . The abridged explanation of this argument is:

> My Lord is the one who makes the sun to rise.
> And the one who makes the sun rise is God.
> So it follows that my Lord is God.
>
> . . . The [operative] logical principle of the Greater Balance is that judgement applying to the more general is a judgement applying to the more particular, and is undoubtedly included therein. (Ghazali, *Al-Qistas al-Mustaqim*, ii–iii)

Of the 'Middle Balance', Ghazali says:

> Its definition is that any two things, one of which is qualified by a quality which is denied by another, are different. . . . Now setting is denied of God and affirmed of the moon [in God's words about Abraham ﷺ: *And when he saw the moon rising, he said, 'This is my Lord'. But when it set he said, 'Unless my Lord guides me, I shall surely become one of the folk who are astray' (Al-An'am, 6:77)*]. So this necessitates a difference between God and the moon, and that moon is not God, and God is not the moon. (Ghazali, *Al-Qistas al-Mustaqim*, iii)

Of the 'Lesser Balance', Ghazali says:

> God says (to the believers, to say to the disbelievers) *either we or you are rightly guided or in manifest error (Saba, 34:24).* . . . The use of this balance is limitless, and perhaps most speculative matters revolve around it. . . it comes down from the restricting of two parts between denial and affirmation. (Ghazali, *Al-Qistas al-Mustaqim*, vi)

The essential point about all this is that reason and the laws of logic, if they are correctly understood, do not have to be opposed to revelation or to Islam, and are not alien to them. On the contrary, they can be used—and in fact *are used in the Qur'an itself*—to point out the truth, and *misused* by Satan to try to obscure it. They are thus an essential tool of correct thinking and help to know the truth (*'Organon'*, the title of Aristotle's works on logic, simply means 'tool' or 'instrument' in Ancient Greek). Indeed, Ghazali sees in God's words: *weigh with a right scale* (*Al-Isra'*, 17:35) and *We sent Our messengers with Scripture and the balance, so that people can uphold justice* (*Al-Hadid*, 57:25), allusions to reason and the laws of logic.

Furthermore, reason was created by God, and the laws of logic are self-evidently true by the nature of things. This 'nature of things' was of course created by God Himself, who is the Truth (6:62; 20:114; 23:116 et al.) and from Whom truth comes (2:147; 3:60; 18:29 et al.). Indeed, the three laws of logic can be seen as theoretic applications of the principles of oneness, self-sufficiency and exclusiveness respectively. And these principles ultimately only exist as qualities belonging to God alone. This is evident in the 112th chapter of the Qur'an (*Surat al-Ikhlas*) as cited earlier: . . . *He, God, is One.* / *God, the Eternally Sufficient unto Himself* / *He did not beget, nor was He begotten.* / *And none is like unto Him.* (*Al-Ikhlas*, 112:1–4). In short, reason and logic—even if first formulated as such by the Ancient Greeks—are not inherently opposed to religion, but on the contrary, can, and should be used in its service. And they are ignored at great peril.

THE ANTI-*USUL* MOVEMENT UP
TO THE PRESENT DAY

The next highly influential figure in the anti-*usul* movement was Ibn Taymiyyah's own student **Ibn al-Qayyim al-Jawziyyah** (d. 751/1350). Whilst disseminating many of his teacher's opinions on *bid'ah*, and railing against Aristotelian metaphysics, astrology, alchemy and other sciences of the day, Ibn Qayyim wrote his classic text on health *The Medicine of the Prophet* 🕌. And whilst castigating Sufi veneration of Muslim 'saints' (*awliya' Allah*), he nevertheless wrote a valuable and lengthy commentary on one of the best-loved of all Sufi texts, 'Abdullah al-Ansari's *Manazil al-Sa'ireen* (*Stations of the Seekers*). **Ibn Kathir** (d. 774/1373) was also one of Ibn Taymiyyah's students but not an anti-*usuli* scholar as such. Ibn Kathir is most noted for his beloved and easy-to-understand commentary on the Qur'an (*Tafsir Ibn Kathir*). Because of his personal connection to Ibn Taymiyyah, later generations of the anti-*usul* movement read, publish and spread his commentary—after selectively editing it, as they do with the Maliki scholar Muhammad al-Qurtubi's (d. 671/1272) commentary, *Al-Jami' li-Ahkam al-Qur'an*.

After Ibn Qayyim, the anti-*usul* movement seems to become more concerned with 'purifying' the religion than the individual soul, and with rules rather than with virtues. It also remained nominally connected to *usul*, and *usuli* scholars, albeit to Hanbali *usul*. This changed with the next significant milestone in this movement, which came over 400 years later with the Nejdi preacher **Muhammad bin 'Abd al-Wahhab al-Tamimi** (d. 1206/1792). With the help of Nejdi tribes—particularly the tribal Chieftain Muhammad bin Saud—Ibn 'Abd al-Wahhab briefly conquered a large section of the Arabian Desert, setting up a proto-state and declaring a *'jihad'* against those Muslims whom he considered had introduced alien elements into Islam. Ibn 'Abd al-Wahhab particularly opposed the Shi'a and those Sufis whom, because of dubious folk practises, he regarded as having transgressed the *shari'ah*. He also wrote a number of short books and treatises, the most famous probably being *Kitab al-Tawhid* (*The Book of the Unity of God*), *Al-Usul al-Thalathah* (*The Three Fundamental Principles*), and *Nawaqid al-Islam* (*The Nullifiers of Islam*). The *Al-Usul al-Thalathah* stresses three principles: *tawhid al-Rububiyyah* (the unity of the Lord); *tawhid al-Asma wa 'l-Sifat* (unity of the Divine Names and Attributes); and *tawhid al-'ubudiyyah* (the unity of worship)—and here Ibn 'Abd al-Wahhab attacked practices such as venerating 'saints' or addressing the Prophet Muhammad ﷺ during devotions. Howbeit, his short text *Nawaqid al-Islam* did, and continues to do, a lot of damage. For example, the tenth 'nullifier' maintains that 'turning away from God's religion, not learning it and not acting upon it' [is unbelief]. This effectively makes all sins of omission a matter of apostasy, punishable by death. The *Nawaqid* also makes sins of commission (without intention of apostasy) and sins of ignorance matters of apostasy punishable by death. It does not stipulate a procedure for punishment, or limit apostasy to individuals—which means that people can be condemned en masse because of popular practices. Clearly, the *Nawaqid* contains problematic claims with dangerous consequences for ordinary Muslims, let alone non-Muslims.

In the twentieth century, the anti-*usul* movement can be seen to have two different main streams. The first is the Saudi Salafi stream (based largely on Ibn Taymiyyah) which often converges with the Saudi

Wahhabi stream ('Wahhabism' being named after Muhammad bin 'Abd al-Wahhab). Salafis sometimes refer to themselves as *'Ahl al-Hadith'* ('the people of *hadith*'), and Wahhabis sometimes call themselves *'Ahl al-'Aqida'* ('the people of the doctrine'—by which they mean Muhammad bin 'Abd al-Wahhab's doctrine). However, the difference today between Salafism and Wahhabism, if any, is a matter of debate. For our purposes, we can distinguish between (1) a mainstream, moderate and tolerant version of the Salafi/Wahhabi movement as typified by the learned scholars of Saudi Arabia; (2) radical Salafi/Wahhabism characterized, in practice, by *takfir* of everyone who is not a Salafi/Wahhabi Muslim—or who is not Salafi/Wahhabi enough for them; and (3) *takfiri-jihadi* Salafi/Wahhabi groups such as Al-Qa'eda, the so-called 'Islamic State' (aka 'ISIS' or 'ISIL' or 'Daesh'), and other late twentieth century and early twenty-first century terrorist movements. These movements are effectively *jihadi* offshoots of radical Salafism/Wahhabism. These have their own dedicated political ideologues (often with little formal Islamic education) who make *jihad* (as they see it) the centre of their activities and even their religious duties. But whilst they *claim* to represent Salafi/Wahhabi thought, in fact mainstream Saudi Salafism/Wahhabism has consistently actively and vigorously opposed—and continues to oppose—them to this day, in word and deed.

Moreover, there has always been, in mainstream Saudi Salafism/Wahhabism, a 'quietist' undercurrent (rooted in the anti-mystical asceticism of Ibn Hanbal, Ibn Taymiyyah and Ibn Qayyim and the writings of Ibn al-Jawzi) which is very influential in people's personal lives but never attracts public attention. For them, adherence to what they perceive as being the pure form of the Qur'an and the *sunnah* as they understand it is basically an expression of their sincerity to God and the message of His Prophet 🙙. So for them, the austerity of Salafi/Wahhabi thought and practice is how they express their devotion to God. This is obviously a noble intention in itself, and no one who is not a scholar can be reasonably blamed for not understanding the hidden consequences and complexities of eliminating the methodologies of *usul*. Moreover, the critical difference between them and radical Salafi/Wahhabis is that whilst they do not agree with or approve of *usul* or of the *madhahib* of Islam, they do not give themselves licence to brand other Muslims as disbelievers (*takfir*), in obedience to the Prophet's 🙙 saying:

Whoever prays our prayers, facing Mecca [as we do] and eats the same
meat that we eat—that person is a Muslim, and is protected God and
by His messenger, so do not break God's [bond of] protection (*Bukhari*).

The two most important figures in the Saudi Salafi stream were arguably
Nasir al-Din al-Albani (d. 1420/1999—Albani was actually a Syrian but
influenced Saudi Salafism deeply) and 'Abd al-'Aziz Bin Baz (d. 1420/1999).
Al-Albani was a famous *hadith* scholar. His redactions of all the major
hadith books—which were taken as definitive by the Salafi movement and
published and distributed everywhere—meant effectively that the Salafi
movement had a differing canon of *hadith* from traditional *usul* thought.
The significance of this should not be underestimated, because it in effect
makes for a difference in *basic sources* between the two. Bin Baz was the
Grand Mufti of Saudi Arabia from 1993–1997 but his influence and *fatwas*
(official juridical judgements) had been critical in the Salafi movement
for decades before that. He was a careful and well-respected scholar who
worked to reform radical Salafi/Wahhabi thought.

The term 'Salafism' is also sometimes applied to certain Islamic modernist thinkers of the beginning of the twentieth century such as the
Egyptian Grand Mufti Muhammad Abduh (1266-1323/1849-1905) and
Rashid Rida (1282-1354/1865-1935). However, whilst these were clearly
influenced by some traditional Salafi thought, and did in turn influence
some twentieth century Salafi writers, this movement was actually much
more a modernist movement than a traditional Salafi movement. In any
case, it has all but died out today.

The second anti-*usul* movement is the Muslim Brotherhood stream.
The Muslim Brotherhood is a huge international Islamic—or rather
'*Islamist*', if what is meant by that term is primarily 'politically-active
Islam'—social, political and religious organization founded by Hasan al-
Banna (1324-1368/1906-1949) in Egypt in 1928. By the end of the twen-
tieth century, it had active branches or members in every Sunni Muslim
country. Its two main ideologues during the twentieth century were the
Egyptians Sayyid Sabiq (d. 1420/2000) and Sayyid Qutb (d. 1386/1966).
In the 1940s Sayyid Sabiq wrote a very popular simplified manual of
Sunni Islamic law (called '*Fiqh al-Sunnah*') which pioneered the way for
cherry-picking from the four Sunni *madhahib* and mixing between them

without regard to keeping an integrated methodology. That is not to say of course, that all members of the Muslim Brotherhood are necessarily anti-*usuli*, but merely that their methodology is so, all the more since many of them anyway adopt Salafi or Wahhabi doctrine or law. Sayyid Qutb was a Muslim Brotherhood intellectual who was eventually executed for plotting to assassinate (then) Egyptian President Gamal Abd al-Nasser. He was influential mainly because of his book *Fi Zhilal al-Qur'an* (*In the Shade of the Qur'an*). In this book, (in his comments on the verses 5:44–50 of the Qur'an) he lays out the *'hakimiyyah'* theory. This theory basically states that anyone who does not implement *only shar'iah* law (as he understood it) becomes an unbeliever (who then must be killed). Accordingly, any state in the modern world that applies *any* non-*shari'ah* laws is an illegitimate and non-Islamic state, and so anyone who works for it in any way (from a policeman to a public school teacher) is also an unbeliever (who then can, or must, be killed—see the annex for more detail). This idea is, in practice, facilitated by the fact that, upon joining, all Muslim Brotherhood members have to swear an oath of allegiance to the organization, which is obviously at odds with an oath of allegiance to their nation's political leader (which is the normal Islamic practice) or an oath of allegiance to their countries or constitutions (which is the normal practice in a modern nation state). Moreover, as regards *jihad* (see Chapter 11), Qutb says the following:

> Many who talk about *jihad* in Islam and quote Qur'anic verses do not take into account this aspect [of progression, stage by stage], nor do they understand the nature of the various stages through which this movement develops, or the relationship of the verses revealed at various occasions to each stage. . . .
>
> This group of thinkers, which is a product of the sorry state of the present Muslim generation, has nothing but the label of Islam and has laid down its spiritual and rational arms in defeat. They say, 'Islam has prescribed only defensive war' and think that they have done some good for their faith by divesting it of its method. . . .
>
> This struggle is not a temporary phase but an eternal state, because truth and falsehood cannot co-exist on this earth. (Sayyid Qutb, *Milestones*, 'Jihad in the Cause of Allah')

Of course, in certain countries, there have always been Muslim Brotherhood thinkers and leaders who have sincerely based their actions and thought primarily on Hasan al-Banna's more peaceful vision of social reform 'from within'. For example, in January 2014 the Tunisian political party Ennahda (which was associated with the Muslim Brotherhood internationally), gracefully stepped away from government after three years of participation in it (albeit after a number of unsolved political assassinations in the country and after a new National Constitution) in order to avoid civil strife. Moreover, most rank and file supporters (and voters for) the Muslim Brotherhood around the world back it because of just reasons that have nothing to do with the *hakimiyyah* theory. These generally include being opposed to removing Islam from the public space in Muslim-majority countries; appreciating the benefits from the Muslim Brotherhood's many active charitable social services; and agreeing with the Muslim Brotherhood's strident public criticism of corruption, social injustice and tyranny. Nevertheless, the core movement as a whole remains overwhelmingly imbued with Qutbi ideology, and Syed Qutb's books *Fi Zhilal al-Qur'an* (*In the Shade of the Qur'an*) and *Ma'alim fil Tariq* (*Milestones*) remain its intellectual heart and soul, whether this is publicly expressed or not. In short, there has been a long struggle between the Banna and the Qutb visions for the Muslim Brotherhood, but it is from Syed Qutb's writings that all damage really comes.

Together these two streams of anti-*usul* thought — Salafism/Wahhabism and the Muslim Brotherhood comprise modern 'Sunni fundamentalism' — if what is meant by 'fundamentalism' is a non-pluralistic religious/ political movement, not based on 'principles of jurisprudence' (which is what '*usul*' means literally, as we have explained). Nevertheless, there are vast differences of opinions within these two streams, particularly within Salafism, which now comprises a considerable range of different ideas.

Over the course of the twentieth century, significant resources have been poured into teaching Salafism all over the Islamic world and especially during *hajj*. Equally, over the course of the twentieth century the Islamic charity-activism of the Muslim Brotherhood benefited millions of lives in the Islamic world. Ironically, both movements also greatly benefited from the rise of secularism and nationalism in the postcolonial age after the Second World War: in many Arab and Islamic countries, secularism and nationalism were trying to stop Islam not only from being politicized (quite rightly) but also trying to ban it (and with it all *shari'ah* law, even personal status law) from the public space altogether (quite wrongly). Salafism/Wahhabism and the Muslim Brotherhood gained a lot from opposing the trends of secularism and nationalism—and indeed seemed to lead the opposition to them—because most Muslims naively conflated the politicization of religion for individual or factional gain with its very presence in the public space. Consequently, over decades, the two movements together completely altered the demographic of *usul* thought in the Islamic world. The following is an estimate of this change based on historical studies and constructed from answers to polls (including Pew's 2015 annual global poll) in many countries.

SUNNI SCHOOLS OF THOUGHT
IN 2016 AND IN 1900

2016:

Usulis: 65%
Anti-usulis: 9%
Modernists: 1%
'Don't knows': 25%

1900:

Usulis: 99%
Anti-usulis: < 1%
Modernists: < 1%
'Don't knows': < 1%

NB: 'Modernists' refers to people who believe that Islam (and not merely Islamic civilisation and culture, but Islamic doctrine and law) should be updated to correspond to Western values. This is universally rejected by all other Muslims.

'Don't knows' refers to people who could not say if they belong to a school of Islamic law and if so, which one. They have become 'don't knows' largely because of the confusion arising from the anti-*usul* movement being mixed up with traditional *usul* influence.

Clearly, the demographics of Sunni Islam have changed tremendously in the last century or so. Even though the anti-*usul* movement itself is still a small minority, it has acquired vast influence through its 'dilution' of the influence of the traditional Sunni *madhhabs*. And even though it still represents a small minority, it is socially and politically much more active than the *usuli* majority.

THE *SHI'I MADHAHIB*

There are three main kinds of Shi'ism. All of them agree that the Prophet Muhammad's ﷺ son-in-law and first cousin, 'Ali ؏, was his 'spiritual successor' and all of them save the Zaydis believe he ؏ should have been his immediate political successor. (In fact, 'Ali ؏ became the fourth caliph, not the first). The very word *'Shi'a'* in Arabic means 'partisans' (of 'Ali ؏)—whereas the word *'Sunni'* means 'followers of the *sunnah*'. However, beyond this allegiance to the Prophet's ﷺ family, the Shi'a groups are each very different from the other. The three main kinds of Shi'ism are:

1. **Ja'fari, 'Twelver' Shi'ism.** This is the main kind of Shi'ism in the sense that perhaps 85 per cent of all Shi'a are Ja'fari. They are named 'Twelver' because of their belief in 12 *'imams'* ('leaders'), who are: (1) 'Ali ؏; (2) his son (and the Prophet's ﷺ grandson, through his daughter Fatimah ؏) Al-Hasan ؏; (3) Al-Husayn ؏ (who was Al-Hasan's brother and the Prophet's ﷺ other grandson); (4) Al-Husayn's son, 'Ali Zayn al-'Abidin; (5) his son, Muhammad al-Baqir; (6) his son, Ja'far al-Sadiq (Ja'far was a great scholar—this branch of Shi'ism is named 'Ja'fari' after him); (7) his son, Musa al-Kadhim; (8) his son, 'Ali al-Rida; (9) his son, Muhammad al-Jawad; (10) his son, 'Ali al-Hadi; (11) his son, Hasan al-'Askari; and (12) his son, Muhammad 'al-Mahdi' (who they believe did not die but went into 'occultation' in 255/868). This means of course that Shi'ism as such crystallized much later than the Sunni *madhahib*.

Twelver Shi'ism is the Shi'ism of Iran, Iraq, Lebanon and minority communities in India, Pakistan, Afghanistan and the Persian Gulf. It differs fundamentally from Sunnism because it regards believing in the 'imamate' as one of the essential tenets of faith (along with believing in God, the angels, the revealed scripture, God's messengers, the Day of Judgement, and Divine Providence). It therefore has not only a different doctrine from Sunnism but also a different *usul*. Its doctrine means that the words of all '12 *imams*' as well as the Prophet's daughter Fatimah ؏ (in addition of course to those of Prophet Muhammad ﷺ) are Divinely-inspired, infallible and therefore legislative. This obviously leads to a completely different canon of *hadith*—and even concept of *hadith*—because *'hadith'* for the Shi'a means the (many) words of any of the '12 *imams*' right up to the ninth century.

The four major Shi'a *'hadith'* books (*'Al-Kutub al-Arba'a'*) are: (1) *Al-Kafi* ('The Sufficient') by Muhammad bin Yaqub Kulayni. It has 15,176 *'ahadith'*; (2) *Man La Yahduruhu al-Faqih* ('[For] one who does not have a jurist present') by Al-Saduq Muhammed bin 'Ali. It has 9044 *'ahadith'*; (3) *Tahdiib al-Ahkam* (*'The Refinement of Laws'*) by Abu Ja'far Tusi. It has 13,590 *'ahadith'*; (4) *Al-Istibsar* ('Foresight') by Abu Ja'far Tusi. It has 5511 *'ahadith'*.

It should be noted that a number of Shi'i scholars—based on narratives found within these books, particularly those from the *'athari'* tradition—do *'takfir'* not only on all Sunnis, but even (retroactively) on the first three caliphs (Abu Bakr ﷺ, 'Umar ﷺ and 'Uthman ﷺ). This is obviously a major source of tension and conflict with Sunnis.

2. **Zaydi, 'Fiver' Shi'ism.** There are about 10 million Zaydis, almost all concentrated in Northern Yemen. They are called 'Zaydis' after their fifth (and last) *imam*, Zayd, the son of 'Ali Zayn al-'Abidin, and the older brother of Muhammad al-Baqir. (Their first four *imams* are the same as the Ja'faris.) But whilst the Zaydis regard these five members of the Prophet's ﷺ family as religious leaders, they do *not* regard them as infallible, nor their words as *hadith* as such. In this sense, their *usul* (or at least that of traditional Zaydis) is actually the same as Sunnis, not Shi'a. For that reason some have debated if they are Shi'a at all, and not Sunnis.

3. **Isma'ili, 'Sevener' Shi'ism.** There are perhaps 10 million Isma'ilis spread all over the world. They are called 'Isma'ilis' after their seventh (and last) *imam*, Isma'il, the son of Ja'far al-Sadiq. (Their first six *imams* are the same as the Ja'faris). There are different types of Isma'ilis: (a) the *Dawudi Bohra* follow *Ja'fari usul* and *fiqh* under the aegis of their leader, the Sultan of the *Bohra*; and (b) the *Nizaris* who follow their 'living *Imam*' and 'speaking Qur'an' the Agha Khan. Accordingly, the Nizaris have no *fiqh* at all as such, and an *usul* that is completely different from all other Muslims. In their view, they are not required to perform the five prayers, fast during the month of Ramadan, or perform the *hajj*.

In short then, there are three major groupings of Shi'ism, but only two *madhahib*: the (majority) Ja'fari, and the (minority) Zaydi.

OTHER *MADHAHIB*

Mention should be made here again of the now extinct (Sunni) *Zhahiri madhhab* which was started in Iraq by Dawud bin 'Ali al-Zhahiri (d. c. 270/883) but which developed in Muslim Andalusia. There are no *Zhahiris* as such alive today but a few scholars still consider the methodology of the *Zhahiri madhhab* as valid or perhaps insightful, and regularly consult it.

There is also a third major ancient division of Islam: *Ibadism*. Today's Ibadi *usul* and *fiqh* are very close to Sunnism. There are, however, only a few million *Ibadis*, mainly in Oman with a few in North and East Africa. These *madhahib* together (the four Sunni, the *Zhahiri*, the two Shi'a and the Ibadi) comprise the so-called 'eight *madhahib*' of traditional Islam (see: Appendix 1: The Big Tent of Islam).

It needs to be stressed here that whatever differences in beliefs there are between Sunni, Shi'a and Ibadi Muslims, these differences are *not* causes or reasons for conflict—no matter what the political situation may be today. Differences of Islamic religious beliefs and opinions in themselves do *not* ever justify religious conflict, and cannot honestly or legitimately be used as a pretext for fighting. The Prophet Muhammad 🌸 himself made this very clear for the future generations of Muslims of all stripes, in his saying:

> Whoever testifies that there is no god but God, and prays in the same direction as us [i.e. towards the Ka'bah in Mecca], and prays like us, and eats what we slaughter, is a Muslim. He [or she] has the same rights as a Muslim and the same obligations as a Muslim. (*Bukhari*; *Muslim*)

CAPITAL AND CORPORAL PUNISHMENT

Returning now to the question of capital and corporal punishment, the first thing to be said is that these form less than one per cent of *shari'ah* laws, and probably less than 0.1 per cent. In the Qur'an itself there are only five offences that warrant capital or corporal punishment (murder, theft, adultery and fornication, corruption upon the earth and calumny against the virtue of women). So capital and corporal punishment are not the essence or the goal of the *shari'ah* as some people seem to think, and as hostile stereotypes depict. It will also be clear that although there is both capital and corporal punishment in Islam, there are legal subtleties about them that make them—and are supposed to make them—far different in practice than they are in theory and very difficult to implement. In theory, there is capital punishment for only three cases: premeditated murder, adultery (of married people) and apostasy with treason. The Prophet Muhammad ﷺ said:

> The blood of a Muslim person who testifies that there is no god but God, and that I am His messenger, is never licit [to shed] except for one of three [cases]: a soul for a soul, married adultery, and passing through religion and leaving the community. (*Bukhari*; *Muslim*)

Capital punishment for murder is akin to the Biblical *lex talionis*. In nations where people will naturally take revenge for the loss of close relatives no matter what any law says, *lex talionis* not only enforces justice and acts as a deterrent, but also saves lives by preventing long blood feuds where many people on both sides are likely to die. Indeed, God says in the Qur'an:

> *In retaliation there is life for you, O people of cores (albab), so that you might fear.* (*Al-Baqarah*, 2:179)

As regards the question of apostasy, this too is a Biblical law (Deuteronomy 13:6–9 and 17:3–5), and Luke 19:27 has been misinterpreted to allude to it. However, despite the classical *usuli* position, some contemporary *usul* scholars have said that the punishment is for high treason, not apostasy alone. There are four reasons for saying this: (a) the punishment is not actually mentioned in the Qur'an as such; (b) the Prophet ﷺ is recorded as having let a Muslim who apostatized go free; (c) prior to the modern nation state system, leaving a religion was actually leaving your state and hence high treason; and (d) the *hadith* quoted above specifies 'leaving the community' together with apostasy.

As regards the punishment for 'married adultery' it is here where the greatest confusion occurs. This punishment (which is also not mentioned in the Qur'an, although it is mentioned in Leviticus 20:10) is accepted by scholars as being stoning to death. The key point here is that under *shari'ah* law, whilst the punishment for adultery is not questioned by scholars, it is virtually *impossible to implement* except if someone voluntarily insists on confessing (and in some traditions even confession per se may not constitute decisive proof).

If we look at the history of Islamic law we see this very clearly. The two places where traditionally *usul*-based *shari'ah* law was implemented over the most number of people for the longest period of time were Egypt (from the seventh to the nineteenth centuries, across various different ruling dynasties), and the Ottoman empire (from 1299 until 1923). During that time Egypt started with a population of eight million and this declined over the centuries for various reasons to around three million. The Ottoman Empire had a population of between 11.7 million and 35 million over its history. During 1200 years of *shari'ah* rule in Egypt there were only two documented cases of stoning for adultery, and both of them were technically illegal and politically motivated. One occurred during Sultan Qaytbay's reign (1422–1438), when a female slave in the sultan's household was hanged for having an affair with a soldier. The other occurred in 1513, when Sultan Qansuh executed a deputy judge and his lover (another judge's wife). The couple were probably guilty, but there was not sufficient evidence to try them with charges of adultery. The sultan at first sentenced them to death by stoning, but the judiciary protested, so he just hanged them, without a basis in law. Similarly, during the entire period of the Ottoman empire there was only one confirmed case of stoning because of adultery. In 1860, a *qadi* (judge) ruled that a Muslim woman should be stoned to death and her Jewish lover should be executed. The scholars protested the judgement, and it was never repeated (see: *Encyclopedia of the Ottoman Empire*, G. Agoston and B. Masters [ed.s], New York, USA, 2008, p. 214).

Why was this? This was because the evidentiary bar that the *shari'ah* has for adultery is so high that it cannot possibly be met unless people voluntarily confess, or deliberately go out of their way to be publicly seen in the act (in which case the act is one of religious and social sedition, not of passion). Specifically, the evidentiary bar is that four male witnesses of upright character (and with no criminal record of even minimal offence) must come forward within a month and testify under oath that they directly witnessed interpenetration (which is physically very difficult to actually see). If they differ on details of the event (such as the colour of the clothes worn) their testimony is rejected. If the witnesses were willingly deliberately watching, they are no longer upright, and so effectively they have to see the act by accident and insist on telling. And if only three witnesses step forward, they are considered liars and are themselves flogged for slander—not much incentive for coming forward! Moreover, film evidence (nowadays), is not permissible as proof since this can theoretically be forged. Even pregnancy in the case of an absent husband is not proof of adultery, because, although highly unlikely, a woman can get pregnant accidentally in a shared bathroom. In fact, as improbable as this sounds, a case like this was clinically proven in Jordan at the beginning of the twentieth century. In the Prophet's ﷺ own time, though one of his Companions, Hilal bin Umayyah, accused his wife of adultery—and her child was later shown by genetic signs not to be Hilal's child—this was not taken as proof of adultery. Moreover, the only recorded cases of stoning in the Prophet's ﷺ own time were due to unsolicited and unwanted voluntary confessions. Even after a confession, someone can withdraw their confession and avoid the penalty, even if it has already started. In short, adultery is a capital crime *in theory* in the *shari'ah* but it is all but impossible to prove, and a hostile accusation has never fairly been proven in Islamic history. This is not a result of un-Islamic legal obfuscation by merciful jurists, it is actually the *sunnah*, for the Prophet ﷺ himself repeatedly turned away or tried to deflect people who wanted to confess. So procedures and conditions *are meant* to soften or ward off the punishments. A jurist is supposed to: (1) exert himself to avoid corporal or capital punishment as much as possible; (2) err on the side of pardoning and not err on the side of punishing; and (3) suspend any punishment in the presence of the slightest doubt. All this is an integral part of the *how* of the law. The Prophet ﷺ said:

> Ward off capital and corporal punishments (*hadd*) as much as you can. . . . (*Tirmidhi*; *Hakim et al*),

and:

> Ward off capital punishments through ambiguities. . . . (*Sunan al-Bayhaqi*)

In the Qur'an we see that even on the Day of Judgement—and despite the fact that God is Omniscient—there are all sorts of juridical procedures and witnesses brought against souls, showing that even in the next world fair procedures are inseparable from justice. So all these *jihadi* terrorists who today, as soon as they grab a foothold in some war-ravaged territory, start stoning women for adultery (and broadcasting it on YouTube), and think they are pious for doing so, show only their barbarism and their profound ignorance of both the letter and spirit of the *shari'ah*.

Why then is there this law in the first place? God says in the Qur'an that He frightens people in order that they may fear Him (for their own good):

> ...*That is what God frightens His servants with, 'So, O servants of Mine, fear Me!'*... (*Al-Zumar*, 39:16)

So Rumi commented (*Mathnawi* I, l.1261):

> It is from loving kindness that He terrifies you,
>   That He may seat you in the kingdom of security.

We said earlier that all the legislations of the Qur'an can be traced to the five aims of the *shari'ah* ('*maqasid al-shari'ah*'). Clearly, the punishment for adultery is to deter people for their own good in order to protect the most fundamental institution of society, the family. So the de jure punishment for adultery relates to protecting the universal right to family, procreation and honour. After all, it is very easy to get divorced in Islam, and if adultery were permitted, that would be the end of the family, and the beginning of the dissolution of Islamic society as a whole.

Finally, it should be noted that capital punishments can be frozen under certain conditions when it would be unfair to implement them, and there are laws that can be suspended by the ruler's authority (*ahkam sultaniyyah*). In a year of famine and plague (638-639), the Caliph 'Umar exempted people from the payment of *jizya* and froze the corporal punishment for theft. Specifically, *usuli* jurists have said that there are no capital punishments in: (a) non-Muslim lands; (b) in travelling during war; (c) when people do not know the rulings; (d) when there is no legitimate ruler; (e) when there are any doubts surrounding the circumstances; and (f) when they cause far more harm than benefit. In short, *shari'ah* punishments are not meant to be tyrannical, but to deter crime and ensure justice.

TAKING IT EASY

We are *supposed to* 'take it easy' in religious matters. God says in the Qur'an:

... God desires ease for you, and He does not desire hardship for you. ... (*Al-Baqarah*, 2:185)
... He has chosen you, and not placed upon you in your religion any hardship. ... (*Al-Hajj*, 22:79)

Likewise, as cited earlier, the Prophet Muhammad ﷺ said:

Make things easy, do not make things difficult. Give good news; do not drive people away. (*Bukhari; Muslim*)

And if there are different options in law or in anything, we are supposed to take the best (*'ahsan'*) and most merciful option. This is what the legal principle and maxim 'hardship calls for ease' (cited earlier) actually means. Indeed, in the Qur'an, God commends those:

Who listen to the words [of God] and follow the best (ahsan) [sense] of it. Those, they are the ones whom God has guided; and those, they are the people of cores. (*Al-Zumar*, 39:18)

Nevertheless, it has to be said that some Muslim scholars do not always take the easiest and most merciful route. Like most people, they unconsciously assume that the most intricate and difficult is the most pious, because it shows the most effort and self-sacrifice. For example, in general everything that is not specifically forbidden in the Qur'an or the *hadith* (or an obvious analogy, such as drugs) is on principle permitted, but ask most scholars about something they do not personally like and they will say 'there is no actual text about it, but. . .' and then proceed to outlaw it. This is not helping. The Prophet Muhammad ﷺ himself warned: 'Perdition shall befall extreme pedants (*mutanatti'un*)' (*Muslim*). Legal pedantry is a problem, especially in our day, when things are changing so fast all the time. And it is a problem even politically. In fact, many of the Islamic world's problems and tensions today—including political problems and conflicts—would be resolved by just relaxing a bit, and letting others relax and leaving them alone. That is the root of pluralism. And that is actually what the *shari'ah* calls for.

~

WHY IS IT IMPORTANT TO KNOW ALL THIS?

It is important to know all this for a number of reasons. First, it is important to know that the *shari'ah* is both a moral code and a legal code. As a legal code it is a plural, not monolithic, body of law and there are usually many different legitimate opinions on a given issue or ruling. Second, it is important to know that with the different opinions within the *shari'ah*, the correct practice and the most pious option is to take the easiest and most merciful available option, not the most difficult. Third, it is important to know that the ultimate goal of the *shari'ah is to help people by instituting justice and mercy, and by looking after their interests.* Specifically, it aims to do this by instituting five basic rights for people, these being: (1) the right to life; (2) the right to religion; (3) the right to family, procreation and honour; (4) the right to reason; and (5) the right to property—with all the freedoms and protections that each of these rights imply—and these reflect the 'spirit of the law'. Fourth, it is important to know that the *shari'ah* has a '*why*', '*what*' and '*how*': and not just a '*what*', and that applying the '*what*' without understanding the '*why*' of intention and the '*how*' of context and of procedure is usually going to lead to a mistake. This is precisely 'the letter that kills'. Fifth, it is important to understand that the *shari'ah is not there so that people should nebulously serve it. On the contrary it is there to help and serve people.* It is not a whimsical or arbitrary set of arcane laws suited only to a different time, nor a reflection of tribal bloodlust, as both hostile stereotypes and ignorant modern Muslims seem to believe. Rather, it is a highly intelligent and carefully crafted system of social laws based both on spiritual principles and the worldly nature of things *for the good of people. It is supposed to* adapt to changing contexts, and *it is supposed to* avoid theoretic capital and corporal punishment in practice if at all possible. Its frequent abuse today is not due to inherent flaws but to individual ignorance, misplaced zealotry and various political factors.

Finally, and perhaps most relevantly today, it is important to understand that modern extremism and terrorism in the name of Islam do not come of traditional *usuli* Islam but rather out of the anti-*usul* movement. No matter what those who commit them say, they are not applications of the *shari'ah* but confusions about it. They are a new phenomenon, alien to the *shari'ah* as it was understood for the first 1300 years of Islamic history. No Muslims who know their *usul* would ever approve of them or commit them. They could not do so in good conscience, even if they wanted to, because they are un-Islamic. There are no *usulis* in the terrorist ranks, no Ash'ari-Maturidis, no Sufis. This is no accident. And whilst only a small percentage of the *anti-usulis* become violent terrorists, all violent terrorists are either ignorant of *usul*, or anti-*usulis*. The *shari'ah* is supposed to be a path to life, not a path to terror and destruction.

$\sim$

Chapter 11

WHAT IS 'JIHAD'?

And fight in the way of God with those who
fight against you, but aggress not; God loves
not the aggressors. (Al-Baqarah, 2:190)

It may seem a bit strange on first reflection that war should be mentioned in the Qur'anic revelation at all, and be associated with any religion. However, war is mentioned in the Bible and in other religious texts (like, for example, the Bhagavad Gita), and there have been countless religious wars that have had nothing to do with Islam. There have also been countless wars that have had nothing to do with any religion. So war, it seems, is an inevitable part of human history, of human society and of human politics—and perhaps even of the human condition itself. And since war involves people dying and killing each other—and there is nothing more consequential than that—it would be perhaps even odder if it were not discussed in the Qur'an. After all, God says in the Qur'an: *And they do not bring you any argument, but that We bring you the truth, and a better exposition (Al-Furqan, 25:33).*

As will be seen in what follows, Islam takes the whole issue of war directly by the horns. By doing that, it actually not only controls and regulates war to make it as merciful as possible—though wars are there to be won—but also gives a higher meaning to the inevitable and necessary sacrifices made in war. In other words, the religion of Islam mitigates war as much as possible and integrates it into religious life. And because of this, history shows there have been less of what we now call 'war crimes' committed by Muslims than by the followers of any other religion except perhaps Hinduism (see *Body Count* by Naveed Sheikh at: www.rissc.jo). This is hardly a perfect situation—because obviously Muslims have not behaved as they should have according to their own religious ethics—but it does show that in the end it is better and more honest to regulate war, and integrate it into ethical behaviour, than to ignore it, deny it or not legislate for it.

THE MEANING OF THE TERM '*JIHAD*'

Many people who do not know Arabic think that '*jihad*' means 'Islamic religious war' or 'holy war'. This is not true and leads to dangerous misconceptions about the nature and purpose of *jihad*, making *jihad* a goal rather than a means. Actually, the term *jihad* in the Arabic language does not in itself originally have anything to do with war. The Arabic term for war is *harb*, and the term for military combat is *qital*. *Jihad* comes from the root *juhd*, meaning making an effort, and consequently 'struggling' and 'contending'. In other words, military combat is not the essence of *jihad*.

THE TWO KINDS OF *JIHAD*: THE 'GREATEST *JIHAD*' AND THE 'LESSER *JIHAD*'

In the Qur'an and the *hadith*, the word *jihad* is used in (at least) two quite different ways, and so there are (at least) two kinds of *jihad*.

The first way refers to the internal struggle against the ego which all believers are called on to wage, and which is the sine qua non of spiritual life. The Prophet Muhammad ﷺ said: 'The [true] warrior [*mujahid*] is the one who wages *jihad* against his own ego in obedience to God Almighty' (*Abu Dawud; Tirmidhi; Ahmad*). And in another *hadith*: 'The [true] emigrant [*muhajir*] is the one who leaves evil, and the [true] warrior [*mujahid*] is the one who wages *jihad* against his passions' (*Hakim*). This inner and peaceful sense of the term *jihad* is used in the Qur'an in verses like: *So do not obey the disbelievers, but struggle against them with it [that is, the Qur'an] a great jihad (Al-Furqan, 25:52); and: And whoever does jihad, does jihad only for his own soul . . . . (Al-'Ankabut, 29:6; see also: 22:78; 29:6; 29:8; 31:15; 66:9)*

This kind of *jihad* is the 'greatest' kind of *jihad*. It is better than the military *jihad* against an enemy, which is a 'lesser *jihad*'. The Prophet Muhammad ﷺ said:

'Shall I tell you about the best of all deeds, the best act of piety in the eyes of your Lord which will elevate your status in the Hereafter and is better for you than spending gold and silver and better than going up in arms against your enemy and striking their necks and their striking your necks?' They said: 'Yes'. The Prophet ﷺ said: 'Remembrance of God'. (Malik, *Al-Muwatta'*; *Tirmidhi*; *Ibn Majah*)

And virtue is an integral part of this 'greatest *jihad*', so that even the virtue of courage is as much part of it as it is part of military combat. Indeed, it involves exposing oneself to danger when one is defenceless. The Prophet Muhammad ﷺ said: 'The best *jihad* is to speak the truth to a tyrannical ruler' (*Abu Dawud*; *Nasa'i*; *Ibn Majah*). So Rumi wrote (*Mathnawi*, I, l.s 1395–1398):

I turned my back upon the outer combat
    I turned my face towards the inner combat.
'Indeed we've come back from the lesser *jihad*'
    and now we're with the Prophet in the greater. . . .
For lions to break the battle lines is easy,
    The true lion breaks the lines of his ego.

THE 'GREATEST *JIHAD*' AS SUCH

As just mentioned, the 'greatest *jihad*' is *jihad* against the ego. It is a *jihad* whose goal is to purify the soul by conquering the ego. Its foundations are the rites of *Islam*, and the demands of *Iman* and *Ihsan* as discussed in Chapter 2. Its great weapon is the remembrance of God, as mentioned in the *hadith* cited in the previous section, and as discussed in the section on polishing the rust from the heart in Chapter 8. The particulars and details of this comprise an immense topic, and represent the central challenge of human life itself. They cannot be fully described here in so short a space, but if there is one short passage in the Qur'an that can be thought of as summarizing the whole 'greatest *jihad*' as such, it is perhaps the following:

> *But as for such who feared standing before their Lord and restrained their soul from base desires / Paradise will be their abode.* (*Al-Nazi'at*, 79: 40–41)

Ghazali elaborates on this principle, and on the whole inner struggle of the 'greatest *jihad*' as follows:

> In every person there is a mixture of these four principles—I mean the divine and the diabolic and the predatory and the beastly—and all that is collected in the [human] heart. It is as if contained within, under a human being's skin are, in total, a pig, a dog, a devil and a wise man. The pig is appetite . . . The dog is anger . . . The pig invites, through greed, to vile and abominable things . . . The dog stirs, [through] anger, to injustice and wrongdoing. And the devil continually stirs up the desires of the pig and the anger of the dog. [The devil] presents to them in a favourable light that to which they are naturally inclined.
>
> The wise person (who symbolizes the intellect) is responsible for repelling the craftiness and cunning of the devil by revealing his deception through piercing insight and clear light. It is also responsible for breaking the greed of the pig by making the dog its master. For the vigour of appetite is broken by anger. The viciousness of the dog is controlled by making the pig its master, and repressing it under its yoke. If the wise person can do that and does it, then there is equilibrium, and justice appears in the kingdom of the body, and all proceed on *the straight path*. . . . But if he is unable to dominate them, then they will dominate him. [Then] he will be continually putting his energy and thought into trying to feed the pig and please the dog. . . .
>
> That is the state of most people whose main concerns are their bellies, their private parts or competing with others. . . (*The Revival of the Religious Sciences*, Book 21, *The Wonders of the Heart*, 5)

THE 'LESSER *JIHAD*' AS SUCH

The 'lesser *jihad*' is military *jihad*. It is combat or war against an enemy under certain conditions (as discussed in what follows). The 'lesser *jihad*' is entirely dependent on the 'greatest *jihad*' and is predicated upon it, for God says in the Qur'an: *O you who believe, when you meet a host, then stand firm and remember God much, that you may succeed* (*Al-Anfal*, 8:45). Accordingly, in an (admittedly weak) *hadith* the Prophet Muhammad ﷺ said, after returning from a military campaign:

> 'We have returned from the lesser *jihad* to the greatest *jihad*'. They said: 'What is the greatest *jihad*, O Messenger of God?' He said ﷺ: 'The struggle against the ego [*nafs*]'. (*Sunan al-Bayhaqi*; Al-Khatib al-Baghdadi, *Tarikh Baghdad*)

It is also extremely instructive to note that whilst everyone is called on to wage the greatest *jihad*, not everyone is called upon to wage the lesser, military *jihad* (see: *Al-Nisa'*, 4:95), and that religious scholars are specifically exempted (see: *Al-Tawbah*, 9:122). Under certain conditions, it is also conditional upon the consent of one's parents. When a man came to the Prophet ﷺ asking him for permission to perform [military] *jihad*, he ﷺ asked him: 'Are your parents alive?', to which the man replied: 'Yes.' And the Prophet ﷺ told him: 'Then perform *jihad* by [serving] them' (*Bukhari*).

THE REASONS BEHIND—AND CONDITIONS NECESSARY FOR—THE 'LESSER *JIHAD*'

The lesser *jihad* is essentially a 'just war' in Islam. This is very clear in the Qur'an and in the *sunnah*. For 13 years the Prophet ﷺ was oppressed, abused, humiliated, threatened, boycotted and persecuted by his tribe in Mecca for preaching Islam after it was revealed to him. His followers from less powerful clans were tortured and killed. Finally, his opponents kept trying to kill him, so he secretly migrated to Medina. But even then, the Meccans did not leave him alone and came to wage war on him. During all that time he was not permitted by God to take up arms in self-defence. Then, finally, in the second year AH, the following revelation came to him:

> *Permission is granted to those who fight because they have been wronged. And God is truly able to help them | those who were expelled from their homes without right, only because they said: 'Our Lord is God'. Were it not for God's causing some people to drive back others, destruction would have befallen the*

monasteries, and churches, and synagogues, and mosques in which God's Name
is mentioned greatly. Assuredly God will help those who help Him. God is
truly Strong, Mighty. (Al-Hajj, 22: 39-40)

So a just war in Islam depends on: (1) being attacked first or being about
to be attacked; (2) being wronged (and having been patient); (3) being
expelled from one's homes and land; (4) being religiously severely persecuted merely for belief in God; (5) having one's holy places (or the holy
places of Jews and Christians) destroyed; and (6) being declared by the
legitimate authority and ruler, so that *jihad* is a communal activity, not an
individual one. The fact that God grants 'permission'—and does not merely
give a commandment to fight—shows that fighting is an exceptional state
which requires a Divine exemption or 'special permission', and is not the
preferred state of affairs. There are also two other, later, verses in the
Qur'an from which scholars derive just reasons for war. The reasons are: (7)
defending (religiously) oppressed men, women and children who pray for
help (*Al-Nisa'*, 4:75); and (8) aggression and the breaking of peace treaties
(*Al-Tawbah*, 9:13). These together make up the only accepted reasons for
justifiable war in the Qur'an. And it is worth noting that every passage in
the Qur'an permitting or ordering war is always followed by a Qur'anic
verse conditioning it, constraining it, showing that it is defensive or urging
peace whenever possible (see Ghazi, Kalin and Kamali (eds), the appendix
to *War and Peace in Islam: the Uses and Abuses of Jihad*).

All this is to say that military *jihad* is strictly tied only to self-defence,
safety, freedom of religion, being oppressed and being evicted from one's
land. These are the *jus ad bellum* rules of military *jihad*. Religious conquest is *not* a reason for *jihad*, and neither is religious conversion. This is
clear from God's words (revealed in Medina, after the military *jihad* had
started): *There is no compulsion in religion...* (*Al-Baqarah*, 2:256). All this
is summed up in the Qur'anic verse cited at the beginning of the chapter:

And fight in the way of God with those who fight against you, but aggress
not; God loves not the aggressors. (Al-Baqarah, 2:190)

In short, military *jihad* is merely a 'just war' defined 600 years before St
Thomas Aquinas formulated his own just war theory.

THE GOAL OF THE 'LESSER *JIHAD*'

Every general in the world worth the title knows that wars cannot be won without first defining what victory is. Without knowing what a 'win' looks like, no one can win a war. A win may or may not be the destruction of the enemy's military or industrial capacity or will to fight. Sometimes completely destroying the enemy's military is a loss, because it leads to a mutual enemy taking over, gaining strength and eventually defeating both other sides. Often the goal of war is political, or seeking a change of behaviour in the enemy, or forcing a peace treaty. So it is necessary for the goal of *jihad* to be defined. At the same time it is important to remember that the goal of *jihad* is something completely different from the reason for *jihad*: confusing the two can lead to disastrous mistakes and unnecessary warfare.

Not everyone understands this, but nevertheless, scholars are in agreement regarding the stated goal of *jihad*, because God says in the Qur'an: *Fight them till there is no sedition, and the religion is for God; then if they desist, there shall be no enmity, save against evildoers'* (Al-Baqarah, 2: 193). This goal is the goal of *jihad* only after war has been waged on Muslims, and even then it is understood in the context of a defensive war in the Arabian Peninsula in the seventh century CE. It defines specifically what victory looks like in the case that Muslims are victorious (and of course they were). It is *not* the cause of *jihad*, the *casus belli*. And it can be forgone if the enemy sues for peace and if it is in the communal interest because God says: '. . . *then if they desist, there shall be no enmity, save against evildoers'* (Al-Baqarah, 2:193). The circumstances and events of the Pact of Hudaybiyah—where the Prophet ﷺ accepted a political compromise with the enemy—are proof of this. And God says in the Qur'an: *And if they incline to peace, then incline to it, and rely on God; truly He is the Hearer, the Knower (Al-Anfal*, 8:61).

IS THE 'LESSER *JIHAD*' OFFENSIVE OR DEFENSIVE?

What does 'offensive' mean as regards war? By 'offensive', we do not mean 'pre-emptive strikes': engaging an enemy who has already unjustly suppressed your brethren, threatened you or made his intentions and preparations to attack you clear—that is arguably 'defensive', even if you manage to attack him before he attacks you. By 'offensive', we mean 'attack a people who are not Muslims or allies but not an enemy', for reasons of conquest in one form or another.

Despite all that we have written above about the goal of military *jihad*, some classical jurists (such as Ibn Taymiyyah and many of the Andalusian scholars) talk about an offensive *jihad*—attacking other nations regularly. This is also the view of some twentieth century Islamic writers (like Syed Qutb) and some contemporary anti-*usulis* (like Abu Mus'ab al-Suri in his *Global Islamic Resistance Call* [2005]). On the other hand, the imams Abu Hanifah, Malik bin Anas, Ibn Hanbal, Sufyan al-Thawri, al-Awza'i and most Shafi'i scholars do not see religious difference in itself as legitimate grounds for *jihad*. And all of the greatest twentieth century *usuli* scholars, of different *madhahib*, who have written on the subject—Shaykh al-Azhar Mahmoud Shaltout, Wahba Zuhayli, Muhammad Sa'id al-Buti, 'Abdullah bin Bayyah, 'Ali Gomaa—say *jihad* is strictly defensive. Now anyone who looks at a map of seventh century Arabia will see that the distance between Mecca and Medina (where the Prophet 🕊 emigrated to in 0/622 to escape the Meccans) is around 210 miles/340 km as the crow flies—a long distance on camelback in the desert (which is how people travelled in those days in Arabia). Yet despite this, the first three battles (*Badr, Uhud* and *Al-Khandaq*) were all waged on the outskirts of Medina, the Meccans having travelled all that distance to attack the Muslims. In other words, the Meccans pursued the Prophet 🕊 and his followers and tried to wipe them out even though he had fled their city. This shows that they were attacking, and he 🕊 was defending. The Muslim sorties against Meccan allies (such as on the tribes of Sulaym and Ghatafan) were to forestall raids on themselves. Moreover, the battles with Arab Jewish Tribes of Medina (and later their allies at Khaybar, with whom they sought refuge) were battles against Medinan citizens who had committed treason against their own city after a written constitution and pact with the Muslims. The campaign against the Byzantines at Tabuk and Mu'tah were of course against a predatory political empire that had amassed a huge army on the borders of (then) Muslim lands and which constantly conquered and absorbed any territories it could. So none of this constitutes offensive war as such. Similarly, the campaign by the first

three Caliphs against the neo-Persian Sassanid empire after the Prophet
Muhammad's ✿ death was a campaign against another predatory empire
which had captured Jerusalem in 614 CE and had, for at least a century prior
to that, been vying for power over Southern Arabia with the Byzantines
and their proxies and allies.

We mentioned in the previous chapter that prior to the formation of the
League of Nations (in 1920), the natural state of political relations between
nations was 'dog eat dog' competition, and 90 per cent of the time nations
were actively or passively at war with each other or with themselves. Ibn
Taymiyyah wrote during the Mongol invasions, a time of savage war on
multiple fronts. These were times when anyone who mustered a strong
enough force would attack whomever they pleased—and who could stop
them? Any nation not strong enough to defend itself would perish. In this
kind of context there is no difference between 'offensive' and 'defensive'
war, because everyone is attacking you all the time. This explains why
some classical Islamic jurists never saw a meaningful distinction between
'offensive' and 'defensive' war. However, after the establishment of the
United Nations, the norm of international state relations became *peace*
by international consensus and UN treaty. So the situation since then is
completely different. The very first article of the first chapter of the UN
Charter (1945) reads:

The Purposes of the United Nations are:

> 1. To maintain international peace and security, and to that end: to take
> effective collective measures for the prevention and removal of threats to
> the peace, and for the suppression of acts of aggression or other breaches
> of the peace, and to bring about by peaceful means, and in conformity
> with the principles of justice and international law, adjustment or set-
> tlement of international disputes or situations which might lead to a
> breach of the peace.

In today's situation, with international peace in place by universally
agreed-upon treaties, even those classical jurists who thought of *jihad* as
offensive in their own times would not sanction an offensive *jihad*, since
God says: *O you who believe, fulfil your obligations.* (*Al-Ma'idah*, 5:1 see
also *Al-Isra'*, 17:34 et al.) In other words, in light of peace being the norm
agreed upon between countries (*'ahd*), the only *jihad* possible today is a

defensive just war after Muslims are attacked and thrown off their lands etc. as outlined in the eight conditions mentioned earlier.

THE INTENTION BEHIND THE 'LESSER *JIHAD*'

All Muslims see the great virtue in the lesser *jihad*. The Prophet 🕌 said that after the acts of the greatest *jihad* (the struggle against the ego), no act is better than the lesser *jihad*:

> Abdullah bin Mas'ud said: I asked God's messenger 🕌, 'O messenger of God! What is the best deed?' He replied, 'To offer the prayers at their early stated fixed times'. I asked, 'What is next in goodness?' He replied, 'To be good and dutiful to your parents'. I further asked, what is next in goodness?' He replied, 'To participate in [military] *jihad* in God's way.' (*Bukhari*)

There are also a number of verses in the Qur'an encouraging Muslims to take up military *jihad* when the need arises. For example, God says: *O you who believe, what is wrong with you that, when it is said to you, 'Go forth in the way of God', you sink down heavily to the ground* (Al-Tawbah, 9:38). Equally, God says:

> *Indeed God has purchased from the believers their lives and their possessions, so that theirs will be [the reward of] paradise: they shall fight in the way of God and they shall kill and be killed; that is a promise which is binding upon Him in the Torah and the Gospel and the Qur'an; and who fulfils his covenant better than God? Rejoice then in this bargain of yours which you have made, for that is the supreme triumph. (Al-Tawbah 9:111)*

This is not a 'cult of death', as both detractors of Islam and misguided neo-*jihadists* seem to think. It is a Divine reward for those prepared to make the ultimate sacrifice. The allusion to the Gospel can be explained by Jesus' 🕌 words: *Greater love has no one than this, than to lay down one's life for one's friends* (John 15:13). Indeed, it is crucial to have a noble motive for military *jihad*, because it is the motive—the '*why*'—that in the end determines *how* it is waged and whether it is accepted by God or not. Intention is key. God says in the Qur'an: '*And that man shall have only what he [himself] strives for'* (*Al-Najm*, 53:39). And the Prophet ﷺ clarified exactly this point in a *hadith*:

> The first to be judged on the Day of Resurrection is the man who died as a martyr. He will be brought forth and [God] will make His favours known to him, which he will recognize. He will be asked: 'What did you do with them?' to which the man will reply: 'I fought for your sake until I was killed.' He [i.e. God] will say: 'You have lied. You fought so that it would be said that you are bold, and so it was said.' He will then be ordered to be dragged on his face and flung into the Fire . . . (*Muslim*)

In other words, martyrs and martyrdom are noble because of love of God, and because of their goodness and self-sacrifice, not because of hatred or revenge. The intention for *jihad* must be one of love, goodness, bravery and self-sacrifice, not a malicious intention of anger, hatred, pride, bloodlust or military adventurism. We honour and admire soldiers and heroes, not killers and bandits. Military *jihad* is essentially a 'good fight'—not terrorism—and so it must be waged in a decent way.

THE RULES OF CONDUCT DURING THE 'LESSER *JIHAD*'

This brings us to the question of the rules of conduct during military *jihad* (*jus in bello*). This is almost as important as the cause for *jihad*. It is important to note here that these rules were revealed at a time when no civilisation before Islam had ever established a methodology for fighting in a humane way, deliberately protecting non-combatants, and even combatants outside a battlefield. We will not go into all the details of these rules here save to say that the Prophet Muhammad ﷺ said:

> Do not kill a feeble old man, or any child or young person, or woman. . . . (*Abu Dawud*)
> Do not act treacherously, do not steal the spoils of war, do not disfigure dead bodies, and do not kill children or priests. . . . (*Ahmad*)
> Wage war but do not be severe, do not be treacherous, do not mutilate. . . . (*Muslim*; *Tirmidhi*)

On the day of the conquest of Mecca, the Prophet ﷺ said:

> Those retreating are not to be killed, nor are the injured to be harmed, and whoever shuts his door is safe. . . . (*Musannaf Ibn Abi Shaybah*)

As regards prisoners of war and captives, God says in the Qur'an: '. . .thereafter either [set them free] by grace or by ransom . . .' (*Muhammad*, 47:4). God also commends providing prisoners of war with their basic needs and treating them with dignity and respect:

> *And they give food, despite [their] love of it to the needy, and the orphan, and the prisoner [of war].* (*Al-Insan*, 76:8)

RELATIONS WITH NON-MUSLIMS OUTSIDE OF THE 'LESSER *JIHAD*'

Outside of military *jihad*, God says:

> *God does not forbid you in regard to those who did not wage war against you on account of religion and did not expel you from your homes, that you should treat them kindly and deal with them justly. Assuredly God loves the just.* (*Al-Mumtahanah*, 60:8)

This means that when people are not waging war on Muslims, and have no intention to do so, Muslims must be kind and just to them, and indeed to everyone. The Prophet Muhammad ﷺ went into more detail:

> By Him in whose hand is my soul, no servant [of God] believes until he loves for his neighbour what he loves for himself. (*Muslim*)

It remains to be stressed that the 'neighbour' here is everyone, no matter what their religion, and no matter how far away (as 'neighbours') they are physically, for the Prophet Muhammad ﷺ also said: 'Love for *people* what you love for yourself' (*Ahmad*). And God Himself confirms this in the Qur'an:

> *And worship God, and associate nothing with Him. Behave with excellence [Ihsan] to parents, and near kindred, and to orphans, and to the needy, and to the neighbour who is near, and to the neighbour who is a stranger, and to the friend at your side, and to the wayfarer. . . .* (*Al-Nisa'*, 4:36)

According to the Qur'anic commentary *Tafsir al-Jalalayn*, *'the neighbour who is near'* means 'the one who is near to you either in terms of residence, or of family ties', and *'the neighbour who is a stranger'* means 'the one who is distant from you, either in terms of residence, or of family ties'. According to the Qur'anic commentary *Tafsir al-Qurtubi*, they mean the 'nearby neighbour', and the 'unknown neighbour' respectively. In other words, 'the neighbour' means every person on the face of the earth, no matter how far away, whether Muslim or not.

Now 'loving' for your neighbour what you love for yourself, *must* be translated into action since the Prophet ﷺ also said:

> Whoever believes in God and the Last Day, let him behave with excellence (*Ihsan*) towards his neighbour. (*Muslim*)

So we have here the Islamic equivalent of both the Second Commandment that *You shall love your neighbour as yourself* (Matthew 22:40; Mark 12:31), and the Golden Rule that *Whatever you want men to do to you, do also to them, for this is the Law and the Prophets* (Matthew 7:12; Luke 6:31). The difference seems to be one of emphasis: Islam stresses the *practice* of *Ihsan* rather than the *emotion* of love.

Practising *Ihsan* towards others is also part of the reason for our creation. As cited earlier, God says:

> *O humankind! We have indeed created you from a male and a female, and made you nations and tribes so that you may come to know one another. Truly the noblest of you in the sight of God is the most God-fearing among you. Truly God is Knower, Aware. (Al-Hujurat, 49:13)*

God created a diverse plurality of nations and tribes—of peoples. By practising *Ihsan* towards people, we come to know them. By coming to know them, we avoid conflict with them and instead can co-operate with them in the best interests of all our societies. Moreover, by knowing others, we know ourselves better. As we have seen, by knowing ourselves better, we come to know God better. By knowing God better, we worship Him better, and that is the reason for our creation, as we have also seen. So the diversity of people *is part of the reason for creation*. Indeed the verse implies precisely this by the causative words *'so that'*. Finally, as the verse above also implies, part of knowing ourselves is precisely understanding that the worth of a person does not depend on who he or she is, what he or she has done, or how much power, money or fame he or she has, but *only* on their piety and *Ihsan* towards others.

~

WHY IS IT IMPORTANT TO KNOW ALL THIS?

Perhaps no word in the English language evokes more dread and mis-understanding than the word *'jihad'*—to non-Muslims at least. So it is important to know all this for a number of reasons. First, it is important to know that *jihad* is not 'holy war', that Muslims do not regard war as such as holy, and that they regard war as a necessary means and not as an end in itself. And they regard it as an end that *should have an end* whenever possible, not as open-ended. That is to say, that there should be peace whenever possible, and that war is a means to peace and not vice versa. Second, it is important to know that military *jihad* is—and has always been—a just war based on the principle of defensive action, for everyone except for a few deluded 'neo-*jihadis*'. Third, it is important to know that military *jihad* is a communal activity decided by states through their leaderships, not by a few angry young men (neither as individuals, nor in gangs calling themselves 'armies'): that only leads to chaos, anarchy and sedition and is strictly forbidden by the *shari'ah*. Fourth, it is important to know that military *jihad* has certain humane rules of conduct, certain legitimate targets and certain legitimate strategies. It is not terrorism, barbarism and savagery—and does not sanction any of these. This remains true in principle despite the horrors the world sees every day perpetrated by deviant, ignorant (mostly) young men and women wrongly attributing their vilest deeds to *jihad* and even recording them and glorying in them. God says in the Qur'an:

> *What about those whose evil deeds are made alluring to them so that they think that they are good?* (*Fatir*, 35:8)

Accordingly (and fifth), it is important to know that the motive for *jihad* cannot be one of revenge, of blood feud, of bloodlust or of adventurism. Those were the emotions which drove pre-Islamic Arabia in its 'Time of

Ignorance' ('*Jahiliyyah*'). The motive for *jihad* has to be a noble one, of duty, dignity, self-sacrifice, courage and love of God and the neighbour, in order for it to be acceptable to God. *Jihad,* then, is just war, made with an intention that is noble but not worldly. Sixth, and finally, it is important to know that outside of *jihad* Muslims are bound by their religion to treat all people with kindness, justice and excellence and that this is obviously the normal and best state of affairs.

~

Chapter 12

WHAT IS GOVERNMENT?

*Verily, God commands you to restore trusts to their rightful
owners. And when you judge between people, that you
judge with justice. Excellent is the instruction God gives
you. God is ever Hearer, Seer.* (Al-Nisa', 4:58)

THE IMPORTANCE OF JUSTICE

As we have seen in Chapter 10, justice is at the root of all rights in Islam,
and the five aims of the *shari'ah*. Justice is also essential in other religions.
For example, in the Torah (and thus the Bible) we read:

> *You shall not distort justice; you shall not be partial, and you shall not take a
> bribe. . . | Justice, and only justice, you shall pursue.* (Deuteronomy 16:19–20)

It remains to be said that all human beings have an instinctive yearning for justice. Children have it, older people have it, and most of all,
young people have it. Even when people cannot put it into words, they
can generally identify it when they see it. In short, justice is a universal
right, essential for the proper functioning of any society, because it is an
innate conviction of the human soul. That is why no government and no
institution can last without justice.

Conversely, the lack of justice—*injustice*—inevitably leads to discontentment, protests, rebellions, revolutions and civil wars. This has been true throughout history. Injustice makes people angry and creates hatred. 'Angry young men' (and women) are usually angry because of an injustice—real or perceived. For example, a large proportion of *takfiri-jihadis* become radicalized because of an injustice: often cruel mistreatment in prison, or the death or mistreatment of one of their relatives or friends (as explained in the annex). Nothing is more dangerous and destabilizing than injustice. God Himself punishes injustice wherever it occurs, even when inflicted on people who do not believe in Him. The Prophet Muhammad ﷺ said, remarkably:

> Beware of the prayer of someone who has been wronged—even if he [or she] be a disbeliever—for there is no veil between it and God. (*Ahmad*)

This *hadith* is remarkable because it is as if to say that even a disbeliever will pray—or at least curse—when wronged, and that God listens to this prayer and answers it because injustice is so inherently wrong. Indeed, God Himself says (in a *hadith qudsi*):

> My servants, I have made injustice forbidden to Myself, and I have forbidden it to you, so do not be unjust. (*Muslim*)

THE 'EXCELLENCE' OF JUSTICE

God says in the Qur'an:

> *Verily, God commands you to restore trusts to their rightful owners. And when you judge between people, that you judge with justice. Excellent is the instruction God gives you. God is ever Hearer, Seer. (Al-Nisa', 4:58)*

This verse is so foundational and conveys so much, of such importance, that entire books have been written on it. Even as recently as 2015, the leading Malaysian philosopher, Syed Naquib Attas, wrote a short book commenting on it. Before attempting to plunge into it, we note that the verse is one of the few times God gives a categorical command ('*amr*') to all people, and this command refers to justice. It is also the only time in the whole Qur'an that God praises His own instruction with the word 'excellent' ('*ni'imma*' literally means 'how fine!', 'how good!', 'how beautiful!', 'how excellent!'), and does so in praise of justice. Moreover, elsewhere in the Qur'an the very point of revelation is identified with justice:

> *We have verily sent Our messengers with clear signs, and We revealed with them the Scripture and the Balance, so that mankind may uphold justice.* (*Al-Hadid,* 57:25)

All this is to indicate the unparalleled importance of justice in the Qur'an. Furthermore, in a well-known *hadith*, 'the Just' is one of God's own 99 Divine Names (*Tirmidhi*). Nothing, then, is more 'excellent' than justice in human affairs.

WHAT IS JUSTICE?

But what exactly is justice? Obviously, it is important to be able to express it clearly in words, in order to clear up confusion and avoid the exploitation of perceived injustices to create greater injustices — as often happens nowadays. So in order to implement justice and convince people of it, it is necessary to be able to say exactly what it is — that is, to *define* it.

There is generally no legal or philosophical agreement on what exactly justice is. The *Oxford English Dictionary* defines justice as 'behaviour or treatment that is morally right and fair'. This of course begs the questions 'What is right?', 'What is fair?' and 'On what is morality based?'. The classical, 'natural' definition of justice is usually taken from Plato's definition of it, or from Cicero's elaboration of Plato. In *The Republic*, the character of Socrates says that justice is: 'doing one's own job and not intruding elsewhere' (433a). Cicero (in *De Natura Deorum*, III, 15) actually puts it more elegantly: it is the 'virtue which assigns each thing its due' (*'suum cuique'*). One of the truly astounding things about the Qur'anic verse which this chapter is based on is that before commanding *And when you judge between people, that you judge with justice, God commands you to restore trusts to their rightful owners.* That is to say that God gives a *definition* of justice before commanding people to enact it. In other words, justice is *to restore trusts to their rightful owners.* This encompasses both the dictionary and classical definitions of justice, since it includes morally fair behaviour or treatment that gives everything its due. But it goes beyond that, by viewing everything as a 'trust' (*'amanah'*). Now a trust is something of intrinsic value and given by God, to be benefited from temporarily, but not wholly owned. It cannot be disposed of at will; we do not have an absolute right to throw it away or waste it. It is something to which we have rights and responsibilities in equal part. So regarding everything as a 'trust' lends to things dignity, inherent rights as well as a reminder of their fragility.

But what specifically are 'trusts'? The Qur'an shows how 'trusts' include everything, even—or perhaps especially—things which are not a matter of law. These start with the trust of the very human state and of human life. God says in the Qur'an, about humanity's creation:

> *Indeed We offered the Trust to the heavens and the earth and the mountains,*
> *but they refused to bear it and were wary of it; but man bore it. Truly he has*
> *proved himself an ignorant wrongdoer. (Al-Ahzab, 33:72)*

The 'trust' here is considered by many commentators to be faith in the One God and knowledge of Him. We have already cited the verse about God's pre-temporal covenant with human beings of knowledge of Him and faith in Him:

> *And when your Lord took from the Children of Adam, from their loins their*
> *seed and made them testify against themselves, 'Am I not your Lord?' They*
> *said, 'Yes, indeed we testify', lest you should say on the Day of Resurrection,*
> *'Truly, of this we were unaware'. (Al-A'raf, 7:172)*

In other words, *the Trust* is 'connected to' God's *Spirit* that He breathed into human beings giving them life *with hearing, sight and hearts* (*Al-Sajdah,* 32:10), in a *dwelling place and a repository* (*Al-An'am,* 6:98) of time and space on the earth. It implies first God's 'right' to be worshipped by human beings, and then the sacredness of human life created by God with an innate knowledge of Him in their deepest spirit. This means that human life itself is the first of all terrestrial trusts. That is why no one may violate human life—not even with suicide—so that:

> *Whoever slays a soul for other than a soul, or for corruption in the earth, it*
> *shall be as if he had slain mankind altogether; and whoever saves the life of one,*
> *it shall be as if he had saved the life of all mankind. . . . (Al-Ma'idah, 5:32)*

'Trusts' also obviously include the five 'aims of the *shari'ah*' as discussed earlier (namely, the fundamental rights to (1) life; (2) religion; (3) family, procreation and honour; (4) reason, and (5) property—with all the freedoms and protection that each of these rights imply). 'Trusts' include all the rights of the neighbour as well—his or her right to *Ihsan* from us as discussed in the previous chapter.

In fact, the concept of 'trust'—and therefore justice itself—also means spending time with family or friends, relaxing, looking after one's body and spending time with one's spouse. The Prophet Muhammad ﷺ said: 'Your family has a right over you; your guest has a right over you; your soul has a right over you' (*Abu Dawud*), and 'Your eye [i.e. sleep] has a right over you; your body has a right over you; your spouse has a right over you' (Al-Khatib al-Baghdadi, *Al-Muttafiq wa 'l-Muftariq*). And of course this concept of 'trust' extends justice to every legitimate aspect of one's personal needs; to social interactions; to one's profession or vocation; to one's time itself (as we have seen), and to every other aspect of human life. Finally, and perhaps most obviously, wealth and money are a 'trust' and not something which we have an absolute right to dispose of—or hoard—without moral responsibility. God makes this crystal clear in the Qur'an:

> *Believe in God and His messenger and spend from that over which He has made you trustees. For those of you who believe and spend theirs shall be a great reward.* (*Al-Hadid*, 57:7)

THE ECOLOGY OF JUSTICE

Beyond that—and, crucially, in our age of climate change and impending environmental collapse—*the Trust* applies to human beings as God's *vicegerents of the earth* (*Al-Naml*, 27:62). This means that justice itself demands that human beings exercise responsible, compassionate and *sustainable* stewardship of the earth and of all the myriad creatures, flora and fauna which inhabit it. Joyce Kilmer (d. 1886) wrote (in 'Trees'):

I think that I shall never see
   A poem as lovely as a tree.
A tree whose hungry mouth is prest
   Against the earth's sweet flowing breast;

A tree that looks at God all day,
    And lifts her leafy arms to pray;
A tree that may in Summer wear
    A nest of robins in her hair;
Upon whose bosom snow has lain;
    Who intimately lives with rain.
Poems are made by fools like me,
    But only God can make a tree.

He was right (except of course the part about being a fool!). Every living thing on earth, including plants, is God's creature and creation, not ours. In a *hadith* in *Bukhari*, a tree stump in Medina was heard to cry by the Companions when the Prophet Muhammad ﷺ left it. So all creatures have their own lives and their own inherent value regardless of their utility to human beings. The Prophet Muhammad ﷺ warned:

> A woman was tormented because of a cat which she had confined until it died and [for this] she entered hellfire. (*Muslim*)

And conversely he said ﷺ:

> A prostitute happened to see a dog on the verge of dying of thirst, circling a well. She removed her shoe, drew water with it, and gave it to the dog to drink. She was pardoned because of this. (*Muslim*)

We may have a right to eat and use some plants, but we don't have a right to destroy them wantonly. We may have a right to eat and domesticate some animals, but we certainly do not have a right to torture them, unnecessarily harm them, annihilate entire species, or destroy their habitats. We do not have a right to hunt them for 'sport'. The fact that over a third of all human food produced is thrown away—to say nothing of overeating and obesity—means that wealthy people at least have no legitimate reason to hunt wild animals or birds for fun, and then eat them and pretend that was the real reason they hunted them. Equally, human beings have no right to despoil, plunder and pollute the earth itself or the mountains or the atmosphere. For we know *the heavens and the earth and the mountains . . . refused to bear* the Trust and *were wary* of being wrongdoers like ourselves. We should then view the earth and the mountains—and by extension the atmosphere which is part of *the heavens* and the seas which cover the earth—as somehow innately conscious in their own way. Consequently, we should consider that nature, the earth, the seas, the mountains, the atmosphere and animals and plants have their own rights, and humanity should think seriously about safeguarding these rights through international legislation—especially since we live off them, and their preservation is essential for our survival. Equally, we should think about universal conventions and legislation for the protection of plant, marine, bird, and even insect life. The Prophet Muhammad 🌸 said:

> An ant had bitten a prophet (one amongst the earlier Prophets) and he ordered that the colony of the ants should be burnt. Then God revealed to him: 'Because of an ant's bite you have burnt a community from amongst the communities which hymns My glory?' (*Muslim*)

And God Himself says in the Qur'an:

> *There is no animal on the earth and no bird that flies with its wings, but they are communities like you. We have neglected nothing in the Book; then to their Lord they shall be gathered. (Al-An'am, 6:38)*

A real community is a group whose members *communicate* with each other. Animals, birds and insects—as we now know—communicate with each other. Even trees communicate (see Colin Tudge's wonderful book *The Secret Life of Trees*), albeit not like us or through sounds. Knowing that animals, birds, insects and perhaps even trees are communities should make us empathize with them and protect them. In doing that, we will also be protecting ourselves. God warns in the Qur'an:

> *Corruption has appeared in the land and in the sea because of what people's hands have perpetrated that He may make them taste something of what they have done that perhaps they may repent. (Al-Rum, 30:41)*

In short, in Islam, human beings have a strict religious obligation to treat animals and all living things—and nature itself—with every possible mercy and consideration, and to avoid unnecessary harm to animals and living beings, as well as to avoid polluting, disturbing or destroying the natural environment. The Prophet Muhammad 🌸 said: 'There is a reward [from God] for [service to] every living animal' (*Bukhari; Muslim*).

WHAT IS GOVERNMENT?

To return to justice and the foundational verse on which this chapter is based, it is clear that the central application of human justice lies in the administration of political government. For after the words *Verily, God commands you to restore trusts to their rightful owners*, God immediately says: *And when you judge between people, that you judge with justice.* First, it will be noted that the command to enact justice here applies to *people*: all people, not just Muslims or believers in religions, but all people, regardless of race or creed or any other distinction. Then it will be noted that the word for 'judge' here ('*hakamta*') also means 'rule' or 'govern' and refers to what we now call the 'executive branch' of government as much as to the 'judiciary branch'. It comes from the root *h-k-m* which means 'to prevent', and hence to prevent oppression and injustice, and their ultimate cause: ignorance. Indeed, the Arabic word for wisdom, '*hikmah*' comes from this same root (*h-k-m*). This is to say, then, that justice applies first of all to government. Government, then, is in itself essentially the wise application of justice to all people, equally. So in the Qur'an God says to the Prophet Muhammad ﷺ: *Say: '... I have been commanded to be just between you. (Al-Shura, 42:15)*, just as He said to the Prophet (and King) David ﷺ: *'O David! ... judge justly between people and do not follow desire that it then lead you astray from the way of God (Sad, 38:26).*

Finally, from the Islamic point of view, it will be noted that government is a reciprocal responsibility shared between the government and the people. It is not based on the whims of individuals and vogues of the day, or the fear or the anger of the moment. Rather, it is based on Islamic teachings as transmitted in the Qur'an and the *hadith*. So the very next verse (after the verse on which this chapter is based) says:

> *O you who believe, obey God, and obey the messenger and those in authority among you. If you should quarrel about anything, refer it to God and the messenger, if you believe in God and the Last Day; that is better and more excellent in interpretation. (Al-Nisa', 4:59)*

This means that people have responsibilities towards their governments just as governments have responsibilities towards their people. In short then, it can perhaps be said that the Islamic conception of government is essentially the wise application of justice to all people equally with reciprocal responsibility between the government and the people, based on Islamic teachings.

POPULAR CONSENSUS AND
GOVERNMENT LEGITIMACY

In the Qur'an, God is the *True King* (*Ta Ha*, 20:114); the *Master of the Kingdom* (*Aal 'Imran*, 3:26); *He in Whose hand is the Sovereignty* (*Al-Mulk*, 67:1); and He who *give[s] the Kingdom to whom [He] will* (*Aal 'Imran*, 3:26). God made some prophets kings (such as David ﷺ and Solomon ﷺ), and God first instituted kingship in answer to the Prophet Samuel's ﷺ prayer (*Al-Baqarah*, 2:246). God made the Prophet Joseph ﷺ serve a (good) king of ancient Egypt—and only the word 'king' is used to describe him in the Qur'an—whereas the tyrants of Egypt who opposed Moses ﷺ are always referred to as 'Pharaoh'. The Prophet Muhammad ﷺ himself confirmed many of the local kings in their roles as kings (such as in Oman, Bahrain and Himyar in Yemen) after they and their people had converted to Islam. The Prophet ﷺ sent a persecuted group of his early Companions (headed by his cousin Ja'far bin Abi Talib ﷺ) to seek refuge with the King of Abyssinia whom he ﷺ referred to as 'a righteous king' (Tabari, *Jami' al-Bayan*, on *Al-Anfal*, 8:38–40). The Prophet also ﷺ said: 'Monarchy (*al-mulk*) is in [his ﷺ tribe of] Quraysh' (*Tirmidhi*; *Ahmad*). And in another *hadith*: 'Leaders (*al-a'immah*) are from Quraysh if they are merciful when asked for mercy, and if they keep pledges when they make them, and they are just when they judge. Whoever (of them) does not do these things, God's curse is on them, as well as that of the Angels and people' (*Ahmad*). Indeed, when the Prophet Muhammad ﷺ died (in 11/632), having no sons, brothers or nephews, he was succeeded by 'Righteous Caliphs' who succeeded him for the next 30 years and were his kinsmen from Quraysh. They were actually also his fathers-in-law (Abu Bakr ﷺ and 'Umar ﷺ) and sons-in-law ('Uthman ﷺ and 'Ali ﷺ) by marriage. The fifth (and last) 'Righteous Caliph' for a few months in 40/661 was the Prophet's ﷺ grandson Al-Hasan bin 'Ali ﷺ. The Prophet ﷺ had prophesied: 'There will be caliphs after me for 30 years, then there will be monarchy' (*Ahmad*; *Sahih Ibn Hibban*). And indeed, throughout Islamic history from 661 CE—until the fall of the Islamic Ottoman Caliphate in 1923—Islamic states were generally local monarchies nominally under one transnational caliphate or another. Some of Islam's greatest heroes and defenders—such as Nur al-Din Zengi and Saladin—were kings. But if there is no Jacobinism in Islam, there is of course no such thing as a 'divine right of kings' or an 'absolute monarchy' in Islam of the type seen in the Middle Ages in Europe either. God says: *Do you not know that to God belongs the kingdom of the heavens and the earth?* (*Al-Ma'idah*, 5:40). Indeed, as mentioned above, the *True King* (*Ta Ha*, 20:114) is God, and so the ruler is always subject to God's laws, and then to human consensus and consultation (as will be discussed below).

Nevertheless, no particular form of government is necessary in Islam, including monarchy or even the caliphate. The Prophet Muhammad ﷺ explained many details of conduct in all sorts of matters ranging from trade to inheritance, yet he ﷺ did not institute a single particular form of government. This must have been deliberate and providential. Presumably the reason behind it is that a form of government is merely a means and not an end, and that God states in the Qur'an what is expected of leaders and government—no matter who they are and what form the government takes—as follows:

> *Those who, if We empower them in the land, maintain the prayer, and pay the alms, and enjoin decency and forbid indecency. And with God rests the outcome of all matters.* (*Al-Hajj*, 22:41)

That then is the ambit of rulers, whoever and whatever they are, and it is clearly founded on the application of (1) 'spiritual justice' ('*maintain the prayer*'); (2) financial justice ('*pay the alms*') and (3–4) social and political justice respectively ('*enjoin decency and forbid indecency*'). In fact, it is only when the prayer is not maintained (i.e. that there is no 'spiritual justice') that a ruler may be overthrown by armed insurrection ('*khuruj*'). The Prophet Muhammad ﷺ pledged Muslims

> not to wrangle with those in power over their power unless you see them involved in open disbelief ('*kufr bawah*'). With regard to this [open disbelief], you need to have clear evidence from God (*Bukhari*).

Beyond that people should be free to determine for themselves the details of what suits them best according to their time, place, circumstances, customs and convictions. What is necessary, however, is the consensus (*ijma'*) of Muslims on the form of government, whatever it be. A ruler or government is legitimate if there is a consensus on them by the people or their leaders. This consensus must be reflected in the two practices of *bay'ah* (a pledge of allegiance) and *shura* (consultation). Both practices are grounded in the Qur'an and the *hadith*. So the *process* of consultation is obligatory in state decisions. God says to the Prophet Muhammad ﷺ in the Qur'an:

> *It was by the mercy of God that you were lenient with them; had you been harsh and fierce of heart, they would have dispersed from about you. So pardon them, and ask forgiveness for them, and consult them in the matter. And when you are resolved, rely on God; for God loves those who rely. (Aal 'Imran, 3:159; see also: Al-Shura, 42:38)*

So a national government is legitimate to the extent that it has been established with the consensus of its people or their representatives and to the extent that the 'overwhelming majority' have given it their allegiance, one way or another. The Prophet Muhammad ﷺ said: 'Follow the overwhelming majority of people' (*Ibn Majah*; *Ahmad*). Some contemporary scholars have said that this can be a consensus on a document like a constitution, and its legitimacy can then be passed on and inherited.

Consensus rule can be said to be a form of democracy, but it is not the same thing as 'majoritarianism'. 'Majoritarianism' is when a plurality or small majority of the electorate—usually under the influence of demagoguery manipulating fear or hate—does something (through 'legal' means and/or by using state apparatus) which oppresses a minority; takes away its fundamental rights, or at least does something which that minority would never freely agree to, and which under consensus rule it would have the power to veto or block. This eventually tends to lead in the long term to a civil war or to secession. New constitutions that are established this way inevitably fail, as we saw after the so-called 'Arab Spring' of 2011 in certain countries in the Middle East. Islam has never accepted majoritarianism as a principle. God says in the Qur'an:

> *If you obey most of those on earth, they will lead you astray from the way of God; they follow only supposition; they are merely guessing. (Al-An'am, 6:116)*

Nevertheless, when a constitution is established by consensus and governments change by majority or plurality vote, this is actually consensus rule not 'majoritarianism'. In *The Social Contract*, Jean-Jacques Rousseau (1712-1778) describes this situation as follows: 'The law of majority-voting itself rests on an agreement and implies that there has been, on at least one occasion, unanimity' (Book 1, Chapter 5).

It is interesting to note that in Western democracies today there is an underlying and unspoken agreement between at least 90 per cent of all people that their form of government is the only kind they will accept. The 1787 US Constitution was adopted and ratified more or less unanimously (only three out of 42 delegates still present in Philadelphia—from the total of 55 who had participated—refused to sign, and all the states eventually ratified it). Consensus is then a potential common ground between Islamic political theory and Western democracy.

In modern terms, consensus provides the ultimate 'check and balance'. In a consensus, no minority (no matter how secular or how religiously radical, no matter what religion, race or ethnic group) is excluded; everyone has a say; everyone has a veto; everyone is protected; everyone is respected; everyone is taken into consideration, and everyone is safe. There can be no tyranny of the majority; no populist or religious demagoguery can lead to the majority infringing upon or victimizing a minority, and so everyone is forced to compromise. By definition, everyone is satisfied.

TEMPORAL STATE

Contrary to what some people seem to think, since the death of the Prophet Muhammad 🕊, the state in Islam is, and has always been (at least in Sunni Islam, and in Shi'i Islam until Ayatollah Khomeini's *Vilayet al-Faqih* doctrine of 1970), a *temporal state*. By this we mean a civil state that is not a theocracy and not run by a clergy or a religious caste, but is not secular either. This is because the Prophet Muhammad 🕊 was the last of the Messengers of God, and when he died, the door of revelation was closed. No one receives revelation after him 🕊, so there can be no theocracy in Islam after the Prophet 🕊. This means both that no person (religious scholar or otherwise) is infallible, and that religious scholars cannot claim temporal authority just because they are religious scholars. God says:

And when there comes to them an issue, be it of security, or of fear, they broadcast
it. If they had referred it to the Messenger and to those in authority among
them; those among them who are able to think it out, would have known it
from them. . . . (Al-Nisa', 4:83)

Those in authority are the rulers of the state. They are the ones responsible
for the security of the state. Politics is a science, and they have observed
it, studied it and know about it. That is why they are better suited to deal
with it. So instead of preachers pretending or aspiring to have some kind
of political authority because they possess a certain religious knowledge,
God tells people to leave it to the legitimate rulers. Obviously religious
scholars can have a moral authority and can say what they think their
religion is and what it demands, but they cannot wield temporal power
or claim executive authority. They also cannot claim absolute Divine
authority for their particular understanding of religion (unless of course
there is a universal consensus of scholars — *ijma'* — on a given point). In fact
historically, great Islamic scholars would do their best to avoid entangle-
ment in affairs of state and politics out of fear of God. Over the course of
Islamic history, religious scholars have almost never been rulers. Indeed,
some scholars, such as Abu Hanifah, suffered imprisonment and flogging
rather than accept a high state post.

CITIZENSHIP

In Islamic government, the basis of citizenship is not religious identity,
ethnicity or race, gender, age, class, wealth or language. It is simply citizenship. Freedom and rights of citizenship in a particular land come — or used
to come — from birth in it. God Himself swears in the Qur'an as follows:

I swear by this land, | and you are free to live in this land. | And [by] parent
and offspring. (Al-Balad, 90:1–3)

So freedom and rights of citizenship are inherent, inalienable rights.
Nevertheless, the basis of the social contract with the *government* of the
state (if there is one) is communal taxes. This contract can also be inherited,
and is usually based on the payment of communal taxes. The first 'constitution' of Medina at the time of the Prophet Muhammad ﷺ identified

Jews and Muslims as one nation. The rights of non-Muslim citizens were the same as the rights of the Muslim citizens. It read:

> The Jews, according to this treaty stand accepted as one nation with the Muslims. As far as their religion is concerned, the Jews will remain on theirs, and the Muslims and their allies on theirs. (Ibn Hisham, *Al-Sirah al-Nabawiyyah*)

In such a context, every citizen is guaranteed the state's protection for their lives, families, properties, honour, privacy, and freedom of religion and thought. Citizens cannot be deprived of their rights on grounds of religion, ethnicity, gender or class. The Prophet Muhammad ﷺ said:

> Beware! Whoever wrongs a non-Muslim citizen, or diminishes any of his [or her] rights, or imposes on him [or her] more than he [or she] can bear, and takes anything from him [or her] without his [or her] consent, I shall plead on the non-Muslim citizen's behalf on the Day of Resurrection. (*Abu Dawud*)

Indeed, every citizen is guaranteed the state's protection for their lives, families, properties, honour, privacy, and freedom of religion and thought. And the state is responsible to see that this is not affected by corruption by its officials or wealthy citizens. God warns in the Qur'an;

> *Consume not your goods between you in deception, and proffer them to the judges, that you may consume a portion of other people's goods in sin while you are aware.* (*Al-Baqarah*, 2:188)

Citizens should also receive state support when needed and possible. The Prophet Muhammad ﷺ said:

> Anyone who (dies and) leaves debts or minors, it is on me. (*Bukhari*; *Muslim*)

Reciprocally, the state is owed loyalty, faithfulness, support from its citizens and its laws are to be obeyed. God says in the Qur'an:

> *And fulfil the pact of God when you made it and do not break [your] oaths after pledging them and having made God a Witness over you. Truly God knows what you do.* (*Al-Nahl*, 16:91)

In short then, citizenship can perhaps be thought of as a fair and equal social contract with the state—and through it, with society in general—based on justice, with God as Witness over it.

~

WHY IS IT IMPORTANT TO KNOW ALL THIS?

It is important to know how crucial justice is because without justice, Muslims—and in fact all people—will be in perpetual revolt, and suffer from terrorism and civil war. Positively speaking, it is important to know that nothing is finer or more excellent than the application of justice in human affairs and for human well-being in general. It is obviously important to know exactly what justice is in order to implement it, and to appreciate that the 'restoration of trusts to their rightful owners' is a concept that encompasses all aspects of social, political, spiritual and even natural and ecological life. It is important to know that government rests upon justice, and that no government can endure long without justice. It is also important to know that governments are only legitimate—and minorities are only protected—when constitutions and states are set up on the basis of consensus, and that this principle is what Islamic governments and Western democracies potentially have in common. It is important to know that religious scholars and preachers have no inherent executive authority and that there cannot be any theocracies in Islam after the death of the Prophet Muhammad ﷺ. Finally it is important to know that there are no religious prerequisites for citizenship under Islamic government; that citizens are citizens, and that an Islamic government is bound to treat all citizens with justice.

All this of course represents traditional *usuli* positions and principles, and everything happening today that does not reflect this is not only wrong but new to Islamic history. So the solution to many of the problems of today lies precisely in Muslims going to these traditional *usuli* principles. And *usuli* principles do not mean replicating all the forms and rules of past ages. Rather, they mean using Muslims' most subtle and careful tools in order to interpret and apply Islamic heritage in the complex and challenging conditions of the modern world. That is real faithfulness to the Qur'an, the *sunnah* and the vision of the early Muslims.

~

Finally, it remains to be said that to everything I have asserted, I add the words 'and God knows best'—'*Wa Allahu a'lam*'. I believe what I have written is correct and right, but of course acknowledge that I could be wrong. I believe those with differing views are wrong, but acknowledge that they could be right. I ask God to accept this effort at explaining and clarifying Islam, and pray that He forgives my shortcomings and errors. *I desire only to set matters right so far as I am able. But my success lies only with God. In Him I trust and to Him I turn.* (*Hud*, 11:88)

GHAZI BIN MUHAMMAD BIN TALAL
Amman, Jordan 1437/2016

Postscript

WHAT IS HAPPINESS?

We started by observing that the purpose of religion is fundamentally 'to *help* people, morally and spiritually'. We noted that '*Islam*' means 'to turn oneself over to; to resign oneself'. And we summarized the function of the religion of Islam as 'an offer of forgiveness and a plan for salvation'. Now salvation means happiness in the next life. However, we saw also how demanding and consuming religion can be. So does all this spiritual effort required for salvation make people *happy* in this life, or does it make them miserable and put happiness 'on hold'? Does religion—and Islam in particular—with all its 'dos!' and 'don'ts!', make life in this world unbearable in order to make the promise of the next world pleasant? In short, is happiness something for the next world, or something for this world as well?

HAPPINESS OR MISERY?

Clearly, religions have caused and do cause a lot of misery in this world. Sadly, this is obvious every day in the news. However, if all religions did was to make people miserable in this life, with a promise of happiness in the next, there would not be many successful or long-lasting religions. Only a few hardy people would actually maintain a religion. But this is not the case. As we noted at the outset, despite the advent of the modern world and modern science, 85 per cent of the world's people belong to a religion.

Therefore religions must in general make people and societies happy, or at least not make them intolerably miserable. This is true for Islam. Indeed, God says to the Prophet Muhammad ﷺ in the Qur'an: *Ta Ha. / We have not revealed the Qur'an to you that you should be miserable* (*Ta Ha*, 20:1–2).

DEFINING HAPPINESS

We all vaguely understand what the word 'happiness' means. However, as we saw with 'justice' (in Chapter 12), in order to find 'happiness'—so that we can truly experience it—we need to *know* exactly what it is. And in order to know something—as Socrates says (in Plato's *Phaedrus*, 277b)—we need 'to learn how to define it as such . . . dividing it until [we] reach something indivisible'. Then we can see it 'backwards and forwards simultaneously' (Plato, *Cratylus*, 428d). Or, in other words, as Albert Einstein supposedly said, 'If you can't explain it simply, you don't understand it well enough'.

In fact, there is a clear and simple definition of happiness in the Qur'an. But in order to understand happiness, it is necessary first of all to know what it is not. So it is necessary to understand three related but distinct concepts, namely: enjoyment, contentment and joy. In the Qur'an, there is a clear distinction between happiness (*sa'adah*) and the three emotions often confused with it: enjoyment (*mut'a*), joy (*farah*) and contentment (*rida*). A close reading of the Qur'an shows that each of these terms has a deliberate, specific and non-interchangeable meaning, and is only used in an appropriate context. Understanding the differences between each of these then becomes the key to answering the all-important question: *what is happiness?* And as we will see, the answer is rather surprising.

ENJOYMENT

In the Qur'an, enjoyment (*mut'a*) tends to denote taking pleasure (*istimta'*) in a stimulus that originates from the physical senses, or that comes via the physical senses. Human beings share this kind of pleasure with animals. God says in the Qur'an:

> . . .*As for those who disbelieve, they take their enjoyment and eat as the cattle eat*. . . . (*Muhammad*, 47:12)

Though powerful, the problem with this kind of pleasure is that it is short-lived, because apart from anything else, the body—and worldly life itself—is brief. Indeed, in the Qur'an, God asks believers:

> ...*Are you so content with the life of this world, rather than with the Hereafter? Yet the enjoyment of the life of this world compared with the Hereafter is but little.* (Al-Tawbah, 9:38)

So pleasure never leads to happiness. It is a *feeling*, and it does not last. As the Scottish poet Robert Burns wrote (in his poem 'Tam O'Shanter', in 1791):

> But pleasures are like poppies spread:
>   You seize the flower, its bloom is shed;
> Or like the snow falls in the river,
>   A moment white—then melts forever. . . .

This perhaps explains why a lot of religious rules—such as fasting—are precisely about controlling physical pleasures, or being patient in the face of their absence or their opposite (pain).

JOY

In Christian theology 'joy' is something spiritual, both amongst people (see for example: 1 Corinthians 13:4–6 and 2 Corinthians 6:4–10) and 'in heaven' (see: Luke 15:7–24 and Matthew 25:23). Perhaps that is why the *Oxford English Dictionary* (2014) defines 'joy' as: *A feeling of great pleasure and happiness*. But in the Qur'an, joy (*farah*) is something slightly different: it is a happy feeling, possibly with great pleasure, but it is not the same as happiness.

In fact there are two kinds of joy in the Qur'an. One is positive, and the other is negative. Negative joy is basically worldly joy. God says in the Qur'an:

> *They rejoice in the life of this world, yet the life of this world in the Hereafter, is but [a brief] enjoyment.* (Al-Ra'd, 13:26)

Positive joy, on the other hand, is rejoicing in God, or because one sees something as coming from God. God says in the Qur'an:

Say: 'In the bounty of God, and in His mercy in that let them rejoice: it is better than what they hoard.' (Yunus, 10:58)

Both kinds of joy seem to depend on being given something: on *getting* or *receiving*. The difference between them is not so much what one receives, but how one sees it. In other words, when one receives something—say food, clothing, a home, a car, or any reasonable material benefit—if one rejoices in it merely for the sake of increasing one's worldly acquisitions, then that is 'negative joy'. If, however, one rejoices in it as a gift from God and for the good it may do, then that is 'positive joy'. But in any case, like pleasure, joy is not permanent. It fades either when the gift fades or when its novelty fades. It is not happiness. As Thomas Gray (d. 1771) wrote (in 'Elegy Written in a Country Churchyard'):

The boast of heraldry, the pomp of power,
    And all that beauty, all that wealth e'er gave,
Awaits alike the inevitable hour.
    The paths of glory lead but to the grave.

CONTENTMENT

The *Oxford English Dictionary* (2014) defines the adjective 'content' as: 'Willing to accept something; satisfied'. This is not very different from contentment (*rida*) as understood in the Qur'an. However, as with joy, there are two kinds of contentment in the Qur'an, one negative and one positive. The negative one is contentment with the world:

Truly those who do not expect to encounter Us, and are content with the life of this world, and feel reassured in it, and those who are heedless of Our signs. . . . (Yunus, 10:7)

The positive one is contentment with what God gives:

If only they had been content with what God and His messenger have given them, and had said, 'Sufficient for us is God. . .'. (Al-Tawbah, 9:59)

Both kinds of contentment depend on a certain situation: on *having* something. Like joy, the difference between them is not so much what one has, but how one sees it. And, like joy, it is dependant on—or at least relative to—something external. Of course if what is external is permanent and wonderful—as it is only in heaven—then contentment means never experiencing fear, suffering, privation or want. God says of the blessed:

> *Their reward with their Lord will be Gardens of Eden underneath which rivers flow, wherein they shall abide forever. God is content with them, and they are content with Him. That is [the reward] for him who fears his Lord.* (*Al-Bayyinah*, 98:8)

But this still does not make contentment exactly the same thing as happiness. Contentment is still something more contingent, and perhaps also more passive.

~

So pleasure is a matter of *feeling*; joy is a matter of *getting*, and contentment is a matter of *having*. And yet none of these are happiness exactly. So what is happiness?

HAPPINESS

The Arabic word for happiness (*sa'adah*)—or rather, its derivatives—occurs only twice in the Qur'an. It describes a permanent state. It never describes a state of human beings in this world. Both times occur in this (already cited) passage, referring to paradise:

> *The day it comes, no soul shall speak except by His permission. Some of them will be wretched, and some happy. | The wretched ones will be in the fire, sighing and groaning. | Remaining there as long as the heavens and the earth endure, unless your Lord wills. Your Lord does what He wills. | And as for those who are happy they shall be in paradise, remaining there for as long as the heavens and the earth endure, unless your Lord wills—uninterrupted giving.* (*Hud*, 11:105–108)

This still leaves us with two great questions: 'What is happiness?', and 'Can we ever experience it here, in this world?'. The answer to both questions also lies in this passage. First we need to note that the happiness here is associated with *uninterrupted giving*. The word for giving ('*ata*'), together with its derivatives, only occurs 14 times in the Qur'an, and nowhere else in the Qur'an is uninterrupted giving mentioned. So we can conclude that happiness comes from uninterrupted giving. But whose uninterrupted giving is the cause of happiness? The context clearly suggests God's, but it does not exclude its being that of human beings as well. Moreover, in Chapter 5 we saw that in paradise *every soul shall be paid in full what it has earned; and they shall not be wronged* (Al-Baqarah, 2:281). So being given *uninterruptedly* is the result of having given *uninterruptedly*—without there being any common measure between God's giving and people's giving. Indeed, God says in the Qur'an:

> *And give good tidings to those who believe and perform righteous deeds that theirs shall be Gardens underneath which rivers run; whenever they are provided with fruits therefrom, they shall say, 'This is what we were provided with before'; they shall be given a likeness of it . . . .* (Al-Baqarah, 2:25)

So what people receive in heaven is a (purified) *likeness* of their provisions on earth. Since a person's true provisions are his or her good deeds, it follows that the *uninterrupted giving* in heaven is the result or the reflection of people's *uninterrupted giving* on earth. In other words, one way or another, *uninterrupted giving* is the cause of happiness. Indeed, you can only be happy if you give. *Feeling* does not make you happy; *getting* does not make you happy; *having* does not make you happy; *giving* makes you happy! It is not just *more blessed to give than to receive*, as Jesus 🕊 purportedly said (Acts, 20:35), it is what makes you happy. In short, *uninterrupted giving* is synonymous with happiness and is its definition.

In a sense this is obvious, because happiness can only come from knowing, loving and 'being with' God—from Whom every perfection and beatitude comes. And what prevents people from knowing, loving and 'being with' God is their own egos and worldliness. God says:

> *Struggle in the way of God with your possessions and your lives: that is better for you, if only you knew.* (Al-Tawbah, 9:41)

So it is only by struggling with one's own ego and worldliness, and ridding oneself of them—the ego is never happy and worldliness is insatiable—that one can be happy. One does this precisely by *uninterrupted giving*, until there is nothing left of the ego or of worldliness. God says in the

Qur'an to the *'soul at peace'* (that is, the soul which has overcome its ego and worldliness, precisely):

> *O soul at peace! | Return to your Lord, pleased, pleasing. | Then enter among My servants! | And enter My paradise! (Al-Fajr, 89:27-30)*

This then brings up the question of whether we can be truly happy in this life—or can happiness only be found in paradise? Now happiness requires the 'giving' to be *uninterrupted*. So we are happy as long as—and to the extent that—we keep giving, in whatever way we can. This can be done actively through constant small acts of giving. The Prophet Muhammad ﷺ said: 'Do not regard any act of charity as trivial, even meeting your brother with a smile' (*Muslim*). Or it can simply be done passively by giving oneself through constant patience and endurance. The Prophet Muhammad ﷺ: 'Happy is whoever avoids tribulations and if he is tried, patiently endures and sighs' (*Abu Dawud*).

This is to say then that happiness depends on *uninterrupted giving*, but because this *giving* can be either active or passive, it requires no money or power or even other people (as recipients). Although in practice this is easier said than done, it can nevertheless be done even in solitude and incapacity—as so many disabled, handicapped, sick and elderly people prove every day. John Milton (d. 1674) expressed precisely this after he lost his eyesight (in his Petrarchan sonnet 'When I consider how my light is spent'):

> When I consider how my light is spent
>   Ere half my days in this dark world and wide,
> And that one talent which is death to hide
>   Lodg'd with me useless, though my soul more bent
> To serve therewith my Maker, and present
>   My true account, lest he returning chide;
> 'Doth God exact day-labour, light denied?'
>   I fondly ask. But Patience to prevent
> That murmur, soon replies: 'God doth not need
>   Either man's work or his own gifts; who best
> Bear his mild yoke, they serve him best. His state
>   Is kingly. Thousands at his bidding speed

191

And post o'er land and ocean without rest:
  They also serve who only stand and wait.'

~

In Chapter 3, we identified love as a 'gift of self'. Is it love, then, that makes you happy through giving? Does love make you happy? The answer is yes and no. Love can make you quite miserable (as every lover knows) when the beloved is absent, or at least perceived to be. So it is not love as such that makes you happy—or even the beloved (if what you love is other than God)—but the gift of self in loving. And even then, the gift must be uninterrupted. That is perhaps why the Qur'an does not specifically mention happiness in this world.

In heaven, of course this is possible, if one loves God. This is known as 'beatitude' ('*ridwan*' in Arabic). It is to be forever with one's beloved. It is the supreme kind of happiness. In it one has given oneself totally and this is never interrupted—and the beloved is never absent nor perceived as absent. It is a state of being. The Prophet Muhammad ﷺ described this as follows:

> God will say to the people of paradise: 'People of paradise!' They will say, 'At Your service and Your pleasure, Lord; all goodness is in Your hands!' He will say: 'Are you content?' They will say: 'How could we not be content, Lord, when You have given us what You never gave any of Your creatures?' He will say: 'Shall I not give you what is better?' They will say: 'Lord, what could be better than that?' He will say: 'I will enfold you in My beatitude, and will never be angry with you thereafter.' (*Bukhari; Muslim*)

~

WHY IS IT NECESSARY TO KNOW ALL THIS?

The 4th of July, 1776, United States of America's *Declaration of Independence*, drafted by Thomas Jefferson, famously says:

> We hold these truths to be self-evident, that all men are created equal,

that they are endowed by their Creator with certain unalienable Rights, that among these are Life, Liberty and the pursuit of Happiness.

Ever since then—and no doubt before—people (Muslims included) have overtly assumed that it is quite natural, if not commendable, to strive to be happy. Many people spend their whole lives chasing happiness. But many people are looking in the wrong places.

As we have said, it is *necessary* to know exactly what happiness is in order to find it. In this sense, accurate definitions are like maps: they help you find your way. Otherwise you could simply just waste your life looking for it—and always be unhappy! In fact, few people can define happiness, even though people have been thinking about it and discussing it seriously at least since Plato's dialogue on happiness, the *Gorgias*. In that dialogue, the character of Socrates says:

> I say the admirable and good person, man or woman, is happy, but the one who is unjust and wicked is miserable (470 e). . . . Happiness evidently isn't a matter of getting rid of evil; it's rather a matter of not contracting it to begin with (478 c). . . . The happiest man, then, is the one who doesn't have evil in his soul . . . And second, I suppose, is the man who gets rid of it (478 d-e). . . . The good man does well and admirably whatever he does, and that the man who does well is blessed and happy, while the corrupt man, the one who does badly, is miserable . . . A person who wants to be happy must evidently pursue and practice self-control. Each of us must flee away from lack of discipline as quickly as his feet will carry him (507 a-d).

This does not contradict the idea of happiness as 'uninterrupted giving', but it also does not actually provide a definition of happiness as such. And whilst it is important to know that passions, material acquisitions and selfish actions never lead to happiness, it is perhaps even more important to know that happiness is simple, if not easy. It is just a matter of giving as much as we can in some way to someone or something that needs it. This means not just money and material things, but time, energy, knowledge and care—in short, yourself, your ego. Everyone can do that, to some extent. As Ellen S. Hooper (d. 1848) wrote (in her poem 'Beauty and Duty'):

I slept and dreamed that life was beauty:
    I woke and found that life was duty:
Was then thy dream a shadowy lie?
    Toil on, sad heart, courageously,
And thou shalt find thy dream to be
    A noonday light and truth to thee.

Mothers, caregivers, aid workers and teachers know this well. They are often among the happiest people because they exhaust themselves in giving. Lovers sense this as well. Love affords them glimpses of happiness. People employed in a job in which they feel productive appreciate this as well: they give themselves in their work, and this leads to 'job satisfaction', which is also a glimmer of happiness. In fact, anyone who gives of themselves or their time in an unselfish way will experience some happiness. For them, being able to define happiness can only help to reinforce what they already know and do. And surely there is no more beautiful moral teaching than this: that happiness, like love, is giving, not taking. In the Qur'an God says (referring to good people):

> And they give food, they love it themselves, to the needy, and the orphan, and the prisoner, | [saying] 'We feed you for the sake of God alone. We do not desire any reward from you, nor any thanks'. (Al-Insan, 76:8–9)

∼

Appendix 1

THE BIG TENT OF ISLAM

THE DIFFERENT KINDS OF MUSLIMS

Throughout this book, and in particular in Chapter 10, we have mentioned the different divisions and beliefs of Muslims that exist today. We restate them here for clarity, with some historical context and proportional percentages.

Thirty years or so after the death of the Prophet Muhammad ☙ (in 11/632), Muslims became politically divided over the caliphate (the supreme political leadership) of Islam. In addition to the political differences, there arose some fundamental ideological differences. Muslims coalesced into two large 'branches' of the religion: *Sunnis*—those who follow the example of the Prophet Muhammad ☙; and *Shi'a*, those who follow the family of the Prophet Muhammad ☙. There was also one small, violent rejectionist group: the *Khawarij*—literally, 'those who "exited" the [mainstream] religion'.

These groups then developed their own integral methodologies ('*madhahib*') for understanding the apparent discrepancies in the two primary sources of Islamic law and thought (the Qur'an and the *hadith*), as well as for dealing with the changes in circumstances of Muslims over time. The *Sunnis* developed many different *madhahib*, but four of them (the *Hanafi, Maliki, Shafi'i* and *Hanbali madhahib*)—dating back to around 800 CE—came to dominate the Sunni world. However, in Muslim

Andalusia, there was also the *'Zhahiri' madhhab*, and although there are no *Zhahiris* as such alive today, some scholars still consider the methodology of that *madhhab* as valid. The *Shi'a* developed two major *madhahib*: the *Ja'faris*—the so-called 'Twelvers', named for the number of their 'infallible *imams*'; and the *Zaydis*—the so-called 'Fivers', likewise named for the number of their 'revered *imams*'. The third branch of *Shi'ism*, (the *Isma'ilis*—the so-called 'Seveners'—named because of the number of their 'infallible imams'), has two branches: (a) the *Dawudi Bohra* who follow the *Ja'fari madhhab* (with some *Shafi'i* laws and some laws drawn from Qadi Nu'man) under the direction of its leader, the Sultan of the *Bohra*, and; (b) the *Nizaris* who follow their 'living imam', the Agha Khan, without Islamic law as such. There is also a separate, smaller branch of Islam— the *Ibadis*—which developed its own *madhhab*, very similar to Sunnism. These together comprise the so-called 'eight *madhahib*' of Islam (*Hanafi, Maliki, Shafi'i, Hanbali, Zhahiri, Zaydi, Ja'fari*, and *Ibadi*). The original *Khawarij* of Islam ceased to exist essentially after their last rebellion in 317/929. Since the religion of Islam is defined by five practised 'pillars', it is an *'ortho-praxy'* (a 'right way of practice') before being a faith defined by *'ortho-doxy'* (a 'right way of thinking'). However, it does have six (or seven in the case of *Ja'fari* Shi'ism) basic articles of faith. This explains why—notwithstanding the Two Testimonies of Faith—*shari'ah* (law) comes before *'aqidah* (doctrine): *'Islam'* ('resigning oneself') comes before *'Iman'* ('faith'), as discussed in Chapter 2.

Within the eight *madhahib* of Islam—which are juridical schools and not necessarily ideological ones—there are different schools of doctrine, theology and thought. Most *Sunnis* of the four *madhahib* follow the *Ash'ari* and *Maturidi* schools of doctrine and theology. Indeed, *Ash'ari* and *Maturidi* doctrines basically only differ on a few issues, most of which are arguably linguistic quibbles, so that these two schools of theology are essentially one tradition. Mention must then be made of Sufism which is an integral part of Sunni Islam, and whose goal is to purify the soul through virtue, prayer, fasting and near-constant invocation of God. Sufism is the mysticism of Sunni Islam, and perhaps a quarter of *Sunnis* are associated with Sufi Orders (*'Turuq'*) in one form or another—and to differing degrees of intensity and commitment. *Shi'ism* has a similar, but less structured, kind of mysticism called *'erfan*. There have been many questionable practices associated with Sufism but orthodox Sunni mysticism, as typified by the writings of Abu Hamid al-Ghazali, was unquestioned until the rise of the contemporary anti-*usul* movements.

During the twentieth century, the whole thousand-plus-year-old edifice of traditional Islamic jurisprudence was shaken by two main ideological challenges: (a) 'modernism' and (b) the anti-*usul* movement. 'Modernism' basically believes that Islam (and not merely Islamic civilisation and culture, but Islamic doctrine and law) should be updated to correspond to Western values. The anti-*usul* movement (basically Salafism/Wahhabism and the Muslim Brotherhood) calls for going back only to the Qur'an and the *hadith* without regard to an integral methodology of jurisprudence. It rejects not only the traditional Sunni *madhahib*, but also, traditional doctrine, theology and mysticism.

Today (1437/2016), the Sunnis comprise around 90 per cent of all Muslims, the *Shi'a* around 10 per cent, and the historical *Khawarij* no longer exist. *Ibadis* are less than one per cent of all Muslims. The *Ibadis* survive only in Oman, East Africa and parts of the Southern Sahara; the *Ja'fari Shi'a* are concentrated in Iran and Iraq (with some minorities in the Persian Gulf, Syria and Lebanon, Pakistan, India and Afghanistan); the *Zaydi Shi'a* are concentrated in northern Yemen, and the Sunnis are everywhere else. Out of a global population of around 7.4 billion people, at least 23 per cent—that is to say, perhaps 1.7 billion—are Muslim: Islam is the world's second largest but fastest-growing religion.

The chart on the next page shows and simplifies all of this.

THE AMMAN MESSAGE (2004–2006)

Despite all of the above, for 1300 years Muslims have managed to quibble about the precise definition of a (true) Muslim. So 12 years ago (in 1425/2004), H.M. King Abdullah II ibn Al-Hussein asked a group of senior Jordanian scholars and thinkers to clarify to the modern world the true nature of Islam and the nature of true Islam. On the eve of the 27th of Ramadan 1425/9th of November 2004, they released what became known as the 'Amman Message'. It sought to declare not only what Islam is but what it is not, and what actions represent it and what actions do not (see: www.ammanmessage.com for all the documents).

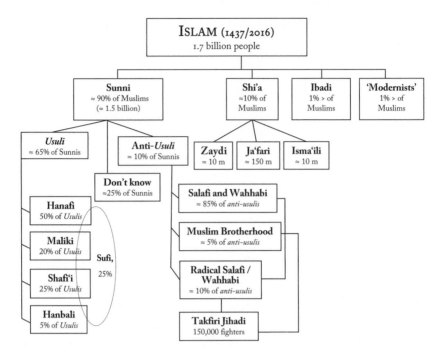

In order to give the Amman Message more religious authority, and act-ing on behalf H.M. King Abdullah II ibn Al-Hussein, I sent the following three questions to 24 of the most senior religious scholars from all around the world representing all the branches and schools of Islam: (1) *Who is a Muslim?*; (2) *Is it permissible to declare someone an apostate (takfir)?*, and (3) *Who has the right to undertake issuing fatwas (legal rulings)?*

In July 2005, based on the *fatwas* provided by these leading scholars (who included the *Shaykh al-Azhar*, Ayatollah Sistani and Shaykh Yusuf Qaradawi), and under H.M. King Abdullah II ibn Al-Hussein, I con-vened an international Islamic conference of 200 of the world's leading Islamic scholars (*'ulama*) from 50 countries. In Amman, these scholars unanimously issued a ruling on three fundamental issues (which became known as the 'Three Articles of the Amman Message'):

1. They specifically recognized the validity of all eight *madhahib* (legal schools) of *Sunni, Shi'a* and *Ibadi* Islam, of traditional Islamic theology (*Ash'arism*), of Islamic mysticism (Sufism), of true *Salafi* thought; and came to a precise definition of who is a Muslim.

2. Based upon this definition they forbade *takfir* (declarations of apostasy) between Muslims.

3. Based upon the *madhahib* they set forth the subjective and objective preconditions for the issuing of *fatwas*, thereby exposing ignorant and illegitimate edicts in the name of Islam.

The actual text agreed upon reads as follows:

In the Name of God, the Compassionate, the Merciful
May peace and blessings be upon the Prophet Muhammad and his pure
and noble family,

1. Whosoever is an adherent to one of the four *Sunni* schools (*madhahib*) of Islamic jurisprudence (*Hanafi, Maliki, Shafi'i* and *Hanbali*), the two *Shi'i* schools of Islamic jurisprudence (*Ja'fari* and *Zaydi*), the *Ibadi* school of Islamic jurisprudence, and the *Zhahiri* school of Islamic jurisprudence, is a Muslim. Declaring that person an apostate is impossible and impermissible. Verily his (or her) blood, honour, and property are inviolable. Moreover, in accordance with the Shaykh al-Azhar's *fatwa*, it is neither possible nor permissible to declare whosoever subscribes to the *Ash'ari* creed or whoever practises real *Tasawwuf* (Sufism) an apostate. Likewise, it is neither possible nor permissible to declare whosoever subscribes to true *Salafi* thought an apostate.

   Equally, it is neither possible nor permissible to declare as apostates any group of Muslims who believe in God, Glorified and Exalted be He, and His messenger ﷺ and the pillars of faith, and acknowledge the five pillars of Islam, and do not deny any necessarily self-evident tenet of religion.

2. There exists more in common between the various schools of Islamic jurisprudence than there is difference between them. The adherents to the eight schools of Islamic jurisprudence are in agreement as regards the basic principles of Islam. All believe in Allah (God), Glorified and Exalted be He, the One and the Unique; that the Noble Qur'an is the Revealed Word of God; and that our master Muhammad ﷺ is a Prophet and messenger unto all mankind. All are in agreement about the five pillars of Islam: the Two Testimonies of Faith (*Shahadatayn*); the ritual prayer (*salat*); almsgiving (*zakat*); fasting the month of Ramadan (*sawm*); and the *hajj* to the sacred house of God (in Mecca). All are also

in agreement about the foundations of belief: belief in Allah (God), His angels, His scriptures, His messengers, in the Day of Judgement, and in Divine Providence in good and in evil. Disagreements between the *'ulama* (scholars) of the eight schools of Islamic jurisprudence are only with respect to the ancillary branches of religion (*furu'*) and not as regards the principles and fundamentals (*usul*) [of the religion of Islam]. Disagreement with respect to the ancillary branches of religion (*furu'*) is a mercy. Long ago it was said that variance in opinion among the *'ulama* (scholars) 'is a good affair'.

3. Acknowledgement of the schools of Islamic jurisprudence (*madhahib*) within Islam means adhering to a fundamental methodology in the issuance of *fatwas*: no one may issue a *fatwa* without the requisite personal qualifications which each school of Islamic jurisprudence determines [for its own adherents]. No one may issue a *fatwa* without adhering to the methodology of the schools of Islamic jurisprudence. No one may claim to do unlimited *ijtihad* and create a new school of Islamic jurisprudence or to issue unacceptable *fatwas* that take Muslims out of the principles and certainties of the *shari'ah* and what has been established in respect of its schools of jurisprudence.

~

These 'Three Articles' were then unanimously adopted by the Islamic world's political and religious leaderships at the Organization of the Islamic Conference summit at Mecca, in December 2005. And over a period of one year—from July 2005 to July 2006—the 'Three Articles' were also unanimously adopted by six other international Islamic scholarly assemblies, culminating with the *International Islamic Fiqh Academy* of Jeddah, in July 2006. In total, over 500 leading Muslim scholars worldwide unanimously endorsed the Amman Message and its 'Three Articles'.

This was a historic, universal and unanimous religious and political consensus (*ijma'*) by Muslims in modern times, and a consolidation of the definition of Islam. The significance of the 'Three Articles' of the Amman Message is that: (1) It is the first time in over 1300 years that Muslims have formally and specifically come to such a pluralistic mutual inter-recognition of *who is a Muslim*. (2) It perhaps made inter-recognition religiously binding on Muslims, since the Prophet Muhammad ﷺ said: 'My ummah will not agree upon an error' (*Ibn Majah*). The *Grand Imam* and *Shaykh al-Azhar* at that time, Shaykh Muhammad Sayyid Tantawi, wrote an introduction to a book about the 'Three Articles' which he described as follows:

> The best resource for all those who wish to travel along the straight path in their words and in their actions, and in their spiritual and religious life.

THE BENEFIT OF THE 'THREE ARTICLES' OF THE AMMAN MESSAGE

God says in the Qur'an:

> *There is no good in much of their secret conferences save (in) whosoever enjoins charity and fairness and peace-making among the people and whoever that, seeking the good pleasure of God, We shall bestow on him a vast reward.* (*Al-Nisa'*, 4:114)

The great benefit of the 'Three Articles' of the Amman Message is that they constitute—*for the first time in Islamic history*—a universal and unanimous religious and political consensus on the part of *Muslims* about who is a Muslim. In other words, they not only give a clear definition of Islam, but also formalize *plurality* and *diversity* within the framework of Islam. Moreover, they also safeguard Islam from distortion and manipulation through ignorant *fatwas* by unqualified or unscrupulous people. In an age when everyone with a BA or an MA in *shari'ah* gives *fatwas*, when there are thousands of television channels, millions of websites and tens of millions of tweets about Islam and Islamic law, the 'Three Articles' point out who actually has the right to issue *fatwas*. So they serve as a unique resource to protect both Islam and Muslims alike. The 'Three Articles' of the Amman Message also provide an authoritative historic text on which laws can be based and that can be taught in education curricula all over the world.

∽

Appendix 2

THREE QUESTIONS
FOR EVERY MUSLIM

After all that has been said in this book, I respectfully ask each and every Muslim reader to consider *honestly* in, and for, himself or herself, the following three questions (or series of questions):

Question One: Do you believe that your view of Islamic doctrine is the absolute Truth? Do you believe that everyone calling themselves 'a Muslim', believing in the five pillars of Islam (the two testimonies of faith; the ritual prayer in the direction of Mecca; almsgiving; fasting the month of Ramadan, and the pilgrimage to Mecca) and the six articles of faith (belief in Allah, His angels, His scriptures, His messengers, in the Day of Judgement, and in Divine Providence in good and in evil) and praying towards Mecca but who otherwise does not hold the same doctrine on matters you view as important (such as for example the meaning of '*God's Hand*') is wrong? Consequently, do you believe if they continue to hold these views they are not true believers and in the end damned to hell? Consequently, is it your personal duty to correct them, and if they argue or refuse to change their view, is it duty to coerce them in so far as this is possible, and even to fight them? Do you believe them then to be really non-Muslims? Are Shi'a non-Muslims? (Or are Sunnis non-Muslims, if you are a Shi'a?) Do you believe Ash'aris to be non-Muslims? Do you believe Sufis to be non-Muslims? Do you believe philosophers like Ibn Rushd and Ibn Tufayl to be non-Muslims? Would you find it impossible to live and let live with such people? Would you find it impossible to love such people?

Question Two: If you are a citizen of a country with a Muslim majority and not all the laws of the country are based on *shari'ah* as you understand it, do you believe it is your duty to take up arms if necessary to implement the *shari'ah* as you see it (rather than work patiently and peacefully within the system to express your views and try to change things within the existing system)? Do you believe a state is a disbelieving state if it does not apply *only shari'ah* laws as you understand them (even if it does apply *some shari'ah* laws, and does not deny the *shari'ah* as such)? Are people who work for such governments then themselves disbelievers? Are people who associate with or benefit from such governments also disbelievers? Can these people then be legitimately attacked and killed? Can their families?

Question Three: If you are a citizen of a country with a non-Muslim-majority and enjoy justice, full freedom of religion and the same rights as non-Muslims, are you, because you are a Muslim and bound by God's laws, not mankind's, above the laws of that country? Are you then unobliged, religiously or even morally, to abide by them (even if they do not impact on your worship of God)? If your country is at war with any Muslims somewhere else in the world, are you then by that fact at war with your own country? Must you—or can you legitimately—then take up arms against targets and people in your own country? Are all your fellow citizens then 'fair game' as targets? Is it impossible to live and let live with non-Muslims in peace, friendship and mutual respect as long as some Muslims in the world have a conflict with them or a grievance against their foreign policy?

~

These are serious questions and need honest answers before God and before other people. They are a litmus test for your understanding of your religion and for your heart.

If any of your answers to *any* of these questions is 'yes' then you are on the radical fringe of the historically new anti-*usul* movement. You will forever be in conflict with at least 90 per cent of other Muslims, plus the 75 per cent of the world which is non-Muslim. You believe that God commands you to impose your understanding of Islam and *shari'ah* on other Muslims, and that Muslims in general should impose their religion and their *shari'ah* on the whole world. If perpetual, offensive *'jihad'* is necessary for this, so be it—this is what you believe is pleasing to God. And you believe that in the end your side will win because God will help it. You believe that you are part of the elite of Muslims, who alone are sincere to God, even if they have historically been a small minority. You believe that the best possible thing—and therefore the very point of your life and its creation—is to fight and kill and be killed for God, but that you yourself, not your country, or the consensus of the religion's scholars, decide the terms of this war.

If all your answers to *all* these questions is 'no', then you hold the same views as 99 per cent of all Muslims until 1900, and you are still within the absolute majority today. You are part of authentic traditional Islam and the Muslim community that spread and built one of the largest, most beautiful, most culturally, scientifically and ethically developed and plural civilisations in the history of humanity that attracted and enthralled so many millions of souls. You can—and you believe that you *must*—live and let live with all people on earth, and you can (and at times must) defend yourself but not attack anyone first. You believe that God created people out of His love and mercy, so that they might know and love Him through worship, and to do that they must also fear Him. You believe not only in obeying the Prophet Muhammad ﷺ, but also in the beauty of his morality and character. You believe that the rules of your religion are not arbitrary, capricious, whimsical or tyrannical but are there for the general good. You believe in mutual respect and tolerance, harmony, pluralism and 'live and let live' between all people. You believe you have a moral duty to be kind and good to everyone on earth and everything on earth. You think and pray that you are right in your beliefs but acknowledge that you could be wrong. You condemn your ego and try to refrain from judging others except if it is your formal job to do so. You believe in consultation and consensus. In principle, you are a person 'from whose tongue and hand all people are safe'.

And if *any* of your answers to these questions are 'I don't know', then read this book again.

God says to Muslims in the Qur'an:

Thus did We make you a middle community that you might be witnesses for mankind; and that the messenger may be a witness to you. . . . (Al-Baqarah, 2:143)

~

Annex

THE CRISIS OF ISIS
A case study of its first two years
(June 2014–June 2016)

OVERVIEW

In this annex we briefly describe the rise and crisis of Daesh—also known as ISIS or ISIL, but calling itself simply the 'Islamic State'—over its first two years (June 2014-June 2016). The name '*Da'esh*' actually comes from the acronym in Arabic for the group's name until June 2014: '*Dawlat al-Islam fil-'Iraq wa 'l-Sham*' ('the Islamic State in Iraq and the Levant', hence the acronym 'ISIL'; which is also translated as 'the Islamic State in Iraq and Syria', hence the acronym 'ISIS'). The word '*da'esh*' does not actually mean anything in Arabic, but it sounds like many words with aggressive meanings in Arabic (*da'asa*—to step on; *dahasha*—to shove or foist; *dahasa*—an abscess in the finger, and hence to sow discord; and even *dahshah*—to baffle or surprise), so it is almost universally used to refer to the group in Arabic—much to its annoyance.

By the time this book is published, Daesh, if still existing, may have morphed into something completely different from what it is today (July 2016), and perhaps (regrettably) even moved its base of operations to Africa. Nevertheless, as distasteful as it may be, it is necessary to analyze Daesh in some depth—mostly (but not entirely) from open source material—in order to understand how it is an extreme manifestation of the larger anti-

usul movement, and how it manipulates selected elements of Islam to harness the latent energies within the religion to create a counterfeit edifice of an Islamic state in both theory and practice—an 'un-Islamic State', precisely. Without clarifying this, the possibility of confusion between *usuli* Islam and Daesh's perversion of it will persist, for 'confusion is the mother of error and discord'.

I. THE ORIGIN OF DAESH

The origin of Daesh is well-known. Regrettably, it was founded by a Jordanian citizen (Ahmad Fadil al-Khalayleh, a.k.a. Abu Mus'ab al-Zarqawi) who was a petty criminal in and out of Jordanian jails in the 1990s, who there 'got religion' and proceeded to commit even worse crimes under the cover of religion. He helped form a group calling itself *Jama'at al-Tawhid wa 'l-Jihad* dedicated to overthrowing Jordan's government and H.M. King Abdullah II ibn Al-Hussein. The group's first ever act was a car bombing on August 7th 2003 targeting the Jordanian embassy in Baghdad (the immediate aftermath was filmed by Australian journalist Michael Ware). In 2004 in Iraq, Al-Zarqawi pledged allegiance to al-Qaeda, and mounted attacks which killed scores of people (mostly civilians) there. This happened during the 'Sunni insurgency' following the 2003 Western-led war against Iraq, which removed Saddam Hussein, but also alienated the Sunni population by institutionally favouring the Shi'a population. The Sunni insurgency was also greatly exacerbated by the sectarian policies of some of the Shi'a-led governments that came into power after the war, and most of all by the notorious clandestine Shi'a militias which tortured and killed tens of thousands of Sunnis whilst ethnically-cleansing Baghdad and most of the southern provinces of Iraq of nearly their entire Sunni populations. On November 9th 2005, whilst based in Iraq, Al-Zarqawi was responsible for bomb attacks in three hotels in Amman, Jordan, which killed 60 innocent civilians and injured 115. In June 2006, he met the justice owed to his many victims and their families in a US airstrike in Iraq.

In August 2011, the group's eventual successor (now calling itself *'Jabhat an-Nusra li-Ahli 'sh-Sham'*) went to Syria to exploit, through terrorism, the situation created by the 'Arab Spring' in the eastern part of

Syria, near the Iraqi border. In 2013 it changed its name to: '*Al-Dawlah al-Islamiyyah fi 'l-Iraq wa 'l-Sham'*. And in 2014, it split from its 'parent', the al-Nusra Front (which was still loyal to the al-Qaeda leader Ayman al-Zawahiri, Osama bin Laden's successor), and began fighting it and expanding and holding territory in Syria. After systematically murdering thousands of people in every way conceivable, and holding territory in Iraq's al-Anbar province for some months, it invaded, in June 2014, with only a few hundred fighters, western Iraq. On June 29th 2014 from the great mosque of Mosul in a televised sermon, it declared itself a 'caliphate' over all Muslims (with an Iraqi man called Dr Ibrahim Awad al-Badri al-Samarrai — aka 'Abu Bakr al-Baghdadi' — as the self-appointed 'caliph') calling for universal '*jihad*' against everyone who did not join them (that is, 99.99 per cent of the Islamic World, plus the rest of the world). Since then it has lost, gained and then lost again a considerable amount of territory in Syria and Iraq. Whilst attempting to establish a functioning administration, it has fought many different opponents in the Syrian civil war, and recruited tens of thousands of foreign fighters (many of whom have now been killed in the fighting). It has tortured and killed thousands of prisoners and civilians and caused untold misery for the millions of people captive in its territory whom it exploits in every conceivable way. Despite this it has also managed to establish toeholds for its terrorism in some 60 countries all over the world, making alliances with some local *takfiri* terrorists (the most notorious and senselessly vicious being Boko Haram in Northern Nigeria), and also exploiting the infighting in Libya to create a larger presence there. Over the course of 2015, Daesh also managed to organize or prompt dozens of terrorist attacks on innocent civilians all over the world, particularly in the Yemen, but also in the West, especially France. Many more plots have been quietly foiled by local authorities, and even ordinary citizens.

When its story is retold in this linear way, it almost seems like there was some sort of master plan, or that its rise was inevitable, whereas in fact it was just one of many groups of hoodlums and murderers active in the chaos in Iraq and Syria in the aftermath of the 2003 Western occupation and the 2011 'Arab Spring' respectively. Daesh happened to rise to the top of the heap by being the lowest, most vicious, most heartless and most active of all the killers there.

2. WHAT IS DAESH?

Daesh is a *takfiri-jihadi* organized gang. That is, it holds an extremist version of radical Salafi/Wahhabi ideology. Yet at its core are former Secularist Ba'athists (that is, Saddam Hussein's old political party). Two of Baghdadi's deputies were colonels in Saddam's military. All of the original '*Shura* Council' members were apparently Iraqis with some Ba'athi connections. Many of them were jailed by US forces or the Iraqi government in Iraq, and may have suffered abuse there. In addition to Iraqi former Ba'athists and *takfiri* foreign recruits, many Daesh supporters are former Muslim Brotherhood members from Iraq or Syria.

Another particular characteristic of Daesh's identity is that its adherents are apocalyptic millenarianists—or at least Islamist 'apocalyptic millenarianists'—according to their understanding of certain *ahadith*. That is to say that they believe that great apocalyptic battles are coming soon between Muslims (by which they mean themselves only) and non-Muslims. They believe that these battles—after unprecedented worldwide death and slaughter—will bring about the coming of the Mahdi (a 'guided' descendant of the Prophet Muhammad ﷺ who will conquer the world and rule for seven years), then the anti-Christ (*al-masih al-dajjal*) and the Second Coming of Jesus Christ ﷺ himself. They see themselves and current events in the light of a *hadith* that says: 'If you see the black flags coming from Khorasan then go to them [and join them] because with them is God's Caliph, the 'Mahdi' (*Ahmad*, and there are two other similar *ahadith* in *Ibn Majah* and *Tirmidhi*). This of course implies that the Mahdi is someone in their army, or who will join their army, and it explains why their flags are black. The area of historical Khorasan comprises much of modern day Iran, Pakistan, Afghanistan, Turkmenistan, Tajikistan, Uzbekistan and south-west Kazakhstan, and so their explanation of this is that their *jihad* started in Afghanistan, and some of their fighters came from there with the original al-Qaeda. It is also worth noting that in 2016 Daesh minted elegant gold and silver coins as their 'currency' bearing the motto '*Khilafah 'ala Minhaj al-Nubuwwah*' meaning 'Caliphate in the Manner of Prophethood'. This shows not only their hubris but also either a misunderstanding of the necessarily temporal nature of government after the death of the Prophet Muhammad ﷺ, or, more likely, their apocalyptic aspirations as per the *hadith* just cited. There is also a *hadith* in *Muslim* predicting an epic battle in '*Dabiq*' or '*A'maq*' between Muslims and Westerners ('*al-Rum*') at the end of which Jesus Christ ☫ will return to lead the Muslims in prayer, and they expect to fight this battle in Syria, because there is a place there called 'Dabiq' (which witnessed a battle between the Ottomans and the Mamluks in 1516). In fact, Daesh has even called one of its online publications '*Dabiq*' and one of its news agencies '*A'maq*'. In short, Daesh sees itself and what it is doing now as the vanguard of a prophesied 'end-time' apocalyptic global war.

3. THE ULTIMATE GOAL OF DAESH

Simply put, Daesh believes that every Muslim is obliged to wage offensive *jihad* on the whole world, at its prompting and to promote its ideas. In Daesh's own words:

> We believe that *jihad* in God's path is an obligation on every individual Muslim, from the fall of al-Andalus until the liberation of [all] Muslim lands, and [that it is an individual obligation] in the presence of a pious person or an impious person. And [we believe that] the greatest of sins after disbelief in God is barring from *jihad* in God's path at the time when it is an individual obligation. Ibn Hazm said: 'No sin after disbelief in God is greater than the sin of forbidding *jihad* against the unbeliev-ers. . . . ('Some of Our Fundamental [Beliefs]', Abu 'Umar al-Baghdadi, March 13, 2007)

We note of course that their 'authority' for this is not a mainstream scholar from one of the four *madhahib*, but the Andalusian *Zhahiri* scholar Ibn Hazm (d. 456/1064) whom they cite out of context, and who lived in distressing times (for Muslims) and saw the decline of the Umayyad Caliphate in Andalusia—which is surely what he had in mind. This is to say then that the ultimate goal of Daesh's '*jihad*' is to conquer and 'own' the world by force of arms, and have it submit to Daesh in particular. This is made clear in the very 'Announcement of the Caliphate' by Daesh spokes-man Abu Muhammad al-Adnani (aka Taha Falahi) on June 29th, 2014.

So rush O Muslims and gather around your caliph, so that you may return as you once were for ages, kings of the earth and knights of war. Come so that you may be honoured and esteemed, living as masters, with dignity. Know that we fight over a religion that God promised to support. We fight for a nation to which God has given honour, esteem, and leadership, promising it with empowerment and strength on the earth. Come O Muslims to your honour, to your victory. By God, if you disbelieve in democracy, secularism, nationalism, as well as all the other garbage and ideas from the West, and rush to your religion and creed, then by God, you will own the earth, and the east and west will submit to you. This is the promise of God to you.

4. WHAT DAESH THINKS AND BELIEVES

Daesh 'thought' is an eclectic combination of the most radical elements of the two basic 'Sunni fundamentalist' streams of 'Islamic' thought: Salafism/Wahhabism and Muslim Brotherhood thought — together with Islamist millenarianism, as discussed above. Even within these two streams of thought, the group always takes the most violent and intolerant opinions it can find, and sometimes makes up new ones. From (i) Salafism/ Wahhabism, (and particularly Muhammad bin Abd al-Wahhab's *Nawaqid al-Islam* [*The Nullifiers of Islam*] Daesh takes the practice of mass *takfir* (anathematizing Muslims who disagree with them, thereby making it licit — or rather obligatory — to kill them; take their money and property and divorce their wives from them). By contrast, Daesh adherents view themselves as the 'elite' folk of '*wala' wa bara'a*' (loyalty to Islam and disassociation from all non-Muslims). From (ii) Muslim Brotherhood thinkers Abul A'la Mawdudi (d. 1979) and Syed Qutb (d. 1966) Daesh takes the '*hakimiyyah* theory' (anathematizing Muslims who do not attack states whose laws they consider to be un-Islamic — see following section). Between these two 'doctrines', as can easily be imagined, the vast majority of *Sunni* Muslims are judged 'unbelievers who must be killed'. Add to these the Iraqi Ba'athi scorn for individual life and freedom and its genocidal efficiency, and al-Qaeda's inheritance of terrorist 'struggle' against the West, and you have the toxic witch's brew that makes up Daesh 'thought'.

5. THE 'HAKIMIYYAH' THEORY

In his books *Fi Zhilal al-Qur'an* (*In the Shade of the Qur'an*) and *Ma'alim fi 'l-Tariq* (*Milestones*), Syed Qutb lays out the '*hakimiyyah*' theory. This theory basically states that anyone who does not implement *only shari'ah* law (as Qutb understood it) becomes an unbeliever (who then must be killed). Equally, any government that does not apply *only shari'ah* law becomes a government of disbelievers, as does anyone supporting that government, voting under that government, working for that govern-ment or even benefiting from that government. And, because they are disbelievers, all of them must be killed (no matter how much they believe in God and Islam's articles of faith, and how piously they practise the pillars of Islam). This monstrous idea has its roots in the fourth '*naqid*' ('nullifier') of Muhammad bin 'Abd al-Wahhab's *Nawaqid al-Islam* as well as Qutb's (and Mawdudi's) new misinterpretation of the Qur'anic phrase '*whoever does not judge according to what God has revealed—it is they who are disbelievers*' (*Al-Ma'idah*, 5:44). All the Qur'anic commentators before him, throughout the ages, (including, but not limited to: Ibn 'Abbas 🙲 and Ibn Mas'ud 🙲, Ibn Hanbal, Tabari, Qurtubi, Baghawi, Nasafi, Ibn 'Atiyyah, Ibn al-Jawzi, Al-Razi [all three by that name: Abd al-Rahman, Ahmad and Fakhr al-Din], Ghazali, Ibn Taymiyyah himself, Ibn Kathir, Ibn Juzayy, Abu Hayyan, Al-Alusi and many oth-ers right up to Ibn 'Ashour, Muhammad Amin Shinqiti and Sha'rawi in the twentieth century) understood it differently. They all said that *if* this verse can be understood in a general context (for it is actually about the Jews of Medina) and *if* it is applied to Muslims, then it means: (i) those who conceal or deliberately change God's words; and/or (ii) those who do not apply *any* of the *shari'ah's* rulings (*if* circumstances allow them to be applied); and/or (iii) those who deny in their hearts and in words the validity of the *shari'ah*, are disbelievers. In short, it does not mean what Syed Qutb said it does.

Ibn 'Abbas 🙲 himself was very specific. He commented that someone who does not apply God's laws 'contains some disbelief, but not disbe-lief in God, His angels, His books and His messengers', and also: 'if he denies what God has said, he is a disbeliever, but if he accepts it but does not do it, then he has committed oppression or wickedness' (Al-Tabari,

Jami' al-Bayan; see also *Hakim*). In other words, as the commentator 'Ata'
bin Abi Rabah added, the verse means 'disbelief that is less than [true]
disbelief; oppression that is less than [true] oppression; wickedness that
is less than [true] wickedness' (Al-Tabari, *Jami' al-Bayan*).

In short, not applying some rules of the *shari'ah* remains a fault and a sin
of omission but not something that undermines the legitimacy of a whole
state, and *not* something that warrants rebellion against it. This is not a
minor or academic quibble. It implies the difference between accepting
the civil authority of every nation state in the twentieth and twenty-first
centuries that have *shari'ah* as a basis or the basis of law—the vast majority
of Muslim-majority countries in the world today—and rejecting them. It
means the difference between perpetual civil war and enlightened change
through state, constitutional and democratic institutions. And it shows
how dangerous wilful tinkering with the meaning of the Qur'an can be.

6. TAKFIR

Takfir is actually a blight that has afflicted the margins of Islam right
from the time of the Companions of the Prophet Muhammad ﷺ. A
group of new Muslims—none of whom had actually known the Prophet
Muhammad ﷺ personally—decided that the fourth caliph 'Ali bin Abi
Talib ﷺ had contravened the Qur'an, and sinned gravely so that he was
no longer a Muslim (i.e. they pronounced '*takfir*' on him). Then they
rebelled against him and tried to overthrow and kill him. Now 'Ali ﷺ
was the Prophet's ﷺ first cousin, his son-in-law, and one of the first three
Muslims. He was described by the Prophet ﷺ as being in the same position related to him ﷺ 'as Aaron was to Moses' (*Ahmad*). It boggles the
mind that they thought they understood Islam more than 'Ali ﷺ simply
by reading (and misinterpreting) the Qur'an. Consequently, they were
known as '*Khawarij*' ('renegades'—literally those who have exited Islam)
according to a *hadith* of the Prophet foretelling their rise:

> There will soon arise a folk who are young in age, sharp-witted and harsh.
> They will recite the Qur'an distinctly and clearly but it will not go beyond
> their throats. So if you encounter them extinguish [their turmoil]; and

if you encounter them slay them, for you will be rewarded [by God] for slaying them. (*Ahmad*)

And indeed they did arise, and they were unspeakably brutal and murderous. Tabari describes the following incident (in his *History*, 'The Events of Year 37 AH') immediately before their battle with 'Ali ﷺ at Nahrawan:

The *Khawarij* entered a village and Abdullah the son of Khabbab the Companion of the Prophet ﷺ came out. . . They asked, 'Are you Abdullah the son of Khabbab the Companion of the Prophet?' and he answered 'yes'. . . .So they brought him to the canal bank where they cut off his head and his blood flowed like the lace of a sandal, and they pierced the womb of the mother of his child and emptied it of its contents.

After 'Ali ﷺ defeated them in battle, small groups of them still went on madly killing unarmed people for some 30 more years. Every century some form of them has reappeared and killed more innocent people. The Companion Ibn 'Umar ﷺ warned: 'They will take the verses revealed about the disbelievers and apply them to the believers' (*Bukhari*).

Of course this is exactly what modern practitioners of *takfir* do: they find excuses and technicalities to declare Muslims who clearly do believe in God, His angels, His books, His messengers, the hereafter and destiny as 'non-Muslims', and then take it upon themselves to persecute them. Radical Salafi/Wahhabis do this to *usuli* Muslims very clearly based on the *Nawaqid al-Islam* and Syed Qutb does this to everyone associated with a nation state; between the two of them they do this to 90 per cent of Sunni Muslims, to say nothing of Shi'a Muslims. In addition, Daesh considers anyone who has not come and pledged allegiance to its leader an unbeliever. Now that includes Daesh's own parent group al-Qaeda and its local franchise in Syria, al-Nusra. Consequently even in the year before Daesh declared its so-called 'caliphate', Daesh and al-Nusra fighters slaughtered thousands of each other, and in fact continue to do so to this day. They are both radical Salafi/Wahhabi *takfiri-jihadis* and they were doing '*takfir*' and '*jihad*' against each other (and of course the rest of the world)! And they pretended to do this in the name of God and the Qur'an. The Prophet Muhammad ﷺ warned about this happening in our times quite precisely:

At the end of time there shall appear a folk, young in age and foolish. They will utter the best of words spoken by people, but they shall pass through Islam just as an arrow passes through hunted game. Whoever encounters them [in war] should kill them, for killing them will be rewarded [by God]. (*Bukhari*)

This explains why the Azhar, the Grand Muftis of Egypt, Saudi Arabia, Nigeria, Jordan and other places and most centres of Islamic learning (including those of mainstream Salafism) have now called Daesh '*Khawarij*'—those who have passed through Islam. Unlike Daesh's condemnation, this does not involve pronouncing *takfir* on them (and calling them 'apostates'), but is merely a pronouncement that they must be fought with force of arms.

7. WHAT DAESH READS

This question is important in order to know how Daesh convinces itself of its views—and how it indoctrinates recruits. Daesh of course reads some of the fine *Hanbali* corpus of the works of Ibn Hanbal, Ibn al-Jawzi, Ibn Taymiyyah and Ibn al-Qayyim. Its members read Salafi *tafsirs* (such as Muhammad Shawkani's [1173-1250/1759-1839] *Fath al-Qadir*) and/or Salafi-edited Ibn Kathir and Qurtubi *tafsirs*. They read Al-Albani-redacted collections of *hadith*. They read also the treatises of Muhammad bin Abd al-Wahhab and his school right up to modern writers like Ibn 'Uthaymeen. Some of them read Syed Qutb and Mawdudi. Then they read (or used to read—they have fallen out with al-Qaeda now) the old al-Qaeda *jihadi* literature like Abu Mus'ab al-Suri's 'Global Islamic Resistance Call' and Abu Muhammad al-Maqdisi's '*Millat Ibrahim*'. Then there are the sinister al-Qaeda operation manuals like Abu Amr al-Qaedi's *A Course in the Art of Recruitment*, and Abu Bakr al-Naji's infamous *The Management of Savagery*. They also have their own in-house writers and spin doctors producing manuals and essays like the group's official spokesman Abu Muhammad al-Adnani's '*Matn Fiqh al-Jihad*'; Abu 'Abdullah al-Muhajir's '*Masa'il fi Fiqh al-Jihad*'; Abu Humam al-Athari's '*Madd al-Ayadi li-Bay'at al-Baghdadi*' and Abu 'Amr al-Shami's '*Itihaf al-Bararah*'. In short, Daesh has its own extensive subculture of radical Salafi/Wahhabi, Muslim Brotherhood, al-Qaeda, and now increasingly home-grown Daesh books, manuals and essays which inculcate its own harsh Weltanschauung and *fatwas* on people who do not know any better.

8. THE ABUSE OF *HADITH*

Daesh and al-Qaeda are not able to manipulate and do much damage through their interpretations of the Qur'an. This is because (as we have seen above with the theory of *'hakimiyyah'*) the Qur'an and the Classical Commentaries do not say and mean what Daesh wants them to mean, and so Daesh's misinterpretations of them have always been easily refuted by traditional *usuli* scholars. However, with the *hadith,* it is different, for two reasons: the first reason, as we have noted, is redactions of the *hadith* corpus. Salafis celebrate the late Nasir al-Din al-Albani (and his students) as if he and his books were pinnacles of objectivity never before seen with regards the *hadith.* But in fact his redactions are deliberate systematic revisions of the *hadith* corpus in line with Salafi thinking. When you hear *'sahhahahu 'l-Albani'* ('Albani says it is true') or *'da"afahu 'l-Albani'* ('Albani says it is not true'), there has likely been a tinkering with a *hadith* in line with Salafi preconceptions and politics—whether consciously or unconsciously. In total, Albani declared some 5,000 traditionally accepted *ahadith* as untrue. Over the last 50 years, Albani's redacted versions of the *hadith* collections have been distributed for free to practically every major library, university and mosque in the Islamic world and countless minor ones—and translated and trumpeted on the internet. In effect, the Salafi *hadith* corpus has drowned out the traditional *hadith* collections that existed until the middle of the twentieth century, to the extent that today few people, even *usulis,* are aware of this.

The second reason why Daesh and others have been able to manipu-late the *hadith* has to do with the sheer vastness of the *hadith* corpus, and because of the accumulated apocrypha, as discussed in Chapter 7 of *The Thinking Person's Guide to Islam.* Reading through all the 200,000 *ahadith* in the two hundred and fifty collections in which they have been compiled (many of them vast multi-volume works that are difficult to find)—let alone studying them with a qualified teacher with an *'ijazah'* (a transmitted teaching warrant)—would take a person two hours a day for perhaps 30 years. Only a limited number of elderly individuals alive today have actually done this. Even fewer know enough about them to be in a position to understand their meanings, their contexts and to be able to assess their authenticity. But what the radical Salafi/Wahhabi and Muslim Brotherhood networks have been doing collectively and indefatigably for at least 70 years is trawling this corpus for *ahadith* that suit them and their views. And they have found some. Not many—they tend to go back to the same 40 or 50 *ahadith* (out of 60,000 or so different, possibly acceptable, *ahadith*)—but seemingly enough to act as a linchpin for their insurrections and their savagery. In *The Thinking Person's Guide to Islam*, we cited the following example:

> I have been ordered to fight people until they say: 'There is no god but God', so whoever says: 'There is no god but God' is safe in himself and his wealth except as permitted by law, and his reckoning is with God. (*Bukhari*; *Muslim*)

We said earlier that this is the goal of *jihad*. It is a goal defined *after war has been waged on Muslims*, and even then it is understood in the context of a defensive war in the Arabian Peninsula in the seventh century CE. It defines specifically what victory looks like in the case that Muslims are victorious (and of course they were). It is *not* the cause of *jihad*, the *casus belli*. The *jihadi* answer to this is that the *hadith* says to fight 'people', and therefore is a general and unlimited command. But of course this is wrong. The Arabic term for 'people' ('*al-nas*') can be general or can be used rhetorically to mean specific people as in the following Qur'anic verse:

> *Those to whom the people said, 'The people have gathered against you, therefore fear them'. But it increased them in faith, and they said, 'God is sufficient for us, an excellent Guardian is He'. (Aal 'Imran, 3:173)*

Now obviously not *all* people had gathered against the believers, and not *all* people said to them: '*fear them*'. Only *some* people did. So the term 'people' has to be looked at in its context, i.e. of who was speaking to them and what they meant. Similarly, the context of the *hadith* quoted is a *defensive* war that the Prophet ﷺ was fighting against the disbelievers of the Quraysh and their allies.

Moreover, Muslim scholars also point out that any fighting which in fact deters people from saying that 'there is no god but God' is obviously excluded from the commandment of the *hadith* cited above. Muslims must act in a way that brings people to witness the unity of God and makes it beloved to them. Terrorism and cruelty obviously drive people away from Islam. So terrorists have turned this *hadith*—even as they themselves understand it— on its head.

All one can say to such a combination of zeal and incomplete understanding is what Alexander Pope (d. 1744) said in his *An Essay on Criticism* (the 'Pierian Spring' is the metaphorical source of knowledge in Ancient Greece):

> Trust not yourself: but your defects to know,
>> Make use of every friend—and every foe
> A little learning is a dangerous thing;
>> Drink deep, or taste not the Pierian spring.
> There, shallow draughts intoxicate the brain,
>> And drinking largely sobers us again.

To give another example, the Prophet Muhammad ﷺ was circumambulating the Ka'bah (in the period before his emigration) and was abused (along with his daughter the Lady Fatimah ﵂) by some of the Quraysh. He ﷺ then said:

> Will you listen, you people of Quraysh, I swear by He in whose Hand Muhammad's soul is, I have brought you slaughter; I have brought you slaughter. (*Ahmad* from *Ibn Ishaq*)

The *hadith* is weak, but 'I have brought you slaughter' ('*ji'tukum bi 'l-dhabh*') has become one of Daesh's favourite phrases. They repeat it whilst they are killing people as some sort of justification. Now of course the Prophet ﷺ did *not* bring the Quraysh slaughter when he finally defeated them at the conquest of Mecca (as discussed in Chapter 7 of *The Thinking Person's Guide to Islam*), but rather he brought forgiveness and honour. And even if one accepts the story but reads the whole story, it becomes clear that the Prophet ﷺ was talking to specific persons who were abusing him and whom he was foretelling would be killed (Abu Jahl and 'Uqbah bin Abi Mu'it who were in fact killed after the battle of Badr—but not by him ﷺ). The Prophet ﷺ certainly was not endorsing the wholesale slaughter of his own tribe, the Quraysh, whom God Himself had honoured and previously secured, with a chapter in the Qur'an named after them. It is as follows:

> For the security of Quraysh, | their security for the journey of winter and of summer, | let them worship the Lord of this House, | Who has fed them against hunger and made them secure from fear. (Quraysh, 106:1–4)

So obviously Daesh's interpretation of the alleged *hadith* runs contrary not only to the *sunnah* of the Prophet ﷺ but to the Qur'an itself! Similar things could be said about the other *ahadith* Daesh misuses and manipulates. But the key point here can be summarised as follows:

> Mere reading of a translation of [even] *Sahih al-Bukhari* will not enable one to determine whether a certain injunction is compulsory, preferable, or permissible. (Muhammad Zakariyya Kandhalawi, *The Differences of the Imams*, trans. Muhammad Kadwa, White Thread Press, 2004, p. 37)

Nevertheless *ahadith* have become Daesh's weapon of choice on Twitter. The reasons are simple: they are short, eloquent, easy to understand, easy to memorize and seemingly authoritative. At one point in 2015, US Under Secretary of State Richard Stengel reported that Daesh and its online 'fanboys' were reportedly producing some 100,000 tweets a day, and in fact many of these started with one of 'their' *ahadith*.

Consequently, anyone wishing to refute Daesh must undertake the study of the *hadith*—or find someone who has already done so—and then proactively communicate a systemic rebuttal of the group's understanding of the *ahadith*, and gather the hundreds of other *ahadith* that contradict them and justify the consensus position of Sunni Islam. In other words, a rebuttal or response to Daesh's abuse of *hadith* literature must have two aspects: *ta'sil* (scriptural basis) and *tawsil* (getting the message out to the masses). Daesh's ideology rests basically on a struggle for the 'soul' of the *ahadith*, fought by abusing, decontextualizing and cherry-picking selected *ahadith*, and then zealously blasting them out via the internet in every way possible.

9. MOTIVATION AND MORALE

Daesh is full of radical zeal. As mentioned, their texts and their shaykhs equate their cause with Islam as such and their opponents with disbelief, and this gives them a big morale boost. Their shaykhs and '*fatwa* councils' justify and give *fatwas* for their every action. This also brings up their morale, and high morale leads to bravery and stamina on the battlefield.

In addition, all fighters are given mandatory religious indoctrination courses as part of their military training. Much of the indoctrination focuses on the glories of getting killed in battle (martyrdom). The rest focuses on the glories of killing others.

The hallmark of Muslim armies throughout the centuries has been a lack of fear of death, and willingness — even eagerness — to die on the battlefield. *Jihad* is an integral part of Islam, as discussed. Moreover, Arabs are inherently a brave warrior people. Of course, this is true of many peoples and armies (including those fighting Daesh, especially the Kurds), and one thing human beings as a species do not lack is courage. Nevertheless, in Arab and Islamic culture, there is no sentiment of '*Dulce et decorum pro patria mori*' ('It is sweet and fitting to die for one's country') being 'an old Lie' as Wilfred Owen (d. 1918) wrote in his poem by that name — not even in the modern world. Daesh has utilized this and capitalized on it, or rather, manipulated it. Lack of fear of death has been one of Daesh's great strengths — as its members are fond of saying — particularly in providing willing suicide bombers.

Nevertheless, as the great Arab historian Ibn Khaldun (732–808/1332–1406) argued in his magnum opus, the *Muqaddimah*, their very victories and gains, and the establishment of their rule, always makes Arab conquerors preoccupied with the world and gradually weakens their zeal. Daesh's establishment of a 'caliphate' is likely subtly having the same effect. Moreover, just as Daesh's morale was buoyed by its many early victories and its supposedly restoring a 'caliphate', a change in its fortunes could easily lead to a loss of morale and then a general collapse. This kind of burnout has happened with almost every fanatical movement over the course of human history.

There are also more prosaic reasons why Daesh fighters have had a high morale. One of them is widespread use of psychostimulant drugs and amphetamines (particularly 'captagon'). Daesh provides these to its fighters, and they can be made in elementary labs. These drugs make people very aggressive, brutal, without conscience or mercy, and increase energy levels with lowered need for sleep and food. Of course, eventually they wear people out, so that after two or three years of constant use, the internal organs begin to collapse, but two or three years with increased chances of survival is a long time on the battlefield. Moreover, World War II studies show that 99% of people suffer serious psychological damage after only 60 days of continuous warfare. So extending the period of 'fighting energy' from two months to two or three whole years—without even the use of combat rotation—through the use of captagon, generally represents a potential 10–20 fold boost in staying power. To be fair, all sides fighting in Syria and Iraq who lack fervour or simply get tired apparently take these drugs. In fact, in the last few years, Jordanian security services have regularly intercepted staggering amounts (20 or 30 million pills in single shipments on convoys) which smugglers try to bring into Jordan from Syria or Iraq.

There is also the terror that Daesh's own fighters experience from their own side and internal intelligence—through the torture and execution they are constantly made to witness—if they slacken or disobey, or begin to doubt the radical doctrines imposed by their leaders. Finally, Daesh employs sophisticated propaganda to keep up morale and bring in new recruits (see below).

10. PROPAGANDA

(a) Daesh has a constant stream of grisly training, fighting and killing videos with emotive music, as well as dedicated music and poetry videos (like *'ya 'asib al-ras, waynak?'*). To further spread its propaganda, the group also has well-produced online magazines, like *Dabiq* (available on the internet) and *A'maq*.

(b) Social media: in addition to countless tweets to reach out and spread its propaganda (to the extent that Daesh is constantly threatening the CEOs of Twitter and other social media and internet giants for taking them down—Twitter, for one, has shut several hundred thousand Daesh accounts in 2015 and 2016), Daesh and its supporters operate hundreds of thousands of Facebook accounts, YouTube channels and various other social media activities. Some, like Kik and online games, are encrypted and untraceable. Western intelligence agencies have begun to work with social media providers to take down Daesh's posts—and its 'fanboy' posts—but throughout 2014 Daesh had a free hand online. It is still (as of 2016) very active, if not winning the internet war, and its postings have become a game of 'whack-a-mole' with social media providers and Western intelligence agencies. Daesh accounts and posts are constantly coming up and then being taken down (mostly after they have already passed their message to their own pre-alerted networks).

(c) The slickness of Daesh's propaganda videos (and use of social media) is now legendary, and is even studied all over the world as a paradigm of effectiveness. These at first shocked the world, which could not believe Islamic militants could produce such slick Hollywood-quality and style footage. Until today everything Daesh releases is, if not shown, extensively reproduced and reported on international media. *This has arguably been Daesh's biggest success and its most important tool* (and has been the main driver of its foreign recruitment).

N.B.: These videos are now finally facing the *law of diminishing returns*, so that every new video has to be more grisly and savage: with more people killed in each video; new more horrible ways to kill people; more perverse situations (such as children performing executions); bigger and more terrifying-looking executioners. Nevertheless, each new video is less interesting to a fatigued and saturated general public (which is now used to them) and less shocking. They also betray Daesh's mockery of Islam and human decency more and more.

II. HOW DAESH IS WRONG

On the 19ᵗʰ of September 2014 (24ᵗʰ Dhul-Qa'da 1435), less than three months after Daesh's so-called 'Announcement of the Caliphate'—just about the time it took to ascertain what was really going on—a group of 126 *usuli* scholars mostly from the Azhar University in Egypt but including the Grand Muftis of Nigeria, Indonesia, Chad, Palestine, Kurdistan, Kosovo, Bulgaria and Egypt wrote an 'Open Letter' to Daesh outlining what they had seen wrong in Daesh's behaviour (see: www.lettertobaghdadi.com). The 'Open Letter' did not get as much attention as it deserved (except in Jordan where it was read in high schools and universities) but was translated into ten languages or so and remains the only collective systematic (albeit simplified) analysis and rebuttal of Daesh's practices from the point of view of traditional *usuli* Islam. Its own executive summary reads as follows:

EXECUTIVE SUMMARY

1. It is forbidden in Islam to issue *fatwas* without all the necessary learning requirements. Even then *fatwas* must follow Islamic legal theory as defined in the Classical texts. It is also forbidden to cite a portion of a verse from the Qur'an — or part of a verse — to derive a ruling without looking at everything that the Qur'an and *hadith* teach related to that matter. In other words, there are strict subjective and objective prerequisites for *fatwas*, and one cannot 'cherry-pick' Qur'anic verses for legal arguments without considering the entire Qur'an and *hadith*.

2. It is forbidden in Islam to issue legal rulings about anything without mastery of the Arabic language.

3. It is forbidden in Islam to oversimplify *shari'ah* matters and ignore established Islamic sciences.

4. It is permissible in Islam [for scholars] to differ on any matter, except those fundamentals of religion that all Muslims must know.

5. It is forbidden in Islam to ignore the reality of contemporary times when deriving legal rulings.

6. It is forbidden in Islam to kill the innocent.

7. It is forbidden in Islam to kill emissaries, ambassadors, and diplomats; hence it is forbidden to kill journalists and aid workers.

8. *Jihad* in Islam is defensive war. It is not permissible without the right cause, the right purpose and without the right rules of conduct.

9. It is forbidden in Islam to declare a person non-Muslim unless he (or she) openly declares disbelief.

10. It is forbidden in Islam to harm or mistreat — in any way — Christians or any 'People of the Scripture'.

11. It is obligatory to consider Yazidis as People of the Scripture.

12. The reintroduction of slavery is forbidden in Islam. It was abolished by universal consensus.
13. It is forbidden in Islam to force people to convert.
14. It is forbidden in Islam to deny women their rights.
15. It is forbidden in Islam to deny children their rights.
16. It is forbidden in Islam to enact legal punishments (*hudud*) without following the correct procedures that ensure justice and mercy.
17. It is forbidden in Islam to torture people.
18. It is forbidden in Islam to disfigure the dead.
19. It is forbidden in Islam to attribute evil acts to God 🐝.
20. It is forbidden in Islam to destroy the graves and shrines of Prophets and Companions.
21. Armed insurrection is forbidden in Islam for any reason other than clear disbelief by the ruler and not allowing people to pray.
22. It is forbidden in Islam to declare a caliphate without consensus from all Muslims.
23. Loyalty to one's nation is permissible in Islam.
24. After the death of the Prophet 🐝, Islam does not require anyone to emigrate anywhere.

Since this letter was issued, Daesh has increased the number of its crimes and added new ones to the list including coercing children into war; making them execute people or conduct suicide bombings; raping captives; burning alive the Jordanian pilot (and hero) Mu'adh al-Kassasbeh; drowning people in steel cages and blowing them up in cars; coercing women to torture and execute other women; coercing a man to kill his own mother (for the 'crime' of trying to get him to leave the group), and mass extortion. It has reportedly even invented a metal contraption — called the 'clipper' — which it uses to cut off small bits of women's skin, if they are deemed indecently dressed. It has also masterminded dozens of terrorist acts all over the world aimed at innocent civilians, and used chemical weapons . . . the list goes on. There regrettably have been, over the course of human history, other groups as savage as Daesh, and even more savage. However, there has never been anyone — certainly not in Islamic history — who has so proudly glorified and documented the 'creativeness' of their savagery with so much enthusiasm. In other words, there have been monsters, but none who have so proudly shown off their own monstrosity. Howbeit, the executive summary of the Open Letter is an adequate summary of Daesh's crimes. It also shows how the ethical standards of *usuli* Islam are a universal norm for most decent human beings, coinciding with primordial human nature (*'fitra'*). Indeed, on September 30th, 2014, the General Secretary of the World Council of Churches (WCC), the Rev. Dr Olav Fykse Tveit, welcomed it with the following statement:

> The meticulous, detailed and scholarly rebuttal of the claims of the IS to represent authentic Islam offered by this letter will be an important resource for Muslim leaders who seek to enable people of all religions to live together with dignity, respecting our common humanity.

12. HOW DAESH OPERATES

A 'normal' nation state in the modern world—and indeed in most pre-modern states including Islamic ones—involves an unspoken social contract of 'justice to all people equally, with reciprocal responsibility between the government and the people' (as discussed in Chapter 12 of *The Thinking Person's Guide to Islam*). Consequently, a state takes taxes but provides justice, order, protection, security, and, in so far as it can, essential services like access to clean food and water, health services, education, jobs, transport, land, housing, energy and so on. It guarantees people certain rights and freedoms. Now if a state gives less than 10 per cent of what it used to give, or is expected to give by its people, there will generally be all kinds of protests and discontent (as anyone advocating austerity measures knows). If a state gives 20 per cent less than what it is expected to—i.e. provides 80 per cent of previous services—there will be very serious disruptions if not insurrections. This is very clearly seen in people's reactions to austerity measures. But as malevolently pointed out in Abu Bakr al-Naji's *The Management of Savagery* (*Idarat al-Tawahhush*), if there has been a brutal war or civil war with social anarchy, anyone who can provide slightly more order will be welcomed. So when a group like Daesh moves in after anarchy and provides some semblance of order, it will be welcomed by most people. So Naji's vile conclusion is to sow pandemonium and anarchy for a while and then impose a brutal social order—and this will be met by welcome (at least initially). And this is precisely what Daesh did in Syria and Iraq.

Moreover, since Daesh is not a state, if it takes the same taxes as a state and provides 40 per cent of basic services to local people, then because they have low expectations, people will think well of it. This is especially so if it cloaks everything it does under the 'religious necessity' of *jihad* (as it sees it). So Daesh is able to extract taxes in return for few effective services, and this is what it has done in Syria and Iraq. In other words, Daesh deliberately exploits a psychological shift in expectations as regards the unspoken social contract between the government and the people. And should anyone realize this shift and speak out, Daesh can always fall back on its unprecedented brutality and sheer terror.

There is another point here which everyone in the world seems unaware of (except, ironically, a few American Libertarians), and that is this: few states in history, including—and perhaps especially the Prophet's ﷺ own state in Medina—were as intrusive into people's private lives as nation states are today, with their endless information and intelligence gathering techniques. However, Daesh's pseudo-caliphate is perhaps the most intrusive of all modern 'states'. Daesh pries as deeply as it can into people's individual private lives, shamelessly using the modern techniques of espionage to enforce the most un-Islamic concept of an all-embracing state.

13. HOW DAESH GROWS

There are at least five paradigmatic differences between Daesh's growth and that of a nation state. Without understanding and interrupting these, no effective progress will be made against Daesh. These represent not only asymmetric warfare, but asymmetric economic competition.

The first is that a normal nation state 'cares' about its people living as long and as safely, happily and healthily as possible—that is its primary function. Through manipulation of all the religious injunctions encouraging *jihad* (as discussed in Chapter 11 of *The Thinking Person's Guide to Islam*), Daesh is able to subsume the lives of people living under its control—and a fortiori the lives of others (whom it anyway sees as unbelievers having no inherent or inalienable rights)—to *jihad* (as it conceives it). For Daesh, effectively, if not in theory as well, human lives are a mere tool to serve *jihad* rather than vice versa. In short, because of the group's misunder-standing or manipulation of the concept of *jihad*, Daesh is able to make human life and welfare, and society itself—even the lives and welfare of its own soldiers—expendable and irrelevant. The only thing its recruits may get is (once they are safely dead) some slick videos and pictures about how they entered Paradise (in order of course to encourage more people to lay down their lives). The upshot of this is that Daesh functionally and effectively does not 'care' about its people living as long and as safely, happily and healthily as possible. All that matters to Daesh is replacing recruits as quickly as it gets them killed, which it does by tapping into the vast personal networks of families and friends of the dead (who naturally want to avenge their dead) and by propaganda (as mentioned above). This means that war does not (at least in theory) hurt Daesh in the way it hurts a nation state, even a losing war. Moreover, whereas any nation state with resource limitations gets worn down and eventually weakened *merely by fighting*, Daesh on the contrary gets stronger by fighting—unless it is choked (by containment and blockade) rather than stoked (by war).

The second point is a consequence of this, pertaining to captive urban and civilian populations. Like Hizbollah, Daesh is not a nation state actor. Just as Hizbollah does not 'care'—or at least is not operationally impacted—if Israel bombs Beirut, Daesh is not affected if the US or Russia flattens Raqqa and Mosul. On the contrary, this merely increases local civilian misery and forces the civilian population to more willingly join its ranks—out of vengeance and despair if nothing else. So Daesh is more or less impervious to aerial obliteration of local populations.

Third, Daesh has a war-booty economy. This means it not only captures and keeps whatever it can of its enemies' actual wealth and weapons, but also taxes all wealth and trade inside captured areas—something a nation state cannot legally do.

Fourth, over and above a war-booty economy, unlike a nation state Daesh sees no obligation to preserve anything. Rather, Daesh appropriates, uses, destroys, torches, sells or cannibalizes anything in its path—making a considerable profit as it does so. Daesh has become known for its partial destruction and sale of Syrian and Iraqi antiquities and archaeological treasures—a trade estimated to bring in tens of millions of dollars a year, if not a month. It also sells land, buildings, houses, farms, livestock, factories, public institutes, natural resources (in particular oil and gas) and human beings themselves (through kidnapping or by selling them into slavery). In short, Daesh is willing to sell or destroy everything from the environment, to culture, to the built environment, to life itself, so that every small expansion of 'its' territory represents a source of income.

Fifth, Daesh operates on the ground by exploiting multiple 'Mexican stand-offs' between its many enemies. Without going into this issue in much detail, it suffices to say that every one of Daesh's enemies in Syria and Iraq (including al-Qaeda/al-Nusra and the US) has one or more other enemies which it is also fighting or concerned about, and so does not commit fully to fighting Daesh. If all the other combatants in these countries were to turn their guns on Daesh (or indeed on any one opponent) that opponent would quickly be destroyed. This of course is simple 'game theory'.

These different paradigms mean that Daesh can be defeated, but it is not going to be *exhausted* by force of arms alone. Since most wars between two determined and competent opponents are ultimately won by marshalling superior resources, defeating Daesh is essentially going to be a matter of observing, understanding, interrupting and countering its operational paradigms, rather than a symmetric military defeat.

14. PERSONNEL AND RECRUITMENT

We will discuss *who* joins Daesh and *why* in later sections. We have also mentioned Daesh's effective online propaganda operations. It remains to be said here that as of June 2016 there were an estimated 25,000 trained (albeit with basic military training) and indoctrinated (every fighter has a month-long religious indoctrination course) fighters in Syria and Iraq compared with over 32,000 in 2015. In all, since the takeover of Mosul in June 2014 to June 2016, Daesh has managed to attract some 30,000 foreign fighters (perhaps a quarter of whom have been killed; some of whom have relocated to other parts of the world; some of whom have returned home with unknown motives; some of whom have defected; and some of whom are still fighting). As of June 2016, foreign recruitment brings in about 200 fighters a month (Daesh has also been directing recruits towards its bases in Libya as a 'Plan B') whereas one year earlier and at the end of 2014, foreign recruitment stood at over 2,000 foreigners a month. No doubt the reasons for this include Western targeting of its funding, the Russian air campaign, more effective restrictions on the Turkish borders, and the gradual rolling back of its military gains—all of which have affected the morale of potential recruits.

Western recruits get a lot of publicity and often are middle-class people with some wealth and a high level of skills (particularly technological skills). However, these recruits do not form the bulk or the strength of Daesh inside Syria and Iraq, and represent less than a quarter of its foreign recruits (the majority of whom actually come from Arab and Islamic countries—particularly Tunisia, Morocco, Saudi Arabia, Turkey and the Islamic regions of Russia). And foreign recruits themselves make up less than half of Daesh's total strength.

Most of Daesh's fighters are in fact local Iraqis and Syrians. The Syrians obviously have decades of genuine grievances against the regimes of Bashar al-Assad and his father Hafez al-Assad. Similarly, the Iraqis have genuine grievances dating back at least to the 2003 Iraq War and to the Shi'i sectarian purges that happened in its aftermath until 2007, when Shi'a politicians and militias grabbed power to take revenge for all the misery inflicted on them under Saddam Hussein. In 2006, the Americans rallied many Sunni tribes to fight (the then) al-Qaeda in Iraq, arming and paying tribesmen under the 'Sahwa initiative'. As soon as the US military presence effectively left Iraq in 2008, the government of Prime Minister Nuri al-Maliki disarmed these tribes and cut their salaries, leaving them to be slaughtered by both al-Qaeda and the Shi'a militias. Consequently, many Sunni Iraqis—even those who fought al-Qaeda in 2006–8—will never again trust the Iraqi government, and when faced with the 'devil or the deep blue sea', will understandably make common cause with Daesh rather than be under a Shi'a-led Baghdad government. For them, only a division of Iraq into Sunni, Kurdish and Shi'a states—or at minimum a federal Iraq with Sunni provinces with their own militias, resources and independent powers guaranteed upfront by law and constitution—will pry them away from Daesh.

Additionally, Daesh imposes general mobilization in the areas it controls (or takes taxes in lieu). Fighters are taken from the age of puberty (14 or 15) to fight. The prepubescent are trained from the ages of six or seven, because, sadly, children make particularly obedient recruits. Since Daesh still controls (as of June 2016) five to six million people in its areas (down from 10 million at its height), this still means it has a vast immediate recruitment pool.

Finally, it is worth noting that Daesh conducts extensive interviews with new recruits (and keeps meticulous records) to examine their motives and networks, and to guard against spying. It does not trust any of them, until, like the worst criminal gangs, it has made them participate in heinous crimes such that they cannot possibly turn against Daesh because of their own guilt and complicity. Daesh does not promote anyone until they have committed their personal share of repugnant crimes.

15. ECONOMY AND FUNDING

We have discussed the difference between the economic paradigms of Daesh and a nation state. At its height in 2015, Daesh was said to have had a two billion dollar a year economy, with revenue from: war booty; farm taxes; kidnapping; extortion; robbery and theft; sympathetic foreign donations; oil and gas (these accounting for up to 80 per cent of Daesh's revenues); taxes and tariffs of every stripe; sales of every asset in 'its' land (including houses, livestock, goods and even people); looted banks and public institutes; sales of public services and other strategies. It has even set up its own local businesses ranging from car dealerships to fish farms. It trades with anyone it can and, bizarrely, even with many of the sides with whom it is still fighting. Its foreign followers also try to arrange trade.

16. HOW RELIGIOUS MESSAGES ARE SPREAD

Religious messages are basically spread in four ways:
1. 'Old ways' (basically 'teaching and preaching').
2. 'New ways' (basically internet-based, particularly social media, or film or audio). These messages are, ironically, always amplified by the world media.
3. 'Carrot ways' (basically financial aid, or services along with a religious message. Groups like the Muslim Brotherhood and Hizbollah, and church-based aid, parochial schools and universities specialize in this).

4. 'Stick ways' (basically legislation-based punishment and social exclusion).

Now all of these ways (except perhaps the second) are the work of entire civilisations over centuries, if not millennia. The time, effort, lives and wealth of countless people, and indeed nations, go into these. It is not easy to understand and monitor—let alone change—what different groups are doing in the name of religion.

This means that people aiming to bring about religious change quickly essentially have to do three things. The first is to examine their motives: the easiest most effective changes occur when the people doing them are sincere. The Arabs have a saying: 'Words that come from the heart reach the heart [of the sincere], but words that come from the tongue, do not go past the ears.' The second is to start with oneself, one's family, one's friends, one's personal networks. People (and especially children) are influenced more by what other people do (in themselves) than what they say. The third—for our day especially—is not to try to reinvent existing institutes, but simply to use existing ones with a different (but religiously authentic) message. This is a question of changing the software, not the hardware—a 'reprogramming strategy'. It does not require very much money, but it does require some things that money cannot buy: namely understanding, intelligence, knowledge, patience, courage and love.

17. HOW YOUNG MUSLIMS ARE INFLUENCED TODAY (2016)

Specific studies have recently been conducted on how young Muslims are influenced. These are particularly important because *religious* people never do something in the name of religion—especially something momentous like joining Daesh or al-Nusra—without finding someone to justify their act (give them a '*fatwa*') usually in accordance with their own inclinations. We reproduce part of perhaps the best of these studies, with the kind permission of Taba Futures Initiatives (UAE). We will not comment on them—they speak for themselves—except to say that anyone seeking to spread or counter a religious message obviously has to take them *all* into consideration.

WHO DO ARAB MUSLIM MILLENNIALS GO TO WHEN THEY
HAVE A QUESTION PERTAINING TO RELIGIOUS AFFAIRS?

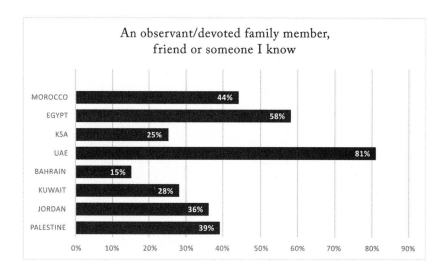

An observant/devoted family member, friend or someone I know

MOROCCO	44%
EGYPT	58%
KSA	25%
UAE	81%
BAHRAIN	15%
KUWAIT	28%
JORDAN	36%
PALESTINE	39%

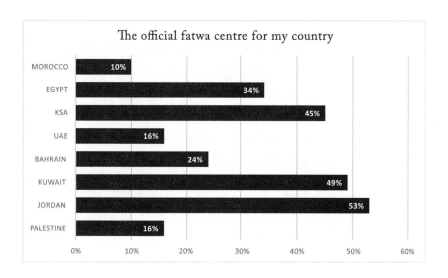

The official fatwa centre for my country

MOROCCO	10%
EGYPT	34%
KSA	45%
UAE	16%
BAHRAIN	24%
KUWAIT	49%
JORDAN	53%
PALESTINE	16%

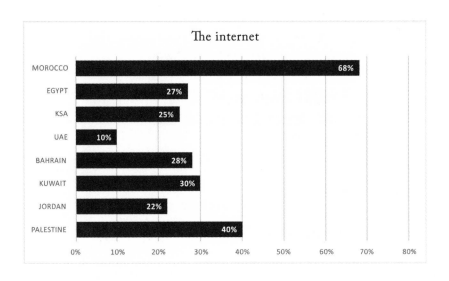

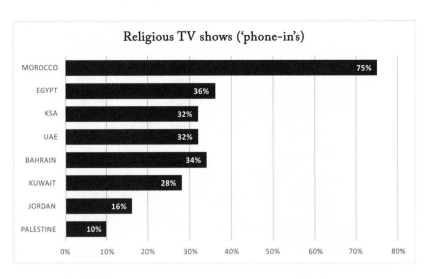

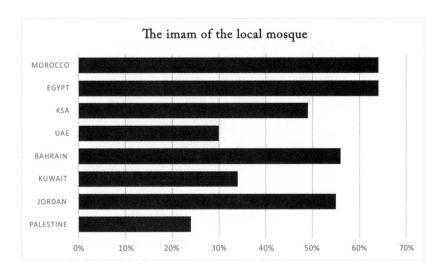

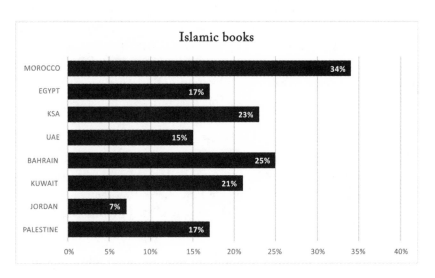

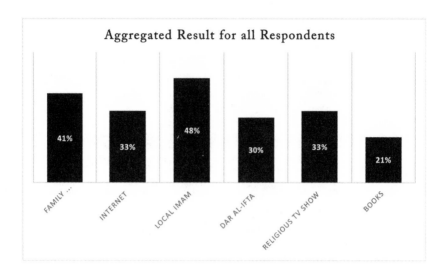

Aggregated Result for all Respondents

41%   33%   48%   30%   33%   21%

FAMILY ···   INTERNET   LOCAL IMAM   DAR AL-IFTA   RELIGIOUS TV SHOW   BOOKS

18. WHO JOINS DAESH?

Despite the above, only certain types of Muslims or people join—or have ever joined—Daesh and its like. The 'sources of influence' (as mentioned above) may change the kind of Muslim someone is, but they do not change what that kind of Muslim will or will not do. This is a subtle but important point that is not well understood. It also means that certain types of Muslims never join Daesh and its like: never do; never have; never will; and could not even if they tried. This is another subtle, and even more important point that is not well understood.

On December 7ᵗʰ, 2015—five days after a US Muslim husband and wife of Pakistani origin randomly murdered 14 people and seriously injured 22 others at a local public health centre in San Bernardino, California in the name of Daesh—the then leading US Republican Presidential contender, businessman Donald J. Trump, publicly announced that he was

> calling for a total and complete shutdown of Muslims entering the United States until our country's representatives can figure out what the hell [sic] is going on. We have no choice! WE HAVE NO CHOICE!

Regardless of Mr Trump's other statements concerning Muslims (including commending a US general's story about shooting Muslims with bullets dipped in pigs' blood), the point he made about the US not understanding which kinds of Muslims may join Daesh—and consequently commit acts of violence, murder and terror—and which will not, is a valid one. It needs to be clarified with introspection, honesty and openness.

In Chapter 10 and Appendix 1 of *The Thinking Person's Guide to Islam*, Sunni Muslims today were described as being divided into the following ideological 'camps':

1. *Usulis* ('traditionalists', literally 'principle-ists'). **Approx. 65 per cent of Sunnis.** These hold to the great Islamic scholarship tradition of the four schools of Islamic Jurisprudence (*madhahib*). For doctrine, they hold to *Ash'arite-Maturidi* theology, and for spirituality they hold to mainstream Sufism (e.g. that of Ghazali). The Azhar in Egypt is a typical *usuli* institute, and is one of the three oldest universities in the world. In 1900, 99 per cent of all Sunnis were *usuli*.

Usulis are by definition and belief not 'politically-minded' unless the state (if it is a Muslim-majority state) bans prayers and enforces 'open disbelief', in which case they are religiously required to overturn it.

2. **Anti-*usulis*. Approx. 10 per cent of Sunnis.** These explicitly reject the methodologies of the *madhahib* or 'mix and match' between them as they see fit. They can be called 'fundamentalist' in English, if it is understood that this refers to political aggressiveness.

'Fundamentalism'—in Islam at least— does not mean textual 'literalism' (as some people seem to think) but rather 'selective literalism'. For example, no fundamentalist takes literally the Verse of Light (24:35), or the Divine Name '*The Outward*' (*Al-Thahir*, 57:3), or God's words: *We are closer to him [the human being] than his jugular vein* (50:16). Rather, fundamentalism is that form of religion that says that not only is it the most authentic form of that religion, but the only form acceptable to God, and then castigates all other forms of the same religion through either intimidation or violence.

There are basically two kinds of Sunni fundamentalism active today. They are: (a) radical Salafism/Wahhabism and; (b) Muslim Brotherhood 'thought'.

3. **'Don't Knows'. Approx. 25 per cent of Sunnis.** Unfortunately, the rise of anti-*usulism* has affected the Islamic world so much that many people could not say if they belong to a school of Islamic law and if so

which one. Even those who do identify with a *madhhab*, adopt, without question, Salafi editions of *hadith* books (mainly Al-Albani's, copies of which are given out for free everywhere). Moreover, the 'demagogic prejudice'—the sentiment that on any issue the most extreme point of view is most sincere—rules supreme everywhere, so that people naturally adopt fundamentalist positions without analysing or understanding them. Finally, apart from ancient universities like the Azhar, most universities in the Islamic world do not teach *madhhab*-based *shari'ah*, but rather (under the pretext of 'Islamic unity') 'comparative *shari'ah*', and this weakens *usul* because it allows fundamentalism to seep in as a credible intellectual narrative.

4. **Modernists. Less than one per cent of Sunnis.** 'Islamic modernism' is the idea that Islam (and not merely Islamic civilisation and culture, but Islamic doctrine and law) should be updated to correspond to Western values. It is universally derided by all other Muslims. Although the West has been encouraging it (together with outright secularism) for several centuries, it is hard to find a *believing* and *practising* Sunni Muslim who adheres to modernism. At any rate, it has less than one per cent following in the Sunni world, and not only no traction but also no potential. When Western powers or institutions try to encourage modernism, this only feeds fundamentalist conspiracy theories.

We should also mention the following group:

5. **Neophytes.** We define 'neophytes' as new converts, or born-Muslims who were lapsed and are now new practitioners (specifically, ones who have only been practising Islam for less than three years). These can never be more than 0.1 per cent of all Sunnis, and probably less than .01 per cent.

The key point about all this is that the only people who join Daesh (from outside of their territories) and its like are anti-usulis or neophytes. All Daesh recruits are anti-*usulis*: they have to take a month-long indoctrination course when they join to make sure of this. Among long-standing Muslims, only anti-*usulis* travel to Syria and Iraq. Certainly not every anti-*usuli* joins or sympathizes with Daesh—only a minority do—but all Daesh members are anti-*usulis*. If they were not, they would never, and could never, join.

Nevertheless, Daesh and al-Qaeda are offshoots of the radical Salafi/ Wahhabi and Muslim Brotherhood movements and thought. Radical Salafi/Wahhabism parted ways with traditional Islam 250 years ago.

Blaming Islam as such for—or even associating Islam with—Daesh is a bit like blaming Britain for the crimes committed against the Native Americans in the 1830s. Those committing these acts stopped being British by definition in 1776. And if they had British ancestry—or if some of them did—the British nevertheless had nothing to do with US actions the following century.

This is important to understand because it reduces the size of the dragnet for Daesh's potential recruits by 90 per cent in one fell swoop. It also clarifies the only possible effective ideological response to Daesh: traditional *usuli* Islam.

Only in areas of actual conflict—or those immediately adjoining them—do local 'don't knows' join Daesh. This is because 'don't knows' can interpret their religion as suits them, and so they can be swayed by money, or pressure to join Daesh. And this is another subtle but important point. Muslims are unlikely to throw away their lives if they have some religious doubts about their cause: this means *both* that they are unlikely to join Daesh if they are not under its rule, and that they are unlikely to oppose them if they are. Hence they do not join from afar. The secret of this lies in understanding the nature of doubt, or at least of uncertainty. It also means that stopping most people from joining Daesh can be as simple as showing them how Daesh's beliefs and practices are contrary to the Qur'an and *sunnah*. In fact, most people who leave Daesh do so precisely because they find out from the inside how un-Islamic the group really is, despite its rhetoric.

It is also worth noting that excited neophytes are perhaps the most vulnerable group of all, and both Daesh and al-Qaeda target these in particular. This is explicitly stated in Abu 'Amr's al-Qaedi's manual *Dawra fi Fann al-Tajnid* ('A Course in the Art of Recruitment'). Many of these recruits are angry or marginalized youth, social fringe groups, or from rebellious youth subcultures. There have been cases in the West of non-Muslims going from one of these groups to Daesh recruit within one month—with no detected warning signs. There have even been cases of non-Muslim university students in countries like Japan trying to join Daesh, without converting to Islam, but as *angry non-Muslims*! In other words, Daesh represents not just a radicalization of Islam, but incorporates an 'Islamization' of radicals: people who would have been Marxists or anarchists 40 years ago today become Daesh. Worse still, there has been even 'an Islamization of crime' and an 'Islamization of sheer lunacy', like the Uzbek nanny who decapitated a disabled child in her care in Moscow in March 2016 because her husband got remarried, and then said she did it 'for Allah' and because she is 'a terrorist'. Arguably, the whole of Boko Haram with its insane wanton arbitrary mass murders, kidnapping and wholesale pillaging is far more an 'Islamization of crime and lunacy' than it is even a *takfiri* movement.

19. WHO DOES NOT JOIN DAESH?

From the above it should also be clear that no committed or knowledgeable *usuli* Muslim joins Daesh—and none ever have, and none ever will. No Ash'ari or Maturidi theologian has ever joined Daesh. No Sufi has ever joined Daesh. No Islamic philosopher has ever joined Daesh. Never have, never will. If they did, they would not be *usulis*, theologians, Sufis or philosophers, since Daesh's practices and beliefs contradict those of *usulis*, theologians, Sufis and philosophers. Even if they tried anyway, for whatever reason, and made their views known, they would soon have their heads sawn off with a blunt knife—or something equally monstrous. Daesh—and in fact all *takfiris*—regard *usulis*, Ash'aris, Maturidis, Sufis and philosophers as apostates who should be killed, even though these constitute the majority of Sunnis, and historically comprise over 99 per cent of all Sunnis. Interestingly also, there is no record of a single major Arabic grammarian or *tafsir* scholar joining Daesh.

All this accounts for and explains the vast discrepancies between the people who join Daesh from different places and countries (as of June 2016). For example, to date there have been some 2,000 foreign fighters from Belgium (with a population of 600,000 Muslims), but only 23 from India with a population of 160 million Muslims. Bulgaria, with an old Muslim community that makes up 10 per cent of the population (that is, around a million Muslims), a country where Muslims were savagely persecuted under communism and are still ostracized and repressed in many local districts—does not currently have a single Daesh fighter. Neither does Oman, with over a million Sunnis. Yet Tunisia, with an overall population of less than 11 million people, has over 3,000 fighters, and European countries like France and the UK with a few million Muslims have up to a few thousand each. Indonesia, with the largest Muslim population in the world with over 220 million Sunnis, has less than 200 fighters with Daesh or al-Nusra. Overall, one in 1,000 of all Western Muslims has joined Daesh compared to 1 in 100,000 from places like Indonesia or Egypt. This means that Western Muslims are one hundred times more likely to become radicalized than Muslims from the Islamic World taken as a whole.

What explains all of this? It is actually quite simple. Places like Bulgaria and India have strong Hanafi institutions and their scholars are well-grounded in Hanafi *fiqh*. Egypt and Indonesia are bastions of Shafi'i *fiqh* and Sufi practice. Europe, by contrast, has been a centre of Muslim Brotherhood and Salafi/Wahhabi activism and institutes for 40 years—particularly those not allowed room to manoeuvre in their home countries. Belgium has a large Salafi/Wahhabi community from North Africa, and in particular from the 'Tetuan triangle'. Under the aggressively secular regimes of Habib Bourguiba (1956–1987) and Zine El Abidine Ben 'Ali (1987–2011), who were busy repressing traditional Maliki *fiqh* and enfeebling one of its great bastions, the oldest university in the world, Al-Zaytuna in Tunis (founded in 120/737), Salafism found a way to seep into Tunisia and replace Maliki *fiqh*. In other words, wherever *usuli fiqh* is strong, Muslims are immune to Daesh, al-Nusra and Salafi/Wahhabi *takfirism* or Muslim Brotherhood 'thought' in general. Wherever anti-*usuli* thinking has taken root, there you have potential for Daesh and its ilk.

One more point needs to be mentioned. Since it is all but impossible for a Sunni *usuli*, Ash'ari or Sufi to join Daesh (it has not happened so far)— and a fortiori a Shi'i Muslim—this means that a discontented or even just bored ethnically European non-Muslim (as will be seen in the section on why people join Daesh), with no ties to Islam, is statistically more likely to join Daesh than an *usuli*! This is not an idle statistical curiosity. It has serious political and security implications particularly for Europe. Hundreds of non-Muslims have wound up joining Daesh. To date, no *usulis* have.

Howbeit, this does not mean that Daesh and *takfiri* ideology are an undetectable and inscrutable force than can suddenly afflict anyone any-where, causing people to suddenly and illogically 'self-radicalize' with no prior warning, as the media sometimes suggests. On the contrary, they work only through very predictable causes and channels. Most of them have been mentioned in the charts above: influence from family and friends/personal networks; the internet; religious programmes; the local imam or mosque; and books and pamphlets (there has yet to be—to our knowledge—a national Grand Mufti or *fatwa* centre to endorse Daesh). However, the most obvious channel (and probably the most influential one) was not mentioned, and that is education, particularly religious education. There is no need to press the point here, because those countries with a problem are aware of it and working on it. The same is true, a fortiori, at certain well-known universities. We should also mention that travel is another source of influence and provides *takfiris* with opportunities for recruitment.

This means that with sound judgement and enough resources, it is possible to know who is at risk of being 'radicalized' and who is not. The first thing that sound judgement and finite resources imply is Occam's razor. Occam's razor means that one need not even consider knowledge-able *usuli* Muslims as being at risk of joining Daesh. Consequently, one should not even speak about Daesh as an Islamic or Muslim phenomenon, but rather a '*takfiri*' one.

20. WHAT IS GOING ON? A *SUNNI* CIVIL WAR

Turning now to the question: 'What the hell [sic] is going on?', we should preface this by saying that early in 2015, H.M. King Abdullah II ibn Al-Hussein of Jordan called the war against Daesh a 'Third World War by other means'. What the king meant by that is, first: that it is going on all over the world (either through terrorist acts, or through full-scale conflict with various Daesh franchises such as in Syria-Iraq, Libya, Nigeria and the surrounding countries, Somalia, the southern part of Yemen, the Sinai and Afghanistan). The king also meant that Daesh's self-declared ambition (as discussed above) is to subjugate the whole world by force of arms, and that it has a strategy for this that (as discussed below) is not quite as insane as it seems. The 'other means' of the 'Third World War' is by starting with a different war, a war that *takfiris* have been waging on and off for hundreds of years. This war is not a religious war against the West. It is not a Huntingtonian 'clash of civilisations'. Nor is it a sectarian war against the Shi'a. It is a Sunni civil war. Or rather, it is a *takfiri* war against *usulis*—since *usulis* do not pronounce '*takfir*' back on *takfiris*. In fact *usulis* never wage war back on *takfiris*, at least not physically. *Usuli*-majority countries occasionally fight back, but no *usuli* scholars have ever—nor would ever, since they recognize the importance of state authority and communal action—organized a '*jihad*' against the *takfiri* onslaught against them.

In short, like the *Khawarij* of the first centuries of Islam, Daesh—and the whole *takfiri* movement—is primarily a war against *usul*. Its first targets are always *usuli* Muslims, in particular Ash'arites and Sufis—all in the name of 'reform'. Only secondarily is it a war against the rest of the world (although now these wars are waged concomitantly). Sometimes this first war is a 'hot' war, with persecution, killing and pillage. Sometimes it is a 'cold' war, where *takfir* is believed, pronounced and taught but not carried out. Sunnis themselves understand this. Anyone in the slightest bit of doubt about this has only to look at the incessant 'straw man' radical Salafi/Wahhabi invectives on Ash'aris and Sufis on the internet—in any language.

Indeed, the first thing that Daesh did when it invaded Mosul was to round up the imams of the mosques. It then put before them the choice of swearing allegiance to its 'caliph' or dying. Those *usuli* scholars who thought this ridiculous and refused were immediately put to death in public, thereby eliminating all *usuli* dissent in the city of Mosul—a city which has had a venerable *usul* tradition dating back to the very first century of Islam. We could mention many instances like this over the last two hundred years, but we will mention only one of the most poignant: the case of the Chechen people of Russia. Since 1817, the Chechen and Ingush peoples have been constantly struggling to maintain independence from Russia. Over the last two hundred years, the Chechen population has literally been decimated seven times (often by mass deportations to Siberia from which few returned). Yet after the breakdown of the Soviet Union in 1991, the Chechen people, under the late President Maskhadov and General Dudayev—and organized largely by Sufi brotherhoods—fought a successful war (1991–1996) for freedom. In this war, they essentially won autonomy from Russia in 1996 under the Khasav-Yurt accord, ratified on

May 12, 1997. This precious autonomy had cost 100,000 Chechen lives and destroyed the country. Yet two years later, they were dragged into a Second Chechen-Russian War (1999–2000) by *takfiri* elements (e.g. Ibn al-Khattab) who started by assassinating the Sufi leadership and liquidating all opposition to themselves and the Russians. The hapless Chechens then lost this war very quickly and their unique hard-fought right to autonomy was completely revoked. Although Russia has worked hard to rebuild Chechnya since, the case represents a typical *takfiri* hijacking of a genuine Muslim cause in order to wage war on *usulis*, which ended in nothing but local destruction and general mayhem. In summary, the *takfiri* war on *usulis* is generally waged through brutal local conflicts all over the world, and if *takfiris* can win these and maintain a unified command, they directly engage the greater 'Third World War' on the rest of the world through 'offensive' *jihad*.

21. DAESH'S GRAND STRATEGY

What exactly is Daesh's 'grand strategy' to take over the world? Earlier we said that it is 'not quite as insane as it seems'. How does it relate to its war on *usulis*? Actually, Daesh itself kindly recently explained all this in its online magazine *Dabiq*, issue no. 7, in an article entitled 'The extinction of the grayzone' [sic]. Roughly speaking, in it, Daesh defines the world as a binary opposition between 'the believers' (by which of course it means its adherents) versus 'the Crusaders' (by which it means the West) and 'the apostates' and 'factions' (by which it means those Muslims opposed to Daesh, or not with Daesh). By increasing attacks on innocent civilians everywhere, and in the West in particular, Daesh members hope to provoke reactions by the far right against *all* Muslims. This would make it impossible for 'neutral' or 'cowardly' Muslims (whom Daesh views as the 'grayzone') to live together with non-Muslims in peace anywhere, and these would be forced to join Daesh. At the same time Daesh also wants to take over all Muslim-majority countries, eliminating all 'apostate regimes' in a 'domino-effect' style and get the masses to join its ranks. This, the group's adherents believe, would deliver Daesh a critical mass of 20 per cent of the world's population (Sunnis alone are 21 per cent of the world's population), which, when geared up for *jihad*, would create a 'tipping point' that would enable them to take over the world. Or perhaps it would lead to an 'end times' epic confrontation between good (themselves, in their opinion) and evil. Here of course they interpret certain prophecies to mean that they would have Divine help and that the Mahdi and then Jesus Christ ﷺ himself would both come at the end of these events. One of the great battles would occur at a place called 'Dabiq' which Daesh takes to be in Syria (hence the name of its magazine).

The critical—but unspoken—calculation in all this is as follows (as can be seen from the diagram in Appendix 1 of *The Thinking Person's Guide to Islam*), schematically speaking:

- There are today roughly 1.5 billion Sunnis.
- Roughly 10 per cent of these Sunnis are anti-*usulis* (that makes 150 million people).
- Roughly 10 per cent of these anti-*usulis* are radical Salafi/Wahhabis (that makes 15 million people).
- Roughly one per cent of these radical Salafi/Wahhabis have taken up arms and are *takfiri-jihadis* (that makes 150,000 fighters).

The ultimate plan is then as follows. If the *usuli* Sunnis can be turned—or forced to turn—into Salafi/Wahhabis; if the Salafi/Wahhabis can be turned into radical Salafi/Wahhabis; if the radical Salafi/Wahhabis can be turned into *takfiri-jihadis*, and if all the *takfiri-jihadis* can be united under Daesh's 'caliphate', this would create the largest militarized society the world has ever seen. It would create an unstoppable transnational empire that is forever growing (as the population of Muslims increases) and conquering its neighbours. In the end, the whole world would inevitably be conquered, no matter how many people died on both sides. That is Daesh's 'grand strategy' and also its 'final solution'.

22. WHY PEOPLE JOIN DAESH

Everyone who joins Daesh must—during the interview process that Daesh conducts internally with new recruits—profess a *takfiri* religious motive for doing so, even before being able to join (even if they are not considered 'true Muslims' by Daesh until after they have been through a month-long indoctrination course). Actually, the vast majority *do* hold some religious motivation: no matter what worldly motives a person also has, it is hard to decide to potentially throw one's life away without the promise of an afterlife. Psychologically speaking, people are complex, and often either hide or harbour more than one motive, of which they may or may not be fully aware, or admit to themselves. Often there is a combination of many motives involved.

Many analysts divide motives into 'push' and 'pull' factors (i.e. motives with psychologically 'external' and 'internal' causes). This is useful only to identify what social causes can be ameliorated. It is not useful in the way it reduces real religious motives and ideology to psychology or pathology.

Some (but not all) of the 42 motives below have been brought to light by interviews with Daesh ex-members and Daesh would-be members in jail in Jordan.

1. A propensity for, and history of, violence, be it social or domestic, or a previous criminal record. (This was actually the most widespread common factor between around 300 Al-Nusra and Daesh ex-members or attempted members in Jordanian jails: some 40 per cent of prisoners had these).

2. Belief in Daesh's cause and *takfiri* thought.

3. Wanting to live under (perceived) Islamic law.

4. A radical Salafi/Wahhabi or Muslim Brotherhood background (one third of prisoners came from these backgrounds).

5. Sincere belief in the virtue of *jihad* and/or martyrdom, and the apparent opportunity for these with Daesh.

6. Angry young men for domestic political reasons (e.g. for Egyptians, the counter-revolution in Egypt after Morsi was elected).

7. Angry young men for domestic personal reasons (e.g. the father gets remarried, neglects his son or his first wife).

8. Angry young men for international political reasons (e.g. the West's stand on Palestine; US foreign policy, etc.).

9. Injustice from a state (e.g. police or intelligence brutality; unfair courts etc.), especially from the Assad regime.

10. Being drawn in by family ties or affection for relatives or friends who are or were Daesh fighters.

11. Revenge: often people fight to avenge people killed whilst fighting for Daesh, or simply killed by Daesh's enemies (on purpose or accidently,

such as in drone strikes in Yemen and Pakistan). There is now apparently a whole cadre of orphaned, trained child soldiers wanting to take revenge for the death of their parents.

12. Poverty (particularly in poor areas controlled by Daesh): Daesh pays its rank-and-file fighters relatively good salaries and also feeds, clothes, equips and houses them.

13. Unemployment and lack of jobs: Daesh provides jobs for its recruits in one way or another.

14. Social alienation in the place they grew up (such as Muslims living in the West).

15. Love/marriage/sex: young people get married late in the West and it is a long and expensive process between two families. In Daesh's lands they get married young and without complications, and are remarried easily when someone dies or when a couple gets divorced.

16. Guilty consciences: many young people have done many things they deeply regret and which Islam views as grave sins (in Muslim societies this of course includes homosexual acts, often in jail). Joining Daesh and a quest for martyrdom seem to provide absolution.

17. Boredom; search for adventure: many young people are just bored, and Daesh's wars and weapons promise endless excitement and adventures. The fondness of many of its fighters for posed personal photographs brandishing weapons is a sign of this.

18. The chance for 'glory', for heroics, and rapid promotion on the battlefield, perhaps promoted via social media.

19. A feeling of personal empowerment.

20. Apparent opportunity for change in the world order, in their home countries, or in personal circumstances.

21. A quest for meaning: Daesh's absolutism reassures some people that there is meaning to their lives and that they matter. It gives them existential purpose.

22. A caliphate: many Muslims nostalgically long for a united caliphate (absent from Islam since the fall of the Ottoman Caliphate in 1924) and for pan-Islamic (militant) brotherhood—Daesh seems (or seemed) to provide one.

23. To spread Monotheism (*'Tawhid'*) as they see it. This of course is deeply ironic because all Muslims are monotheists and Daesh members consider

all non-*takfiris* as being unbelievers. Moreover, the horror and revulsion they inspire puts off far more people from Monotheism than it does attract people to Monotheism (leaving aside the question of non-Muslim Monotheists). So in the name of spreading Monotheism, they consider 99% of Muslims not Monontheists, and make sure that few other non-Muslims will ever accept Monotheism.

24. For the 'honour' of Islam. This too is deeply ironic, since nothing actually dishonours Islam more than their cruelty and barbarity.

25. The chance to make history, to be involved in something important.

26. The American invasion of Iraq in 2003.

27. Inter-Islamic, or inter-sectarian tensions and resentments; particularly anti-Shi'i resentment in Iraq after the pogroms against Sunnis committed by the Shi'i death squads after the 2003 war.

28. The presence of Western troops in Muslim lands, real or imagined.

29. Veneration and lionizing of *jihadi* fighters. This is an important attraction, because when Daesh's textual narrative does not stand up to hermeneutic scrutiny by *usuli* Islamic scholarship, Daesh's 'fallback position' is some-times to attempt to claim authenticity and even legitimacy by having a reputation for being fighters ('*mujahidin*'), for having been imprisoned, for having suffered and having sacrificed (as they portray it). In short, their 'street credibility' is, emotionally speaking (as they portray it at least), one of 'actions, not words'—even though their actions are barbaric and the words they do not actually measure up to are those of God (the Qur'an) and the Prophet Muhammad ﷺ (the *hadith*).

30. Resentment against the apparent rise of Western values, moeurs or eco-nomic systems in Muslim lands.

31. Suppression of Islamic values (as they see them) in their home countries, or promotion of secular values by the state in a Muslim-majority country.

32. Perceived corruption of Arab rulers and governments.

33. Anger at the injustice of the occupation of Palestine and Jerusalem, and the diaspora of the Palestinian people. This is in fact the central grievance of Muslims worldwide (or at least is perceived as such by them) because Palestinians are oppressed there and their land—or what is left of it—is being taken on a daily basis by illegal (according to international law) Israeli settlements. Moreover, whereas others areas of the world are, Islamically speaking, the responsibility of the local or regional Muslim

community ('*fard kifayah*'), Jerusalem concerns *every single Muslim everywhere in the world* ('*fard 'ayn*'). This is because the Aqsa Mosque/Haram Sharif—or rather its area, since the current structure was not yet then constructed as such—is specifically mentioned in the Qur'an as being the place to which the Prophet Muhammad ﷺ miraculously travelled to from Mecca, and the place from which he ﷺ ascended to heaven in his 'nocturnal voyage' (*isra' wa mi'raj*). God says in the Qur'an:

> *Glory be to He who took His servant by night from the inviolable place of worship to the far distant place of worship [al-masjid al-aqsa], whose surroundings We have blessed, that We might show him some of Our signs! He Alone is the Hearer, the Seer.* (*Al-Isra*, 17:1)

Moreover, Jerusalem was the first direction of prayer ('*qibla*') for Muslims (*Al-Baqarah*, 2:142-5), and the Prophet Muhammad ﷺ said:

> Do not set out for pilgrimage except for three [mosques]: al-Masjid al-Haram [in Mecca], the mosque of God's messenger [in Medina] and the mosque of al-Aqsa. (*Bukhari*)

So the key point about all this is that justice denied in Palestine for the Palestinians, and the occupation and interference with the Aqsa Mosque/Haram Sharif (all 144,000 m² of it—491m west, 462m east, 310m north and 281m south—including the Dome of the Rock Mosque, the Qibli and Marwani mosques and all the other mosques in it as well as its buildings, walls, courtyards, plazas, esplanades, pathways, libraries, museums, water cisterns and channels, bathrooms, offices and all the other *waqf* properties attached to it above and under the ground—all of which are an integral part of it) create a legitimate grievance *based on faith* for all 1.7 billion Muslims everywhere in the world. This is why the issues of Jerusalem and Palestine are more important to resolve than any other single issue in the Islamic world, and why there absolutely must be a just and fair resolution to the rambling Peace Process.

34. Anger at the genocides against Muslims, particularly in Bosnia, Kosovo, Myanmar (against Rohingya Muslims) and the Central African Republic.

35. Anger at various other instances of oppression against Muslim people or minorities such as in Thailand and the Philippines.

36. Coercion (in Daesh-controlled areas): Daesh forces the millions of people

under its control to fight for it (or else pay a lot of money instead, which many people do not have).

37. Peer pressure and influence (in pro-Daesh) communities.

38. Madness or mental instability.

39. Victory: Daesh's string of victories has caused people to join it in order to be on the 'winning side' (or so they believe). Entire battalions and fighting groups (as well as tribes) in Syria have flipped and joined it because of its victories.

40. Brainwashing; many young people and children are simply brainwashed by Daesh members or by Daesh propaganda.

41. Desperation, starvation or shell shock (for people in conflict zones): being incessantly bombed from the air by the allies, the Russians or the Syrian regime, starved or deprived, is enough to drive anyone to anything.

42. 'Cannot explain it': many Daesh recruits cannot explain or put into words why they joined it: in other words, they are just confused.

To list so many motives may give the (mis)impression that the impulse for joining Daesh is overwhelming and is going to attract more and more young people. In reality, this is not the case. If someone were to conduct a proper analysis of why thousands of young people join, for example, any given job or profession, they would find at least 40 different motives. Any given person might harbour five or six of them together. So it is with Daesh, and one should not be fooled by the apparent variety of motives they have. In the long run, many of these motives become sources of weakness, and ultimately, dissatisfaction and defection.

23. ARE THEY EVIL?

The question is of course melodramatic and self-righteous. Indeed, Muslims do not judge other people's souls, because only God has the right to do this and only God truly knows people's real inner states. But Muslims do judge people's outward acts, and obviously Daesh has a long list of well-known crimes that are completely wrong if not evil (as outlined in section 11, and they have increased considerably since then).

Nevertheless, Daesh recruits—with the exception of some criminals or mentally unstable individuals—generally do *not* start out with evil intentions. If one thinks about the motives mentioned above, only five or so are evil. Things like going to war out of love of fighting or for adventure, for glory or to be on the winning side, are clearly base motives for going to war, which, after all, involves killing and being killed. Other motives like wanting to avenge one's family or friends, being coerced, and anger at genocides or injustices are natural motives. As W.H. Auden (d. 1973) wrote (in his poem 'September 1st, 1939'):

> I and all the public know
>> What all schoolchildren learn
> Those to whom evil is done
>> Do evil in return.

Still other motives are actually noble—if naïve—like a commitment to self-sacrifice and martyrdom, to a perceived caliphate, or wanting to live under perceived Islamic law. For Muslims, this is perhaps the most tragic thing of all: to see earnest young people with good intentions lured and duped into Daesh's web of crimes in the name of religion.

The Prophet Muhammad ﷺ helped people understand this situation by setting down a 'gold standard' for wrongdoings in the name of religion. He ﷺ said: 'A believer remains firmly attached to his religion as long as he has not spilt forbidden blood' (*Bukhari*; *Muslim*). That is to say then, that short of murder there is hope for everyone. Of course Daesh itself precisely does not fully trust its recruits until it has made them participate in the murder or execution of innocents. So until this 'initiation of evil' has occurred, recruits are not beyond redemption and are not 'trusted' members of Daesh. They are in the process of taking 'baby steps' on the slippery slope of a long and unseen series of inner negotiations and compromises. God warns all believers in the Qur'an of this precisely:

> *O you who believe, do not follow in the steps of Satan. For whoever follows in the steps of Satan, assuredly he enjoins indecency and wrong. And were it not for God's bounty to you and His mercy not one of you would ever have attained purity. But God purifies whom He will, and God is Hearer, Knower.* (*Al-Nur*, 24:21)

24. DAESH'S BRUTALITY

We will turn shortly to Daesh's other tactics, but it is important to note that its primary tactics are fear, terror, brutality and intimidation—'Just Terror', as it proudly claimed on the cover of *Dabiq* no.12. Not since the Crusades or the moment the Mongols swept through the Middle East (and the world) in the mid-13th Century CE (or Tamerlane the following century), has anyone in the Arab Levant made such use of international terror and intimidation as Daesh. In addition to mass executions of thousands of defenceless prisoners, Daesh has proudly filmed the public execution of prisoners by: shooting them in the head; chopping their heads off with swords; sawing off their heads with knives; burning them alive; crucifying them; stringing them up with chains; blowing them up; drowning them in steel cages; stoning them; pushing them off tall buildings; stabbing them in the heart; burying them alive; lowering them into tubs of acid; having women kill women; having children shoot adults; having children saw off the heads of adults; having children kill their parents; making siblings kill their siblings; making friends kill friends; and all manner of other senseless, evil, brutal and inhuman forms of murder.

Now the immediate purpose of this is terror and intimidation, but in fact it goes far beyond that to wanton psychopathic bloodlust dressed up as religion. Of course, Daesh videos are very slick and always contain false religious and absurd political justifications for these acts (accompanied by gloating, triumphalist a capella singing and clever graphics). However, quite apart from the unpardonable crimes of murder, all of this glorying in—and enjoying inflicting torture—is the very opposite of anything to do with *sunnah*. The Prophet ﷺ said: 'if you slaughter [animals in order to eat them], make the slaughter as perfect [i.e. painless] as possible' (*Bukhari*). This applies a fortiori to human beings in cases of justifiable capital punishments (which these murders are not). In short, in terms of cruelty, Daesh is as cruel as Saddam Hussein's Ba'athi state at its worst—but flaunts it more shamelessly—and uses all the same brutality (and perhaps some of the same personnel) to try to terrorize local populations into submission.

Earlier we mentioned how this tactic has hit the 'law of diminishing returns', so that people are so used to all this horror that it scares them less, and in fact can repulse them so much it gives them determination to resist. It remains to be said, however, that we suspect that this will be Daesh's legacy. When its adherents are consigned to the darkest footnotes of history, as they thoroughly deserve, they will have left an indelible and historical stain of mass murder and cruelty on the image of Islam, and an apparent confirmation of the worst caricatures of the religion.

25. DAESH TACTICS

It is important to understand Daesh's military tactics in order to defeat it. This means not belittling its military achievements, and recognizing that the group has been able to hold a good deal of territory for two years against a vast and powerful international coalition. After all, God says in the Qur'an: . . . *Let not hatred of a people cause you not to be just . . .* (*Al-Ma'idah*, 5:8). Moreover, it is necessary to objectively analyze how Daesh has managed to do this. The following are general observations from open source materials. They do not represent any kind of classified information or military secrets.

(a) *Leadership and Command*
  (i) *Unity of Command*: In their view, declaring a 'caliphate' means a unified command that has the unquestioned 'right' to kill any internal opposition or external opponents through summary execution (which Daesh commonly does). This obviously makes for strong unity of command.
  (ii) *Young and Flexible Operational Commanders*: Daesh has no stultifying bureaucracy, no automatic promotion of bad officers. Weak or incompetent officers are literally killed in the war through survival of the (militarily) fittest.
  (iii) *Decentralization*: Daesh has well-empowered regional emirs, all under 'caliphate' control.

(b) *Strategy and Operational Mentality*
  Daesh combines a number of 'morphing' and/or interchangeable operating mentalities: it combines the fervour, secrecy and absolutism of a New Age cult; the extortion rackets of the mafia; the bombs, booby traps, discord and demoralizing tactics of terrorism; the assassination hit-

and-run tactics of guerilla warfare; the industry and purpose of an all-out conventional war; the rural door-to-door coercion of Maoist rebellions; the scorched earth tactics and disdain for rules of war and conventions of religious warfare; and the ruthless no-holds-barred mentality of Ba'athi genocide.

(c) *Tactics and Combat Experience*

(i) Daesh has continuous combat experience. Some Daesh fighters have been operating continuously since the 1980s in Afghanistan and then from the 2003 war in Iraq. Some of the Iraqi leadership have combat experience not only from the 1991 and the 2003 Iraqi wars, but from as far back as the eight-year 1980–1988 Iran-Iraq war. Some Daesh fighters started as Free Syrian Army rebels, received training from the allied coalition itself at the beginning of the Syrian Crisis from 2011 to 2013 in order to fight the Assad regime, and then 'flipped' and joined Daesh. Moreover, many of Daesh's fighters come from armies all over the world and are veterans of many wars, and these too have brought their combat experience with them. Few armies in the world today (including Western armies) have had as much actual recent combat experience as the Daesh *jihadis*. Moreover, Daesh has experience in every type of weaponry imaginable, and not merely NATO or Russian weaponry.

(ii) *Combined Arms*: Daesh uses a combined-arms attack approach. It is capable of many-pronged, many-sided attacks. It is capable of unexpected attacks in disguised uniforms, even through Turkey.

(iii) *Experienced shots*: veteran Daesh fighters are now good shots and accurate snipers. Practised Daesh fighters must have shot tens if not hundreds of thousands of rounds every year, as opposed to the few hundred (if not few dozen) rounds fired by soldiers in standing armies in the region.

(iv) *Improvisation*: Daesh improvises cheap equipment, repairs, suicide belts, IEDs (improvised explosive devices), VBIEDs (vehicle-borne improvised explosive devices), tunnel bombs and even remote IEDs.

(v) *Urban Warfare*: Daesh boasts that it now specializes in urban warfare, and this is perhaps true. Certainly its use of tunnel bombs is unprecedented both in terms of scope and effectiveness. 'Tunnel bombs' are when one digs a tunnel—usually in an urban battlefield—up to one or even two kilometres underground to reach important enemy installations and place explosives underneath them. They are extremely difficult, dangerous, labour-intensive, and time-consuming to set up. Nevertheless, Daesh—and to a certain extent al-Nusra—have used them to devastating effect, because once set up, there is almost no limit to how much explosives one can use. They are also obviously extremely difficult to detect, being deep underground. Moreover, Daesh has even anticipated battlefield losses and effectively left tunnel bombs under sites its enemies would use in the future. Consequently, Daesh and al-Nusra have occasionally been able to take out entire enemy units and city blocks (albeit after months of digging) even when pinned down by aerial bombardment.

(vi) Daesh uses the lightning-fast, small, mobile units with adapted commercial vehicles to perform the hit-and-run tactics first pioneered by Ahmad Shah Massoud in Afghanistan (via the Afghani *mujahidin*, presumably).

(vii) *Sudden, massive shocks*: Daesh specializes in sending multiple, co-ordinated improvised 1,000lb + ammonium-nitrate bombs placed in armed Humvees or armed SUVs with suicide-bomber drivers to destroy enemy defences, outposts and barracks. It selects sites through drones or human intelligence, and can attack at night or dawn. The ammonium nitrate (which is ordinary fertilizer) seems to be acquired via Turkey and can take out an entire city block from 100 metres away. This is Daesh's most effective military weapon: it is so fast, it is effectively an air force. In city blocks or close battle lines, it is all but impossible to stop. The suicide trucks are armoured so they cannot be stopped by machine gun fire or even RPGs and they can come at over 100+ mph. Nevertheless, Kurdish troops have been able to stop them in their tracks through a combination of constant vigilance, clear battle vision in desert and mountainous areas; ditches; spike strips; night vision equipment and guided anti-tank missiles at the ready.

(d) *Weaponry, Supply and Procurement*

(i) Daesh started with large quantities of weaponry and ammunition that it captured from the Iraqi or Syrian armies. Since then it has bought or been supplied with enough ammunition to keep its wars going. Given the number of fighters and fronts it is fighting on, and the time that has elapsed (two years so far) this means it has somehow been able to get a hold of at least a billion rounds of small calibre ammo alone over the last two years(25,000 fighters shooting 200 bullets a day for 730 days would require 3.65 billion bullets). Since Daesh is landlocked and hemmed in by enemies on all sides, and since it does not have any ammunition factories in the areas it controls, this begs the question: where do these supplies come from, and how does Daesh receive them?

Open source information shows that in addition to countless small arms, Daesh weaponry includes: SA-7 and Stinger surface-to-air missiles, M79 Osa, HJ-8 and AT-4 Spigot anti-tank weapons, Type 59 field guns and M198 Howitzers, (over 2,000) Humvees, T-54/55, T-72, and M1 Abrams main battle tanks, M1117 armoured cars, truck-mounted DShK guns, ZU-23-2 anti-aircraft guns, BM-21 Grad multiple rocket launchers, and at least one Scud missile. It has better armaments than the Kurds or the actual Iraqi Army. More worrying still is that in March 2016, 20,000 uniforms coming from Spain were intercepted on their way to Daesh.

(ii) Daesh mounts its own heavy machine guns on SUVs. If an army leadership does not care about casualties, these are cheaper, quicker and more effective than APCs.

(iii) Daesh makes a large array of improvised bombs, ranging from remote bombs to pipe bombs, tunnel bombs, suicide belts, mortars, crude cannons and (as mentioned above) SUVs and Humvees armed with 1,000+ lb bombs and suicide bombers.

(iv) Daesh has tried to make use of dams as weapons of war (through flooding or cutting downstream water supplies).

(e) *Maintenance and Repair*
Daesh is apparently able to conduct maintenance and repair of its equipment—Cuban-style—through clandestine supplies, improvisation and cannibalization.

(f) *Military Engineering; Industry and Construction*
Daesh has commandeered and recruited extensive local engineering and construction, and taken over or co-opted all the local industry it wants in its areas.

(e) *Defences*

(i) Whilst Daesh is essentially still helpless against airstrikes from high-altitude bombers, towns recaptured from it show vast underground tunnelling. These include tunnel defences; underground living quarters; tunnels for movement and supply; and tunnels for escape and reinforcement. No doubt Baghdadi and his top henchmen have been holed up in such tunnels and underground caves for the last two years.

(ii) Daesh relies on civilian appearance to protect its fighters and their movements.

(iii) Daesh has learnt to rely on secrecy and information blackout (or selective blackout) to conceal itself. Low-ranking fighters are not given access to phones or the internet, and all internet communications in Daesh areas are watched.

(iv) The area Daesh controls is (in Syria and Iraq alone) large (albeit now reduced), and this obviously helps conceal its forces.

(f) *Technology; Scientific Research and Development*

Daesh has no high-tech industry or serious scientific research, but continually conducts its own R&D military experimentation, and has managed to come up with a number of technical military adaptations, notably commercial drones (its followers try to buy every drone they can on the international market) which it uses effectively for live battlefield intelligence.

(g) *Communications*

Daesh makes use of captured military equipment; of 'low-tech' al-Qaeda-type operational communications; and also (even on the battlefield) of encrypted and untraceable social media messaging such as Kik and WhatsApp.

(h) *Movement and Transportation*

Daesh's land-fighting speed and mobility are rapid, mainly because its fighters are unencumbered by heavy armour and bureaucratized logistics.

(i) *Intelligence, Counter-intelligence and Infiltration*

(i) Radical Salafi/Wahhabis — and a fortiori *takfiri-jihadis* — have their own subculture within Sunni Islam; their own rulings, habits, customs, attitudes and words that they use. This makes them impenetrable from the outside, like a cult. Living with them and spying on them is very difficult for that reason.

(ii) So much information is now available on the net that clever trawling of open sources leads to excellent information for anyone looking for it. When Daesh released its internet instructions to kill Jordanian pilots, it used Google maps to point out the pilots' houses.

(iii) Daesh has many Ba'athi intelligence officers within its ranks, and has reconstructed an effective but repressive state intelligence system.

(j) *Battlefields*

(i) Daesh has extensive local knowledge and battle experience, so it picks its battlefields well. In June 2014, with fewer than 2,000 fighters, Daesh overran Mosul, a city in Iraq of two million people with 25,000 to 30,000 troops and police then stationed there.

(ii) The Iraq-Syria battlefield is joined to those of Libya and Somalia through sea routes and commercial planes via Turkey and/or smuggling routes. Libya is vast and opens up to the Sahara and from there to all of North Africa and Sub-Saharan Africa. In other words, via Turkey, Daesh is connected to the whole of Africa and the Middle East. So for Daesh, the Middle East is effectively one battlefield, and it can move with relative impunity anywhere it likes in this 'one battlefield'.

26. DAESH ADMINISTRATION

(a) *Occupation*

(i) The big difference here between al-Qaeda and Daesh is that Daesh from the beginning sought to hold territory, and not merely move freely through it. This is perhaps because Daesh was born in urban areas, whereas al-Qaeda was born in the vast and rough Afghan countryside.

(ii) Daesh holds its occupied territory with a grip of terror, worse than the most dictatorial nation state.

(b) *Food, Water and Sanitation; Medical Care*

(i) Daesh has apparently maintained basic food, water and sanitation in the areas it controls. There have been no reports of mass famine or starvation.

(ii) Daesh has taken over hospitals in its areas and keeps them open (with priority for its fighters). It has even set up its own medical degree. It has made a slick online medical video asking for foreign medical personnel volunteers and claiming it has all the equipment it needs. Medical services are rudimentary at best, but arguably they were the same before Daesh's occupation. It has started human organ trafficking for cash, selling the organs of prisoners and even its own wounded fighters.

(c) *Organization; Logistics and Administration*

(i) Daesh has made use of Ba'athi party expertise in organization, and in setting up the trappings of a modern nation state.

(ii) Daesh seems able to organize logistics and deliver supplies wherever its fighters need them.

(iii) Daesh now has extensive record-keeping to the extent that it has started to issue identity cards to 'citizens'.

(iv) Daesh has benefited enormously from local knowledge, especially in Iraq (as its leadership is Iraqi).

27. DAESH'S WEAKNESSES

On the other hand, Daesh suffers from many important military, political and religious weaknesses. These include:

(i) Lack of an air force and a navy and really sophisticated equipment.

(ii) A lack of any real R&D, as noted.

(iii) A lack of real industry.

(iv) Nobody outside of the group likes it. Despite the terror its adherents inspire, Daesh has a high defection rate; people in its areas generally live a miserable, short, brutal life. Services in Daesh areas are poor, and its members treat people badly, and constantly enforce weird new religious rules (such as banning congregational *tarawih* prayers in Ramadan, and the destruction of the graves belonging to Islamic Prophets and their Companions). Daesh does not have a sustained, consistent goodwill campaign for populations under its control, and it has already shed too much blood amongst these. Natives resent foreign fighters, and many resent Iraqi dominance in the organization. All this is in stark contrast to al-Nusra, whose members are largely local Syrians and try to be as respectful as possible of the local people (and consequently are better-liked and respected). Daesh defectors reveal some corruption and considerable discontentment in the ranks. Simply put: people do not like them and know they are bad.

(v) Daesh's religious arguments are not only specious but weak, not only from the *usuli* point of view, but even from the mainstream Salafi point of view. The group has its own texts, as mentioned, but these can be easily demolished by knowledgeable scholars and no Muslim scholar of repute has endorsed them. So Daesh members have now been called heretics ('*Khawarij*'—literally 'outsiders', 'renegades') by the Azhar, and by the Grand Muftis of nearly every country from Saudi Arabia to Nigeria. In fact, the only thing they seem to mind—as seen in Baghdadi's address *Even if the Disbelievers Despise Such* (May 15th, 2015)—is being called '*khawarij*' and having their religious credentials questioned.

(vi) Daesh adherents have happily killed (or executed) so many other *jihadis* of the same schools of thought as them (i.e. fellow 'Muslims'). Reportedly, at least 12,000 fighters have been killed in fighting Daesh and al-Nusra in the last few years. In Afghanistan they have declared war on the Taliban. This gives the lie to Daesh's 'pan-jihadist' claims. Moreover, they are ideologically at war with their own original *jihadi* ideologues like Abu Muhammad al-Maqdisi and Abu Qatada, and with the al-Qaeda chief, Ayman al-Zawahiri.

(vii) Daesh is perceived to be not concerned with Israel, attacking the same enemies as Israel in Syria and Iraq (i.e. the Assad regime and Iran). Israeli officials have publicly said that they see Daesh as less of a threat than Hizbollah or the Syrian regime. At the same time, Daesh is busy killing other Muslims and Arab Christians. One of the first (and perhaps) most successful spoof videos about Daesh (by *Watan 'a Watar*) satirizes them hilariously for just that. Moreover, there are some 10 million Palestinians in diaspora all over the world, and Israel keeps building more and more settlements in the West Bank every week and so this, combined with occupied Jerusalem's sacred significance in Islam, undermines Daesh's claims of representing Islam.

(viii) As mentioned, much of Daesh's success relies upon the disarray and disunity between its many enemies: increased co-ordination between these (especially the US and Russia) can seriously undermine this.

(ix) Daesh's land is surrounded on all sides by enemies, and it is entirely dependent on Turkey for supplies. If Turkey were to be able to truly close and patrol its borders, Daesh would quickly be starved out.

(x) Daesh's electronic surveillance is weak, and its social media communication is at the mercy of those who control the internet nodes of the communication and social media giants.

(xi) For all their slickness and shock value in propaganda, Daesh's videos have no story and no individual charismatic champion that its viewers can identify with. They have no normal human interest narrative. Ironically, it is always the Western media which researches and tells the 'story' of its members to create interest in the stories about them. Daesh's videos are basically just 'circuses of death', and so the scope of their appeal is ultimately limited—in addition to the law of diminishing returns mentioned earlier.

(xii) The Iraqi Sunni tribes: these regard Daesh as upstarts and barbarians. Recent polls show that 95 per cent of Iraqi Sunnis (and all Iraqi Shi'is) oppose Daesh. As mentioned, if they were not between 'the devil' (to them—Daesh) and 'the deep blue sea' (the sectarian Shia-dominated government and state of Iraq), they might turn more convincingly against Daesh. In other words, if the Iraqi parliament granted the Iraqi Sunnis armed autonomy up front, by law, in their three or four provinces (like the Kurds), or if Iraq were amicably (especially with the Kurds with whom Baghdad would have to have resource-sharing agreements) confederated into three states, the Sunnis would more likely fight Daesh.

28. COUNTERING DAESH'S STRATEGY

Countering Daesh's strategy first requires properly understanding how it works—as described in this annex and other studies. It then requires actively interrupting or starving its strategies for growth (as described in sections 13 and 21). It requires a military and intelligence component. But most of all it requires a holistic 'soft power' component, because without a soft power strategy, Daesh will continue to try to enlist the world's 150

million anti-*usulis* (and their resources), and then the rest of the world's
1.5 billion Sunnis. The number of Sunnis is constantly growing as Islam
is the world's fastest-growing religion. This means that without a global
'soft power' strategy, fighting Daesh and *takfiri-jihadism* is just going to
be at best a game of global whack-a-mole and at worst a case of whistling
in the wind while the whole world burns.

This is not as difficult as it seems. It is not simply a question of eliminating all legitimate grievances in the Islamic world (although this would
help). It is not a question of eliminating anti-*usuli* thought, or even of
educating the 'don't knows' (although the latter would be immeasurably
beneficial). Rather, it is a question of tackling *'takfiri-jihadi'* thought at
its roots and source texts. In other words, it is not a question of destroying
its 'hardware' but rather 'tweaking its software' on three critical issues
that will allow all people to live together in peace and justice. These issues
have been outlined in Appendix 2 of *The Thinking Person's Guide to Islam*,
so there is no need to repeat them here.

As H.M King Abdullah II ibn Al-Hussein has repeatedly said, this is
a challenge for all Muslims. In particular, Muslim scholars, from *usulis*
to Salafis. These scholars must point out and make clear again and again,
constantly, everywhere—based on the Qur'an and the *Sunnah*—through
every means available ('old', 'new', 'carrot' and 'stick') the mistakes and
flaws of *takfiri* thought. Muslims, have collectively and over generations,
through apathy and lack of vigilance, allowed Islam to be hijacked by people with apparently more zeal than them. They must reclaim their religion
with an equal or greater zeal for God, for the Prophet Muhammad ﷺ and
for the beauty, love, goodness and truth that true Islam brings. As W.B.
Yeats expressed it in his poem 'The Second Coming' (in 1919):

> Turning and turning in the widening gyre
>> The falcon cannot hear the falconer;
>> Things fall apart; the centre cannot hold;
>> Mere anarchy is loosed upon the world,
> The blood-dimmed tide is loosed, and everywhere
>> The ceremony of innocence is drowned;
> The best lack all conviction, while the worst
>> Are full of passionate intensity.

One more thing: today's enemy, with some kindness and proper Islamic scholarship, may become tomorrow's friend, and may abandon *takfiri* thought, and even become an ambassador against it (as so many ex-*jihadis* have). This requires Muslim-majority countries (especially those with *takfiri-jihadis* already in jails) to put into place a road to repentance. It must be combined with a generous 'de-radicalization and reconciliation' educational programme either in jails or in mosques. Then, people with a level of involvement in radicalization or even terrorism can find an attractive route back into society, with dignity, not find themselves stigmatized by society or the state for the rest of their lives. As recent experience in Algeria has shown, the prevention of radicalization is much easier and more effective than 'de-radicalization', but there must be a path to 'de-radicalization', whether in secret or in the open.

For the rest of the world it means not overreacting to terrorist outrages or sensationalizing them, and above all not targeting all Muslims as such.

That is the task at hand—no other plan will work.

29. THE END OF DAESH

Daesh's slogan is '*baqiyah wa mutamaddidah*', which means 'lasting and expanding', and this is precisely what it will not do, God willing. In addition to exploiting Daesh's weakness and using the counter-strategies we have mentioned, the end of Daesh will likely come about suddenly through internal collapse and infighting once a critical mass of pressure has been applied. T.S. Elliot (d. 1965) wrote (in 'The Hollow Men'):

> *This is the way the world ends*
> *This is the way the world ends*
> *This is the way the world ends*
> *Not with a bang but a whimper.*

This is because Daesh has committed so much injustice towards the local populations and even to its own adherents that its internal cohesion is fragile, and as mentioned in *The Thinking Person's Guide to Islam*, 'injustice always leads to discontentment, protests, rebellions, revolutions and civil wars'.

At this stage in Syria and Iraq, entire battalions are likely to defect to al-Nusra or other Salafi/Wahhabi fighting groups like *Ahrar al-Sham* (who may succeed in establishing their own emirate in Northern Syria—but that is a different question). The core leadership (and the global leadership of the pseudo-caliphate) is likely to move to Libya, where it has been trying to establish a 'plan B'. Libya is a much bigger territory, and it is open to the whole Mediterranean Sea and the whole of Africa and therefore is more difficult to contain, so there will likely be another campaign there. Furthermore, like a Mexican drug cartel when the drug baron is removed, the destruction of Daesh's central leadership may leave local commanders with a free hand. This can mean even more unpredictable trouble at local levels. These, like the mythical Lernean hydra, have to have their heads 'scorched' or 'potted' systematically, one by one. And of course this has to be done in co-ordination with the full soft-power strategy at the local level.

30. THE CRISIS OF ISIS

From all of the above it should be obvious that every religion has a *ghoul* that follows it around, misquoting and misusing its texts for its own purposes. All religions have had these throughout their history, and every religion has them even today (like for example Joseph Kony's 'Lord's Resistance Army' in Uganda, or the Buddhist monk Ashin Wirathu in Myanmar), but few have achieved the kind of publicity and military success that Daesh has.

The word 'ghoul' in fact is very telling: it is of Arabic origin. It literally means a 'horrible monster' or 'ogre' (from the desert) that attacks and snatches things or people when a community has its guard down. Now this is precisely what movements like Daesh do. After the weakening of *usuli* knowledge, and even of traditional Salafi knowledge, Muslims had their 'religious guard' down, and *takfirism* was able to attack. Clearly Daesh is one of Islam's ghouls, although perhaps not its worst ever (that would have to be the original *Khawarij* movement).

But more than that, Daesh is the ghoul of the 'impostor apocalypse'. We have already touched on its messianic pretensions of being the vanguard of the awaited Mahdi's army—its use of black flags alludes to this—and its pretending to lead an 'end times' Manichean epic struggle that will culminate with the battle of Dabiq. So, as a corrective, let us consider an alternative prediction from 'Ali bin Abi Talib ﷺ to be found in *Kitab al-Fitan* of Bukhari's own teacher Nu'aym bin Hammad (1,200 years ago):

> When you see the black flags, remain where you are and do not move your hands or your feet. Thereafter there shall appear a feeble insignificant folk. Their hearts will be like fragments of iron. They will have 'the state'. They will fulfil neither covenant nor agreement. They will call to the truth, but they will not be people of the truth. Their names will be parental attributions, and their aliases will be derived from towns. Their hair will be free-flowing like that of women. This situation will remain until they differ among themselves. Thereafter, God will bring forth the Truth through whomever He wills.

The authors of the 'Open Letter to Baghdadi' on 19th of September 2014 (see: www.lettertobaghdadi.com) mentioned above suggest the following reading of it:

'When you see the black flags': The flags of the 'Islamic State' are black.
'Remain where you are': i.e. stay where you are, O Muslims, and do not join them'.
'And do not move your hands or your feet': i.e. 'do not help them financially or with equipment'.
'Thereafter there shall appear a feeble insignificant folk': i.e. 'weak' and 'insignificant' in terms of understanding of religion, morality and religious practice.
'Their hearts will be like fragments of iron': i.e. they will ruthlessly kill prisoners of war and cruelly torture people.
'They will have the state': For almost a century, no one has claimed to be an Islamic caliphate other than the current 'Islamic State' in Iraq and the Levant.
'They will fulfil neither covenant nor agreement': The 'Islamic State' did not fulfil its agreement with the Sha'etat tribe after the tribe pledged allegiance to it; indeed the 'Islamic State' slaughtered them by the hundreds. They also killed journalists.
'They will call to the truth': The 'Islamic State' calls to Islam.
'But they will not be people of the truth': The people of the truth are

merciful. The Prophet Muhammad ﷺ said: 'Have mercy and you will be shown mercy.'

'Their names will be parental attributions': Like: 'Abu Muthanna', 'Abu Muhammad', 'Abu Muslim' and so on.

'And their aliases will be derived from towns': Like: 'Al-Baghdadi', 'Al-Zarqawi', 'Al-Tunisi' and so on.

'Their hair will be free-flowing like that of women': 'Islamic State' fighters have hair like this precisely.

'Until they differ among themselves': Like the differences between the 'Islamic State' and its parent, the al-Nusra Front (al-Qaeda in Syria). The fighting between these two has led to around 10,000 deaths in a single year.

'Thereafter, God will bring forth the truth through whomever He wills': through a clear and correct Islamic proclamation (like this Open Letter).

This is to say then that Daesh is not the predicted revival of Islam, but merely a predicted glitch. And God knows best.

～

Index

~

GENERAL INDEX

Index

INDEX OF *AHADITH* CITED

INDEX OF QUR'ANIC VERSES CITED

INDEX OF POETRY

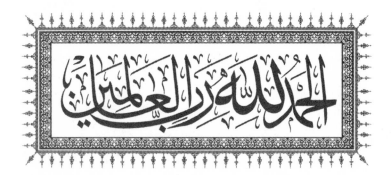